ORGANIZE YOUR HOME!

How to store clothing, kitchen items, tools, and other clutter efficiently and with no wasted space

DEBRA MELCHIOR

BOB ADAMS, INC.
PUBLISHERS
Holbrook, Massachusetts

Published by Bob Adams, Inc.
260 Center Street, Holbrook, MA 02343

ISBN: 1-55850-119-3

Printed in the United States of America

C   D   E   F   G   H   I   J

This publication is designed to provide accurate and authoritative information with regard to the subject matter covered. It is sold with the understanding that the publisher is not engaged in rendering legal, accounting, or other professional advice. If legal advice or other expert assistance is required, the services of a qualified professional person should be sought.
— From a *Declaration of Principles* jointly adopted by a Committee of the American Bar Association and a Committee of Publishers and Associations.

Illustrations: Laura Crew and Debra Melchior

This book is available at quantity discounts for bulk purchases.
For information, call 1-800-872-5627.

IT'S TIME TO GET YOUR LIFE IN ORDER IF
YOU'RE SERIOUSLY ASKING YOURSELF:

1. Would I rather go naked or open the closet door?

2. Would I rather get a divorce or straighten up my half of the closet?

3. Would I rather throw it away or find a place to put it?

4. Would I rather buy a new one or find the one I have?

5. Would I rather move to a bigger house or reassemble this one?

6. Would I rather swallow poison or let an outsider see my closet?

IF YOU OPT FOR ORDER, YOU ASK YOURSELF:

1. Where do I start?

2. Do I draw up plans first or jump right in?

3. Do I need to purchase anything? Gadgets or gizmos?

4. Can I really double the space?

5. Do I need to install anything?

6. How do I know what to keep and what to pitch?

7. Can I keep it organized after I organize it?

8. If it's so easy to do, why haven't I done it?

TABLE OF CONTENTS

READ THIS FIRST: A NOTE ON ORGANIZATION AND BUDGETS

We'll be working together very closely as we progress from closet to kitchen, bathroom to garage in this organizing overhaul of the entire house, so perhaps I should introduce myself.

If you've looked at anything more than the title of this book and a few random pages, you'll realize my name is Debbie. I'd much prefer that you address me this way and not as "**#%#@@*%!! Debbie," which is a possibility when your head's stuck under the kitchen sink or underneath the clothes in your closet as you attempt to measure and assess each disastrous situation.

My mind's eye sees the chaotic conditions that exist inside most homes as though they were the pieces of a jigsaw puzzle to be taken apart, examined, evaluated, and then improved, renovated, and restored. I'm very good at establishing order and systems for organizing all the pieces.

I planned "systems" for my friends for years, until I decided to widen my horizons by opening my own business, which would enable me to bring these same skills and solutions to the general public.

Business prospered, my reputation grew, and word of my expertise was spread throughout my town and the surrounding areas. I was consulted when all other treatments had failed. And then, out of the clear blue sky, I was a mother for the first time at age 38. Serious and painful decisions had to be made and I opted for Mommyhood over Big Businesshood. Now, nearly four years later, I find myself playing space-management games: inventing clutter problems so I can challenge myself; seeking upbeat, innovative yet practical and logical solutions to everyday hassles. It became quite obvious to me and my family that I was devoted, obsessed, and committed to organizing, so I guess I'll continue to probe the recesses of every dark closet I encounter in order to provide you with a composite picture of the resources, recourses, and rehabilitations that are feasible and worthwhile, especially in our fast-paced, erratic, sporadic, and time-restricted lifestyles.

You will find a wealth of suggestions here. Some are of the "ingenious brainstorm" variety—others require the purchase of new storage equipment. I've taken a generous approach to the issue of budgeting, opting to lay all the approaches out on the table and let you choose the organizational method that best suits your pocketbook. Where appropriate, I've given estimated retail prices. Beware, however; these will vary by region. Check your local hardware, sundry, or department store. (These are places you'll probably be visiting soon!)

Debra K. Melchior
Cincinnati, Ohio

CHAPTER ONE

The Clothes Closet

COMPONENTS

✔ How to Mastermind Measurements

✔ How to Compare Costs

✔ How to Select a System

✔ How to Count Clothes

How to Mastermind Measurements

The single most important component to consider when organizing a closet is its size and shape, since obviously it's the one element within the closet that can't be changed without funneling a ridiculous amount of our time, money, and energy into its reconstruction. Reconstructing a closet seldom justifies the expenditure, nor does it satisfy our expectations, especially if we envisioned our closet as a permanently and perpetually tidy and delightful depository for our belongings.

A spacious and accomodating closet isn't achieved by simply increasing its size, since it's our erratic, ineffectual, and uninformed behavior that creates the conditions we're concerned with. Even given the biggest closet imaginable, we'd soon have it victimized and violated unless we gain some insight into the art of organizing it.

Organizing implies cosmetic restructuring and rearranging, yet this oversimplified terminology should never fool us into believing the process attains merely superficial results. For, in reality, organizing establishes not only improved patterns of behavior in our own dealings with the closet, but it also helps us to recognize and therefore conquer our fear of all those misunderstood but overwhelmingly chaotic conditions that live and breathe within the limited boundaries of our existing closet.

We've been looking at our closet in its entirety; it's no wonder we've procrastinated, for a face-to-face confrontation with such a wildly confused and complex beast would scare anyone off. We've also postponed this project, perceived as a dreaded ordeal that's doomed to failure before it's begun, because we can't picture our meagerly sized, nightmarish closet being transformed into our dream closet. We've been so intimidated by the prospect that we've allowed the closet to control us rather than the more reasonable reverse.

The reasonable course of action is to break the closet down into snippets of pertainent information, thereby putting them in understandable and manageable perspective. By graphically explaining each fundamental principle and every option, organizing the closet becomes nothing more than a few simple, logical steps and stages to be chosen and executed based on personal preferences. The individually masterminded closet is a tribute in itself, but gloating is premissible on those occasions when the joy and wonder can't be contained.

The first step furnishes the most vital statistics: the width, the depth, the height, the door space, and the wall space(s) adjoining the door, hereafter known as the lip of the closet.

Measure every little nook and cranny, allowing not a single inch to escape the yardstick's intention, and then record these precise figures on the fill-in-the-blank form following. Please notice however that the blank space labeled "DOOR" isn't properly answered with a yes or no unless there is indeed simply a doorframe without a shutting mechanism of any type. Otherwise the information needed is more descriptive: bi-fold, sliding, open-out, shuttered, pocket, louvered, or draped.

A word to the wise: accuracy and exactness work for us or against us when we install the products or the hardware and when we return the clothes to the closet. If we've made drastic errors, we might decide to hang our neck from the closet rod, since the rod's not going to hang the clothes we'd planned.

Illustration 1 is a bird's-eye view of a standard closet.

The rod occupies more than its length and diameter, since the clothes on it take up much space. The rod is also attached to the two opposide side walls, which reduce the walls into much smaller sections of useable space, decreasing their potential.

Illustration 2 shows a standard 6-foot closet laid out in a traditional way, meaning the rod is attached to each side wall. These side walls average 24 inches deep and even though the rod is commonly positioned 10 to 12 inches from the back wall for adequate clearance, the clothes often brush against the front or back wall or both.

Illustration 3 portrays the identical closet, except the rods are attached to the front and back walls, which reduces hanging space but nearly doubles the shelf space. This illustrates why we need to be able to recognize our specific needs (based on the characteristics of our belongings) to decide whether shelf space or hanging space is more

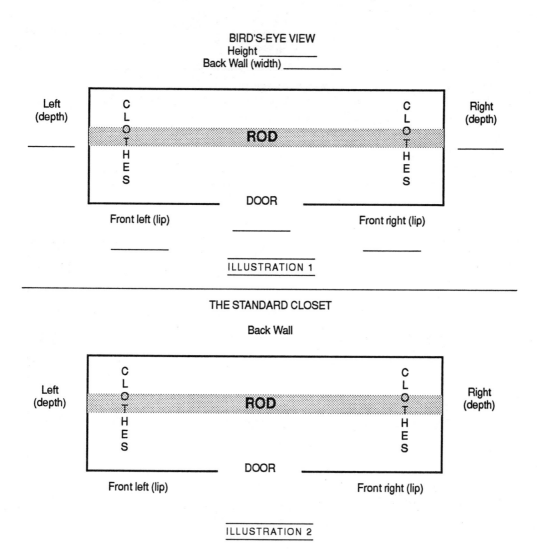

BIRD'S-EYE VIEW
Height _____
Back Wall (width) _____

ILLUSTRATION 1

THE STANDARD CLOSET

ILLUSTRATION 2

beneficial. Only then can we design the closet.

Two major points are demonstrated by this comparison. First, deviating from the norm is encouraged, and second, by engaging in this practice we develop a feel for the better possibilities, which oftentimes are not the more conservative and traditional approaches.

Illustration 4 shows typical walk-in closets, which always place the rods and shelves on the largest uninterrupted walls. The wall containing the door is never utilized, yet using it can substantially increase the closet's capacity.

Illustration 5 shows a walk-in closet that uses the space near the doors.. Shelves

THE STANDARD CLOSET
Back Wall

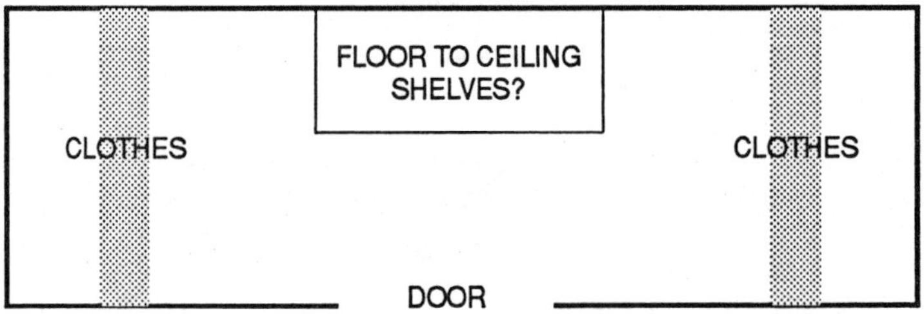

```
        ┌─────────────────────────────────────────────┐
        │       ▓       ┌──────────────────┐    ▓      │
        │       ▓       │ FLOOR TO CEILING │    ▓      │
        │       ▓       │     SHELVES?     │    ▓      │
        │   CLOTHES     └──────────────────┘  CLOTHES  │
        │       ▓                              ▓      │
        │       ▓                              ▓      │
        └───────────────────  DOOR  ──────────────────┘
```

ILLUSTRATION 3

MEASUREMENTS
THE WALK-IN CLOSET

Height   _____

Back Wall _____

Left Wall _____

Right Wall _____

Left Lip _____

Right Lip _____

Door _____

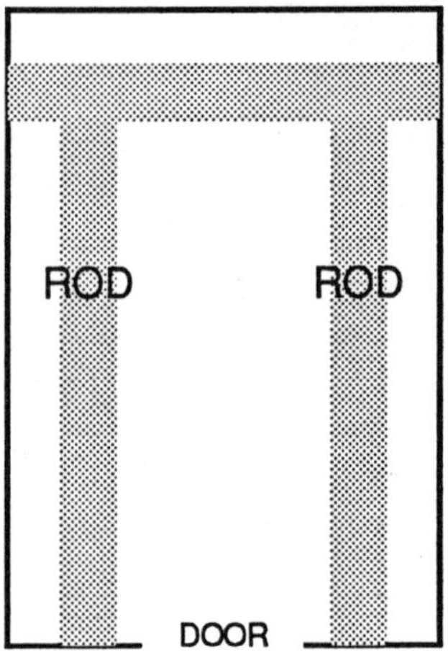

ROD   ROD

DOOR

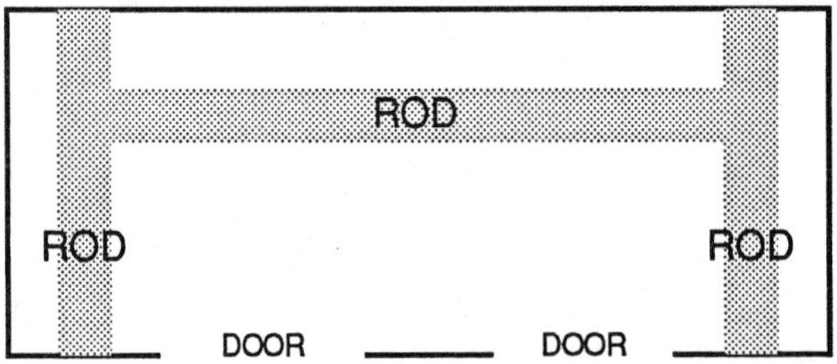

ROD

ROD   ROD

DOOR   DOOR

ILLUSTRATION 4

were installed floor-to-ceiling on the wall between the two door openings, providing an additional twenty feet of storage space.

Illustration 6 shows the same closet with two rods instead of the shelves.

Illustration 7 shows the same closet with only one rod.

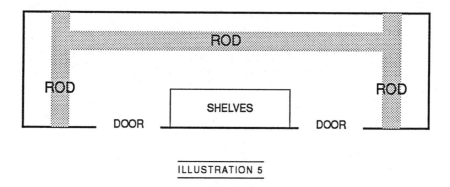

ILLUSTRATION 5

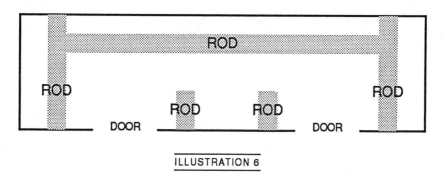

ILLUSTRATION 6

While the bird's-eye view heightened our awareness of the closet by presenting essential elements we need to know in order to place objects in the closet, the dead-ahead view (illustration 8) is an accurate rendition of the perspective we see every day, minus of course, the personal appointments and tasteful touches we've lavishly added to the interior of our own closet.

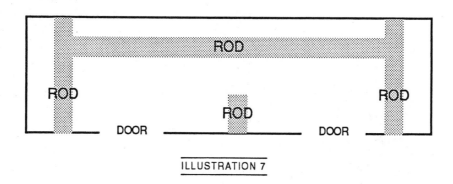

ILLUSTRATION 7

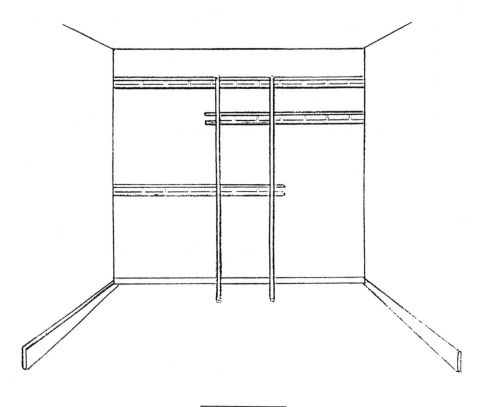

ILLUSTRATION 8

This looks like the kind of promotional literature we receive in the mail advertising well-known closet or shelving companies, and it inspires us to believe we can achieve the same clean and inviting closet. It lacks however a very valuable piece of information: it doesn't explain *how* to fill the spaces with our belongings. Obviously, our problem isn't that we can't fill the space (we've done that all too well), but rather *how* to fit our belongings into the space effectively, efficiently, and in an orderly manner.

How do we measure odd-ball closets with sloped ceilings, curved corners, and off-beat walls? These guidelines will make the measuring of those wretched walls much easier.

1. Stand at the door opening. Whatever is seen straight ahead is the back wall.

2. Look to your left. That is the left side (depth).

3. On your right is the right side (depth), and so on.

Getting the height of an odd closet can be confusing, since ceilings slant into or away from the walls. Walls that peak, point, or curve at their ceiling juncture can be best approached by using the dotted-line method for measuring successive increments. See illustrations 9, 10, and 11.

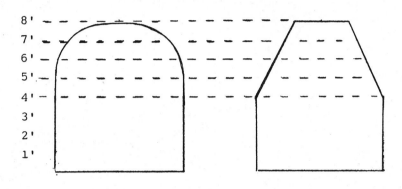

ILLUSTRATION 9

The dotted lines not only help us get the exact measurements, but they also help to transpose the precise shape onto our graph paper. Grossly disproportioned walls may need 6-inch increments rather than 12-inch increments as our eye and yardstick travel up the complete height of the wall.

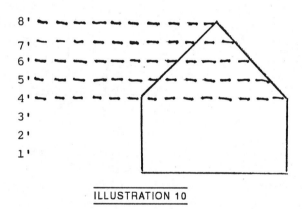

ILLUSTRATION 10

A perfectly square or a perfectly rectangular closet is not a prerequisite for serviceability, which is good news when we're stuck with triangular or odd-ball walls. Forethought and careful planning are critical, but the results are oftentimes astonishingly functional. See illustrations 12 and 13.

Needless to say, the odd closet carries with it the distinction of being the exception to the rule, since it follows no pattern for either lengthier side walls or a shorter back wall, nor does it even have the same height throughout.

What is suitably assigned to a low wall (18 inches to 44 inches high), and what benefits can be had from a ceiling that's nine feet tall?

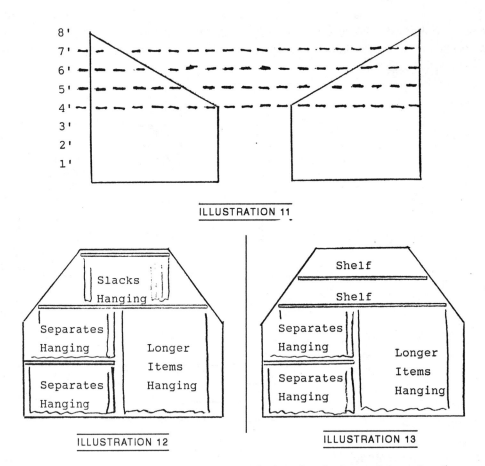

ILLUSTRATION 11

ILLUSTRATION 12

ILLUSTRATION 13

Using a process of elimination is essential when developing and assessing the potential of an odd closet. Accessories, sweaters, or shoes belong on the low walls either on shelves we install or on specialty racks for ties/belts. The longer items like dresses, robes, or coats need to be hung from rods running along the tallest wall in the closet.

Odd closets offer an advantage in that they set limitations, making it easier to assign possessions because we have less choice. A regular closet is open to all suggestions, which can sometimes cause us to act impulsively, thereby defeating our intention to evaluate our situation step by step.

Illustration 14 shows possibilities for designing an odd closet.

How the blankity-blank-blank are rods and shelves supposed to be installed on a curved wall? How can a rod or a shelf be installed when there aren't two parallel side walls to attach it to?

Sounds insurmountable, yet a little effort spent in investigating products and hardware may just resolve the difficulties, or consider improvising to custom-fit the

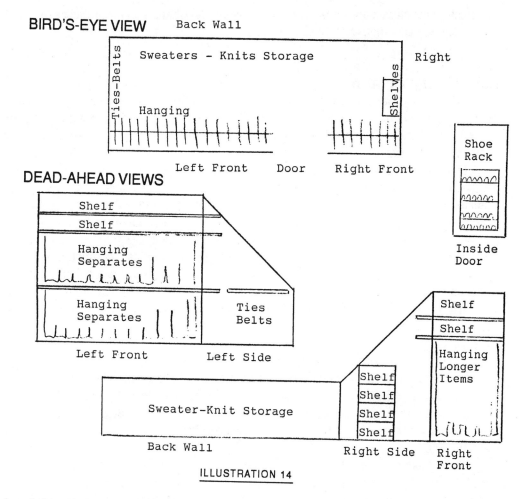

BIRD'S-EYE VIEW

Back Wall

Ties-Belts

Sweaters - Knits Storage

Right

Shelves

Hanging

Left Front   Door   Right Front

DEAD-AHEAD VIEWS

Shelf

Shelf

Hanging
Separates

Hanging
Separates

Ties
Belts

Left Front   Left Side

Shoe
Rack

Inside
Door

Shelf

Shelf

Hanging
Longer
Items

Sweater-Knit Storage

Shelf

Shelf

Shelf

Shelf

Back Wall

Right Side

Right
Front

ILLUSTRATION 14

closet's less-than-perfect offerings.

Adhering to only one closet material, be it a ventilated system or wood could undermine the project since sticking with one system seldom meets all of the closet's demands.

When there isn't a flat level wall, ventilated systems are useless, and regular rods will have to do. When there aren't two opposite walls for a rod to be installed, ventilated systems will stand free without a wall. Ventilated systems function as a shelf and rod united in one struc-

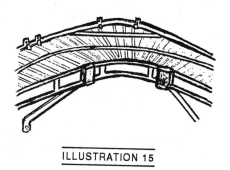

ILLUSTRATION 15

tured unit. This curved corner piece either butts into adjoining ventilated pieces or it can stand alone in the corner. (See illustration 15.)

How to Compare Costs

Want to know what it's going to cost? Cost depends not only on the closet components and products selected but also on the amount of personal participation you're willing to give the project. Certainly the estimated cost, whether it's manual labor or cash, is a major component to consider.

First, we'll look at the economical route in which we salvage as much of the existing hardware and rods as we can. Although brand new shelves and rods update the closet's appearance, they don't make the closet organized. It's our planning of their arrangement that actually organizes the closet. We have the freedom to specify the amount of shelf space we want the closet to have as well as regulate the size and shape of the hanging space we want.

This option requires that we carefully scrutinize our old closet components, and if anything sags, bends, swags, dips, or is beyond repair, toss it. Make a detailed list of the pieces and parts that were saved and a shopping list of the dilapidated items to be replaced.

After reviewing the parts and pieces of our closet, we may be compelled out of curiosity to visit the nearest hardware, lumber, or custom closet company to secure their price lists.

At the store will be a vast array of either ventilated shelf/rod, laminated modular systems or the standard wooden shelves and metal closet rods, depending on the store's area of expertise. Take the time to ask questions about each mode and examine the quality and qualifications of each, so that you feel qualified to make an educated choice. They are each distinctly different and, therefore, the decision is based solely on personal judgment and preference.

The upcoming illustrations and explanations are helpful for the home shopper who views the merchandise on TV, reads consumer reports, or bones up at the bookstore or library. Gather together the pertinent facts before 1) making a final decision, 2) making a phone call to have it delivered, or 3) begrudgingly going to the store to see it face-to-face.

The costs not only vary because of the different qualities of the materials themselves, but also because some materials require extra vertical support walls, which means additional materials must be purchased, inflating the overall cost of the project. Illustration 17 depicts the following:

> SEPARATE SHELF/SEPARATE ROD SYSTEM—furnished one rod and two shelves.

> MODULAR SYSTEM—allowed three rods and two shelves, but an extra vertical wall had to constructed

As an exercise in placement, mentally picture your belongings in each closet; add, subtract, shorten, lengthen, or embellish each specific aspect as needed.

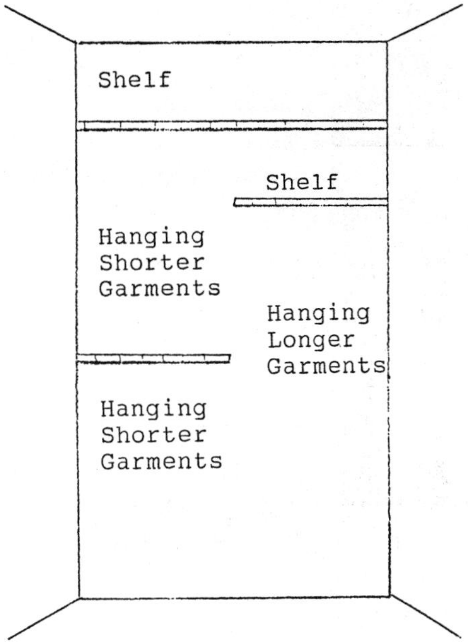

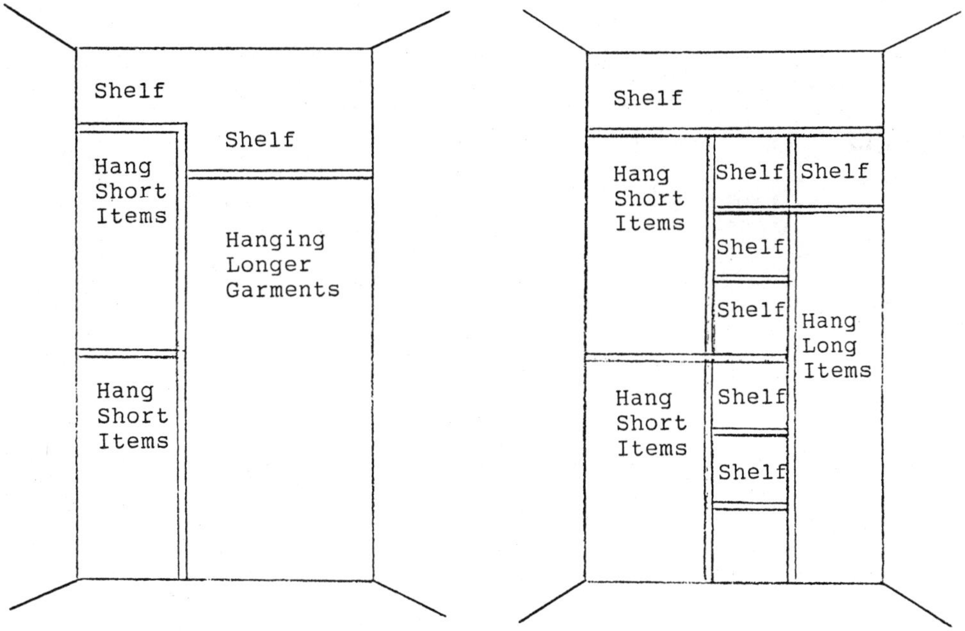

Shelf

Shelf

Hanging
Shorter
Garments

Hanging
Longer
Garments

Hanging
Shorter
Garments

Shelf

Shelf

Hang
Short
Items

Hanging
Longer
Garments

Hang
Short
Items

Shelf

Shelf

Hang
Short
Items

Shelf

Shelf

Shelf

Shelf

Hang
Long
Items

Hang
Short
Items

Shelf

Shelf

ILLUSTRATION 16

21

COSTS

These costs are based on a standard-sized closet with a width of between 4 feet and 5 feet.

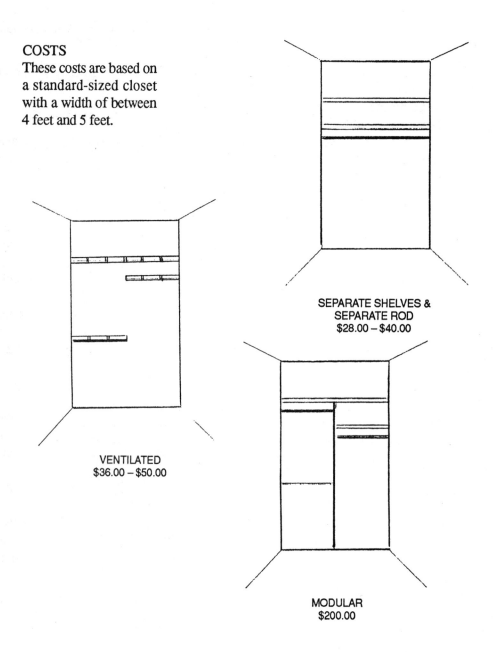

SEPARATE SHELVES &
SEPARATE ROD
$28.00 – $40.00

VENTILATED
$36.00 – $50.00

MODULAR
$200.00

ILLUSTRATION 17

VENTILATED SHELF/ROD SYSTEM—yielded three of each because it's able to "free-stand" anywhere.

Perhaps a clearer definition of the three main systems is necessary at this point, since you may not have the slightest knowledge of them.

Separate shelf/separate rod system

These are the old-fashioned wooden or metal shelves and rods found in a typical closet. The price depends on the quality of the wood, but this system generally costs more than a ventilated system and less than a modular system.

Modular system

These are presized cubicles that sit in the closet, dividing the space into preconceived sizes the manufacturer thought we ought to have. They are usually of particle board that's laminated with a white, beige, or simulated wood. For the true connoisseur, solid wood ones will quadruple the already exorbitant price on these units, which are usually purchased separately, since few of us could afford to buy all of them at the same time. To use these in a walk-in closet would cost a small fortune so its feasibility is usually limited to a smaller standard closet. And because these units are perfectly square or rectangular, they seldom suit the unnatural terrain of odd closets, even though they are the most attractive system of all.

Ventilated shelf/rod system

A ventilated system costs approximately one–third less than a laminated modular system, and it is more versatile, adaptable, adjustable, and requires the least amount of space. This is primarily due to the fact that ventilated systems combine both the shelf and the rod together in one compact unit.

Having a generalized overview of the components, in particular their effect on the cost to renovate the closet, is a worthwhile revelation. However this knowledge doesn't supply enough information about each system's abilities and capabilities, both positive and negative, so that a final decision can be made. To that end, each of the options are evaluated and explained in greater detail in the next section, giving us the insight to competently and consciously choose our closet's future appearance.

How to Select a System

The inquisitive types want to know everything there is to know on a given subject so as to be absolutely certain they've made the smartest selection and also so they can pat themselves on the back when the finished product is revealed to the world in all its splendor—a job well done, well researched, and well received.

The advantage gained by using a ventilated shelf/rod system in the closet is its all-in-one serviceability. It is constructed from metal rods, layered with a vinyl or epoxied chip-resistant coating. Its overhanging lip forms an edge on the front that is used as the closet rod for hanging clothes. By combining both functions, a mere 2 inches of closet space is needed, whereas both the other methods need a minimum of four inches to do the same job. (See illustration 18.)

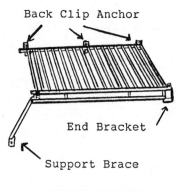

ILLUSTRATION 18

The modular system in illustration 19 looks great, doesn't it? But looks can be deceiving, especially when we are more concerned with conserving closet space than we are with creating a showpiece.

Illustration 19 exemplifies the wasted space between the shelf and the closet rod below it. The three inches that are squandered may seem insignificant, but they could be vital in a critical design situation, when one more inch would allow the creation of a masterpiece. Double-rodding loses six inches—enough to hold an extra shelf.

Here's how the six-inch figure was derived.

A wooden shelf is ¾ to 1-inch thick; add to that the two inches of open space that's needed for the hanger to clear the rod, and then add the diameter of the rod itself, which is ordinarily two inches. We must therefore have on hand five inches to install a separate shelf and separate rod system in a closet.

Subtract the two inches we needed for the ventilated shelf/ rod

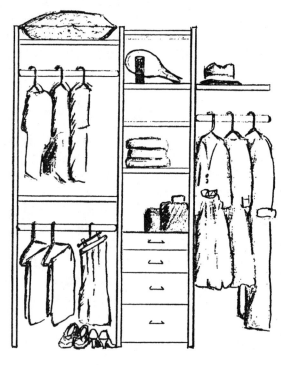

ILLUSTRATION 19

system and there's the big, big, big three-inch difference.

When ventilated systems arrived on the scene and we discovered their beneficial differences, we had for the first time a choice. Unexpectedly and unexplainably, the manufacturers of ventilated systems began marketing a product that took the advantages away again. (See illustration 20.) Ventilated systems vary in strength and durability, as does the hardware for installing it. As a rule of thumb, the larger the rod's diameter inside the protective coating, the stronger the product.

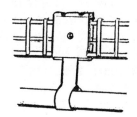

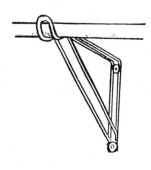

The hardware shown in illustration 21 is not drawn to scale; it is simply a representation of the various kinds available. The pieces that are preloaded with the screws and anchor plugs are more reliable than those without (and they eliminate the necessity to supply our own).

One reason for the popularity of ventilated systems is their ability to freely stand without support walls on either side; however they are disfavored because of the intersecting struts that are built in every 12 inches along the front edge.

It is sometimes said that these struts inhibit the hanger's movements on the rod; yet when a closet is properly organized, there should be no reason to push clothes from one end of the rod to the other.

ILLUSTRATION 20

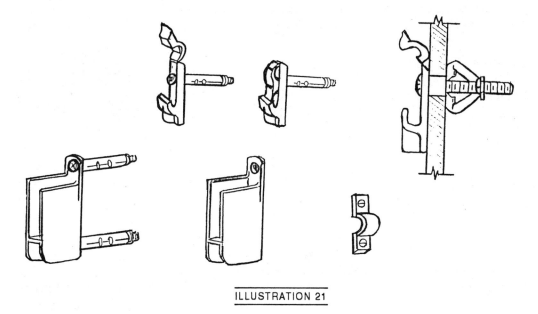

ILLUSTRATION 21

The support braces installed on the wall are attached to the lip every 12 inches as well and they could cause stop-gaps. View A in illustration 22 shows a brace that wraps itself around the entire front edge, while View B shows an improved version that touches only the top of the front edge of the strut, thereby allowing the hangers to freely slide below.

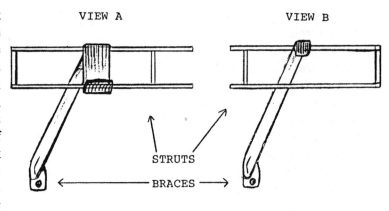

ILLUSTRATION 22

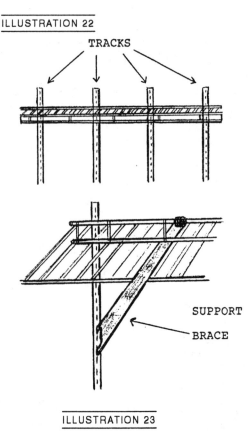

ILLUSTRATION 23

The newest feature available in the ventilated line is a track system which allows adjustable shelf heights. This is often advantageous when switching garments from one closet to another or for the fluctuations experienced with growing children.

The manufacturers of ventilated systems also offer a pole system, which uses supporting vertical shafts as dividers, much as the modular units incorporate an extra supporting wall to split the space for specifically defined functions. The poles usually run floor-to-ceiling, although some systems stop short of that height. (See illustration 23.)

The poles are meant to strengthen the unit by giving it more support than the brackets or braces alone can provide, and they also allow the manufacturers to promote accessories, like wire baskets, shoe racks, and tie/belt racks that are cleverly attached at various locations up and down the poles.

Last of all in the production of ventilated closet compatibles are the prepackaged kits, known as instant closets, which are simply assembled in any large and open area of the house and then through a series of manipulations and maneuvers inserted into the closet. As a free-standing unit, instant closets require little if any installation, but assembly is labor intensive.

Some versions of the instant closet are not freestanding. It is partially preassembled prior to insertion into the closet, but once there, holes are drilled and screws are tightened to secure the unit to the wall. Either of the styles will usually use a tension pole for front-end support, pictured in illustration 24, and they usually, but not always, include a free instruction manual.

Notice in illustra-

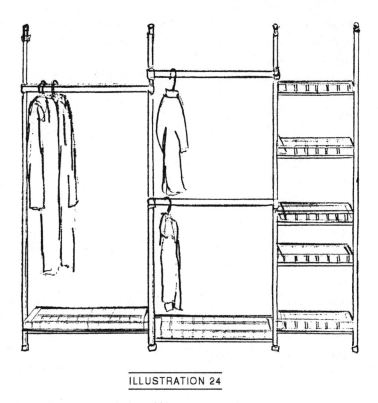

ILLUSTRATION 24

tion 24 the huge amount of space that has been sacrificed between the shelves and pull-out wire baskets on the right side of the unit.

What do you have in your closet that could possibly require that much height?

Would you stack your folded sweaters that high, just to occupy the space and if you did, how long would they stay in that stack before they came tumbling down around your ears?

The instant closet or prefab kit offers such a limited choice of configurations that our choices are correspondingly and instantly limited as well, especially when our belongings don't fit the manufacturers. Instant closets seldom accomodate our own unique and individual specifications. If we opt for this seemingly easy way out, we'll soon rue the day once it sinks in that we let some complete stranger prescribe the amount of space that will be allotted to our belongings as well as where they will be positioned within the closet.

An instant closet is an inferior substitute for a modular system. Although the kits are economically more feasible, they are prohibitive because of their preconceived shapes and sizes.

How to Count Clothes

The last of the closet components are the clothes and accessories we've been shuffling around for eons, a constant source of irritation and frustration. As a component, they must be dealt with on three levels.

They are the culprits that create the chaos. They are a time-consuming and energy-eating nuisance to maintain, and whatever remedy is finally used to cure their ills should have long lasting effects, so that the benefits are felt long after the initial project is completed.

The first move toward resolving these issues is a real eye-opener, since most people are unaware of just how much they've managed to accumulate in their closet when most of it's hidden and lost somewhere within.

They think they own about eight pairs of slacks, but after spending the day in the closet trying to find them all, they will eventually emerge with twice that number. Try it yourself. Imagine, without looking, how many pants are in your closet. On your next day off, count them and compare the number with your original estimate.

No further explanation is required as to why we are going to physically count all of our articles of clothing.

Notice, not a word was written about all those other extra special treasures we've been sheltering in our closet, like gardening tools, used shopping bags, broken clocks and telephones, window shades, wrapping paper, and paperback books. That's because they don't belong in the clothes closet. They'll have to find a warm and loving home somewhere else in the house.

Eliminate those wayward items from the closet. And weed through the clothes themselves to distinguish between the rejects and the wearables. Suitable places for the items that are barred from the closet are briefly mentioned in this section, but detailed accounts are forthcoming in later chapters, based on the description and category of the merchandise we've reluctantly removed.

The number one, irrefutable, basic law of closet space is that hanging space is the most valuable resource in the closet; therefore it must be protected at all costs. Since it is in such short supply and because the majority of our garments are meant to be hung from a hanger, there is little room for argument as to why it's been placed on the list of endangered species.

Numerous chapters are devoted to organizing the accessories contained in our closet. Until those chapters are read, suffice it to say that accessories are never, ever hung from the closet rod. Period.

This section deals strictly and matter-of-factly with the hanging garments. The questions that must be asked are whether all of our clothes are currently present and accounted for in the main clothes closet, or are they scattered about in every closet, on every drainpipe, and on every doorjamb upstairs and downstairs throughout the entire house? Are the clothes that are in the main clothes closet worthy of it's space, or should they be consigned elsewhere because of their unworthiness to occupy our primary clothes closet?

These may appear to be paradoxical points, but they are sensible questions that need a logical response, since they are basically implying that on one hand, we're going to remove some things from the closet, while on the other hand, we're going to add something else.

Remove everything that isn't essential to daily survival. Sort through these discarded articles, place them in groups of similar items and determine where each group might best be stored. For instance, an umbrella in a coat closet or near the door where we enter and exit makes far more sense than keeping it in the closet in the bedroom, which just happens to be located the farthest distance from the doors. Our books are readily at hand in a nightstand or under the bed or near the recliner, if that's where we frequently read, but reading in the closet is indefensible, since the quality of the light there is bound to impair our vision. Perhaps the most sensible spot in the whole house for our reading material, however, is in a bookcase along with all our other books, unless the majority of reading in your house is done in the bathroom.

The point being made is simply that by appointing each group of items to one and only one convenient location, we'll save time, energy, and frustration, especially when we go looking for something.

Gather together the seasonal and scattered clothes from around the house and incorporate them into the existing wardrobe, but make sure to include them on the inventory you've been so diligently compiling.

With the closet redesigned for increased capacity, it can receive these additions. So for the very first time in recorded history, you can look inside the closet and review your entire wardrobe at a glance.

This puts a stop to seasonal exchanges and transfers and questions like: Is this autumn apparel? Should it stay? Is it spring apparel? Take it out? With clothing more accessible, it actually gets worn more often rather than lingering in our minds as a lovely garment that would have been just perfect for today's unseasonable warmth, but oops, it's somewhere in a trunk in either the basement or attic and you can't quite remember which or where.

With the cost of a wardrobe nowadays, wardrobes should be able to take care of themselves.

The all-in-one-closet concept might be discomforting to those clothes freaks who have three closets at their disposal, but if they have three, they probably aren't feeling the pinch quite as much as those of us with only one closet and the same scandalous volume of clothes. The one-closet combatant has no choice but to establish priorities and to set limits on what specific articles will occupy the closet space. By complying with this practice, the closet will contain only the best of the possessions and only the particular items that are worn routinely (not ones that are worn once every couple of years).

While contemplating the destination of the clothes, figuring out whether they belong in the elsewhere bin, the closet bin, or the rubbish pile, many of the garments will be automatically understood and quickly dealt with, while others are less easily pigeonholed.

Many of our garments will likely fall under the miscellaneous classification. These items are the ones that are difficult to properly place.

How should we classify leotards, workout garments, tights, tennis shorts, jogging shorts, walking shorts, leg warmers, shawls, knit scarves, lingerie, unmentionables, socks, undies, visors, jock straps, sunglasses, driving gloves, camera equipment, and the rest of the almost endless list of closet paraphernalia?

This list may repeat many of the items on your original list of items in the closet, but the items on the first list were immediately recognizable as clutter, whereas this list states quite a number of valuable and useful objects that aren't as easily brushed aside, nor are they as easily removed from the closet. The same applies to the clothing articles on this list, since they oftentimes are stored in the closet with our everyday street clothes because we wear many of them everyday as well.

These items do however deserve consideration, and decisions as to their placement must be made, even though the task isn't simple.

To make this process palatable, base your choices on this premise. If it's paramount to daily survival, then it's given priority clearance and it goes in the closet. If it's worn, used, or surveyed fairly regularly, it goes in the closet. Each of these closet items must now be itemized, categorized, inventoried, and assigned a place on the closet's design that's slowly developing.

Those items that aren't used enough must be categorized as well and assigned to a place somewhere else in the house.

We've been devising our definitive inventory step-by-step so that we can begin visualizing those items in the closet in order to calculate their space requirements, but now it's time to face a few facts, often unpleasant and certainly unacknowledged and unknown, that will greatly influence the shape of things to come.

These facts pertain to a person's proportions, since our general shape and size is rarely described as pee-wee or petite. Smaller, shorter people because of their miniature garments and accessories gain a distinct advantage that permits and approves extensity and originality in their closet design, whereas taller, wider folks forfeit creativity because the mere size of their clothes puts some of the planning process beyond their control.

There are some very important points of reference that lie hidden and unacknowledged within average-sized people and their average, run-of-the-mill clothes. The first important question is, obviously, what's average and how much space does it take? To determine this, garments are measured for their length. The correct way to do this is to place the 0 of the tape measure at the top of the closet rod, extend it down to the bottom edge of the garment. That number is the exact one you'll use for calculating the closet design. To satisfy your curiosity, here are the average lengths of the kinds of clothes we commonly put on our bodies, when current fashion isn't dictating mini, mid-calf, tea-length, butt-level, or sailor-style styles.

MEN'S SUITS AND SPORTSCOATS: 40–42"

MEN'S SHIRTS: 39"

MEN'S OR WOMEN'S SLACKS: Folded over the hanger, 29"

MEN'S OR WOMEN'S SLACKS: Perpendicular/lengthwise, 46"

WOMEN'S BLOUSES: 30–34"

WOMEN'S SUIT SKIRTS: 34"

WOMEN'S BLAZERS OR JACKETS: 32–34"

DRESSES: 50"

Oddball and faddish fashions with extremely short or long tails, are the exceptions to the rule and as such cast no vote in majority decisions which affect the whole.

There are quite a number of unknown and unusual factors that you should be aware of, since they too affect the inventory as well as how the inventory affects design possibilities. As you may have noticed in the list of average lengths, a choice was presented for how to hang slacks. If your particular preference was perpendicular, go back to this list and take a good, hard look at the extra inches you'll use. Then weigh the unnecessary expenditure of space against the strength of your desire to hang slacks lengthwise.

To put this loss of space in perspective, the lengthwise mode totally eliminates the ability to double-rod that area of the closet. In reality it isn't merely indulging a whim at the expense of a marginal amount of inches. It's undermining the objective. The clothes that are crowded and crammed on the rod no longer have a means of escape, since the second rod they could have had is nonexistent.

Another area of interest is that in taking the measurement for the length of the garment, it's important to realize that there are different kinds of hangers. Each different style of hanger produces a different length. This is discussed in detail in the hangers chapter, yet it needed to be mentioned here and now, before the actual measuring begins. You'd hate to have to go back and remeasure after discovering you wanted something other than a wire hanger in your closet.

An inventory chart is provided next, although one restriction applies: suits are for men; women should count their jackets and skirts as separates.

INVENTORY CHART

	FEMALE			MALE
BELTS	_____			_____
BLAZERS/JACKETS	_____	___ in	___ in	_____
BLOUSES/SHIRTS	_____	___ in	___ in	_____
BOOTS (TALL)	_____	___ in	___ in	_____
BOOTS (SHORT)	_____	___ in		_____
DRESSES (FORMAL)	_____	___ in		_____
DRESSES (STREET)	_____	___ in		_____
HATS/VISORS	_____			_____
JOGGING/SWEATS	_____			_____
JUMPSUITS	_____	___ in		_____
PURSES	_____			_____
ROBES (NIGHTIES)	_____	___ in	___ in	_____
SHOES	_____			_____
SKIRTS	_____	___ in		_____
SLACKS	_____	___ in	___ in	_____
SUITS	_____		___ in	_____
TIES/SCARVES	_____			_____
SUPER BULKY SWEATERS	_____			_____
REG. BULK SWEATERS	_____			_____
T-SHIRTS (Polos, Turtles)	_____			_____

CHAPTER TWO

THE CLOTHES CLOSET

PRINCIPLES

✔ How to Recognize the Realities

✔ How to Plan Placement

✔ How to Spend Less Money, Time, and Tantrums

How to Recognize the Realities

The Jigsaw Puzzle Effect as it relates to the organization of closet space is explained as follows:

Once a single category is assigned its place in the closet, the remaining categories are forced in certain directions. When the second category is positioned, those that remain follow the course that has been established. Sequentially, as each category is assigned, there are fewer places remaining for assigning the remaining categories. The goal then for this procedure is to focus on each individual category, placing it in the most effective area possible without forfeiting the overall objective of having the entire closet as organized as possible.

Each piece of the puzzle is important. It is vital that it be joined correctly with the other pieces of the puzzle to complete the picture. The picture couldn't stand complete and whole without the contribution of each individual piece.

The individual pieces we'll initially discuss are fundamentals that enhance the closet's ability to function smoothly by putting everything within easy reach.

The first piece of the puzzle is so elementary, we'll wonder why we didn't think of it ourselves.

The result of not having thought of this sensible little convenience is that the top shelf of our closet becomes the world's largest lost-and-found depository. Since we can't reach it we find ourselves consistently and constantly using it for "pitching" practice.

With the top shelf being a perfectly practical and centrally located area of extensive potential, it's a shame we've willfully drummed it out of business and misused its vast resources without reaping any rewards whatsoever.

By simply putting a step stool in or near the closet, we're back in business.

Selecting the appropriate stool might be riskier than cleaning off the shelf, since we've never done either of them before. Small closets can't accomodate large stools, unless they're collapsible. But if we add an extra activity to our daily routine we guarantee that we'll soon "pitch" again. The molded stool (illustration 25), gives the best all-around

ILLUSTRATION 25   ILLUSTRATION 26

serviceability. The larger stools, folding or not, should remain open at all times when they're in a larger closet. Draw the chosen stool on the design and view it as a permanent closet fixture.

This hassock stool (illustration 26) with removeable lid, supplies it s own built-in storage. Toy stores offer a variety of small molded chairs and stools that adapt wonderfully to closets. A ladder-chair, better known as a bachelor's chair, swiftly converts from seating to stepping, but it would naturally find little room in a closet the size of a double bed.

The top shelf is awesome, and awful, due to its height. It's the shelf's height that caused us to pitch, thereby wasting its functionability, but we also waste space by positioning the shelves inappropriately.

Illustration 27 shows a huge area of empty wall above the shelf, which is typical of most closets. It forces us to build stacks and mounds as we attempt to utilize the excessive height.

Illustration 28 overcorrects the wrong by adding more than was necessary, but the idea comes across loud and clear.

In this case, the original shelf was lowered, which automatically prohibits double-rodding. Also stacking is nearly impossible now, since the height between the shelves is reduced to admitting only single-layer storage.

We also waste the space below our hanging garments. In illustration 29, the top shelves were raised even higher,

ILLUSTRATION 27

ILLUSTRATION 28

which allows the installation of extra shelves at a lower level (or the space could be double-rodded).

This was an exercise in realizing how we inadvertently and unintentionally mismanage our closet space. Resolving our space problems involves nothing more difficult than simply dividing the space differently, so that the sections we create correspond to our needs for hanging space or shelf space.

Divide space into smaller compartments, making sure the items in each compartment are similar in size; otherwise we're facing our old enemy wasted space, which is vividly demonstrated in illustration 30.

Compare this modular unit with its twin (illustration 31) to see how easy it is to nearly double the capacity without squandering a square inch of space.

When the capabilities of this unit were increased by simply inserting shelves between the original ones, the unit's length, depth and height didn't need to be increased even a fraction of an inch to neatly handle double the number of belongings.

ILLUSTRATION 29

How to Plan Placement

Assigned placement is simply a shorter way of saying, "a place for everything and everything in its place." It's extremely irritating when we come to a screeching halt, with some object or another clasped tightly to our chest, muttering and mumbling to ourselves, "Where in the world am I going to put this?" Or we've hesitated halfway up the stairs, trying to remember if we really left it upstairs last time we used it or was it dropped off downstairs instead.

ILLUSTRATION 30

We're victims of the random placement syndrome, meaning we've never taken the time to think about putting a certain category in a certain place. This disheveled level of living isn't really living at all, since it not only affects our possessions and our home, but it causes major flares of temper and discontent with ourselves, our home, and our lifestyle.

This principle might better be called the "permanent home" principle. We shouldn't enter any home, most especially our own, without first seeing that these corrections, alterations, and adjustments have been properly attended to. The end result is twofold: the systematic elimination of clutter and mastering our destiny.

In finding permanent places for our belongings, certain gray areas defy description and therefore undermine our ability to properly classify. These belongings are usually secreted away in bags, boxes, trunks, and in the corners hither and yon. In all likelihood, they'll never again see the light of day.

ILLUSTRATION 31

Even though you intended to eventually dig them out for the following reasons— 1) I'll wear it after I've lost weight, 2) I'll get it to the Salvation Army as soon as I can, 3) I'll keep this because it's a classic that'll be back in style someday, or 4) there'll be another garage sale next year— you never do retrieve them.

Seriously consider establishing a recycling center, giving a home to these reprobates and getting them out of the way. Assign them to a place that's located as near as possible to the car, van, boat, airplane, or bicycle, making it possible to haul them away quickly, conveniently, and forever.

Maximized space is a principle that polishes and fine-tunes the Jigsaw Puzzle Effect. To master maximized space management, a few fundamental points need to be presented. These separate entities work in unison to achieve an arrangement that functions best in the least amount of space.

A lot of "mental" movement will occur as the pieces of the puzzle are placed and then replaced and then fitted somewhere else again. Planning these moves on paper is physically and mentally less tiresome than manual labor.

Each category can be handled in a variety of ways: hung, stacked, shelved, boxed, rolled, nailed, hooked, displayed, concealed, abandoned, removed, or thrown away! Some of these methods are uncompromising and demand large areas, but the value is in deciding which categories deserve it and which categories should be cut down to size.

Unless you're unusually perceptive and can automatically calculate the areas of space occupied by each category in different storage modes, then the process begins with measuring each method. If it's too difficult to visualize each of the alternative designs, make it real by drawing it to scale on graph paper.

For instance, let's suppose you're partial to the idea of storing your twenty-one pairs of shoes in boxes on the shelf, which means they occupy forty-two inches of horizontal shelf space. What if I told you that you could put a shoe rack on the door, store all 21 pairs of shoes there, and still be left with every inch of your original shelf. And since the door was probably either empty or misused, the closet area itself is the same as it was before you started (except it's really more, because the shoes won't enter it anymore).

This example exemplifies effective space utilization, and it depicted an extremely impressive situation, because it's nearly impossible to maintain this high level of efficiency for every single category "as it finds its place in the closet."

"As it finds its place in the closet" is a key statement that should be investigated further. Each move we make with one kind of item limits the space that's left for another. When we place this second category, there's even less space for the third category, and so on and so on.

Maximized space then, is the process of combining all the categories as effectively as possible while striving to achieve the best we can for each one individually.

In reading the upcoming chapters that detail the various methods and products for storing the specific categories, keep an open mind. People have a tendency to wear blinders, hating to relinquish their habitual way of doing things because any change makes them uncomfortable.

Category has been used repeatedly, and illustration 32 puts the common closet categories in plain view.

Converting the closet to this system conserves so much time and energy, our fingers do the walking through each small section instead of galloping through the whole closet, examining it from end-to-end and top-to-bottom in order to lay our hands on whatever it was we wanted.

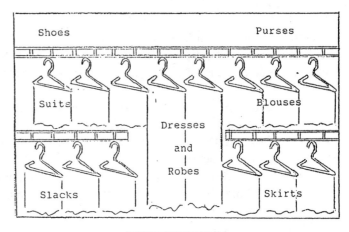

ILLUSTRATION 32

The one and only absolute and nonnegotiable trait in organizing closets is that clothes that have to hang, have to hang. There isn't an alternative method. The first, foremost, and primary objective then, is allotting a sufficient supply of rod space. After that obligation has been met, we can begin to consider the demands of the clothes that don't need to hang.

Most closet rods are jammed and crammed and there's little reason applied to the clothes that hang there. If this is a fair and accurate portrayal of your closet rod, open it up, give it visibility and accessibility, and put your clothes in their rightful place by putting them in categories.

What if you don't know what you want to wear and you're not looking forward to pulling out a separate here and a separate there in a vain attempt to coordinate an outfit. Why don't you choose whatever strikes your fancy first and hold it against the category that contains its coordinating opposite and see the possibilities for mixing, matching, or blending as if by magic. After deciding on the two pieces, you opt for a third piece for the outfit, too. Simply hold both selections near the appropriate corresponding category and make your final choice.

Categorizing highlights your clothing and increases their potential wearability because they aren't hidden, but more importantly because different combinations become

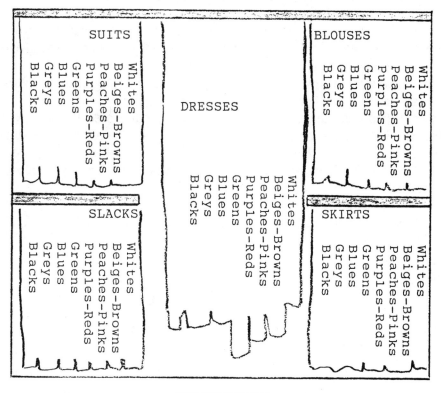

ILLUSTRATION 33

apparent. The procedure outlined is probably extreme, since clothes that hang in an arrangement of tops on a top rod and bottoms on a bottom rod, as shown previously, let your eyes roam the full expanse of the closet to automatically focus on perfect prospects.

Clothing is easier to find now that it's being cared for by category, but believe it or not, this method can still be improved upon. Each category is broken down into color and that makes the clothing even more distinguishable and that means it's even easier to find the one and only garment you wish to wear. See illustration 33.

A fairly complete range of colors is shown, although your personal preferences will shift proportions into one color spectrum or another more heavily.

Starting with white on the right and ending with black on the left, the in-between colors are arrayed by their intensity. The lightest-hue progresses to gradually darker tints as they are placed from right to left. Due to the fact that navy blue and black are often mistaken, gray is the color next to black in the sequence.

The obvious advantage to color-ranging is that you see at a glance all of your belongings. For the first time in your life, you can say with conviction that you do indeed know just what your closet contains. To add to the already delightful aspects of this system, the maintenance is so easy you can practically do it in the dark, especially after it becomes habit-forming and customary to replace items in their designated category and within their proper color range. Getting your hands on any given item at any given moment is a dream come true in organizing.

As if those weren't enough good reasons to incorporate categories and colors into the closet system, let's try a few more for added incentive.

It's a help to also hang tops above bottoms, but in either case, the newly created visibility puts the spotlight on versatility, so that even though you're seeing the same old garments, it's almost as though you're seeing them for the first time because your perspective is better. It furnishes an opportunity to try combinations that you never before even contemplated.

When shoes are stored in boxes on a shelf, the coloring process could be implemented either vertically or horizontally. Illustration 34 depicts the colors in a vertical arrangement not only because it looks nicer, but also because a vertical arrangement accomodates boxes in a configuration that adapts

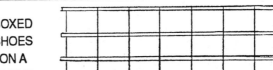

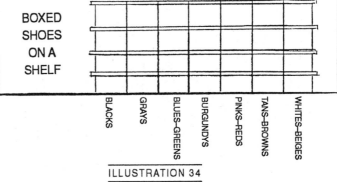

COLOR-RANGING FOR SHOES

BOXED SHOES ON A SHELF

BLACKS • GRAYS • BLUES-GREENS • BURGUNDYS • PINKS-REDS • TANS-BROWNS • WHITES-BEIGES

ILLUSTRATION 34

to the height of the shelf. To handle shoes with less handling, it's advisable to identify the boxes as sandal, sling, pump, sneaker, loafer, or flat, although there's no need to I.D. color because you can tell this by where the box is placed.

Illustration 35 of the door shoe rack shows white and beige on the bottom, which is contrary to the typical color lineup where white always starts at the top. I do this because there is often little light penetrating closet shoe racks. By placing black at the top, black catches the most available light. This prevents your from grabbing navy blue shoes when you really want black.

The color-ranging process for articles stored on a shelf can be varied at your discretion, but purses need to stand up as pictured in illustration 36. Dividers are inserted periodically to support the handbags.

Handbags should be lined up, all facing in the same direction, with the straps placed inside and the closure buckled, snapped, velcroed, or tied shut. Placing them in strict confinement keeps them from roping, snagging, or latching onto other stuff in the closet. Their all-time favorite targets are clothes hangers.

COLOR-RANGING FOR SHOES

ILLUSTRATION 35

COLOR-RANGING FOR PURSES

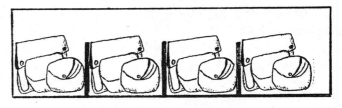

ILLUSTRATION 36

Sweaters can't be lumped together as one. Polos, T-shirts, sweatshirts, turtlenecks, bulky knits, medium weight, and dressy sweaters are each treated as a subcategory, and each subcategory is color-ranged.

Illustration 37 is not meant as an accurate portrayal of effective utilization of space, only as a representation of color-ranging within each subcategory under the main sweater category.

CATEGORIZING AND COLOR-RANGING SWEATERS

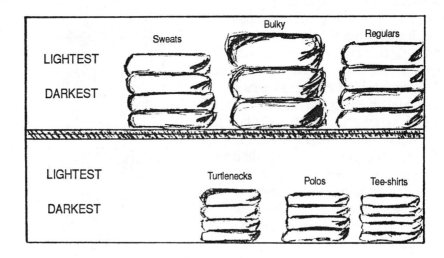

ILLUSTRATION 37

How to Spend Less Money, Time, and Tantrums

After discarding our undesirables and restructuring our outlook on organizing closet space, we're proud of ourselves and rightfully so, but we've also reaped other benefits.

For one, purchases made in the future will be more proficient now that we've made an inventory of the clothes we own. The "on-sale," "discounted," "going-out-of-business" buy isn't much of a bargain if it bears a striking resemblance to five other such items that were unearthed while sorting through the closet.

Categorizing and color-ranging also exposes the impulsive faux pas committed on past shopping expeditions so that repeat performances can be avoided. Implementing category and color techniques brings seemingly lost and forgotten clothing to the forefront, just as it opens our eyes to which garments are seldom, if ever worn. Our inclinations in the future will lead us to purchase a coordinating piece rather than a piece purchased on an impulse.

Smarter shopping enhances a wardrobe by providing clothing that complements and blends into the existing elements to attain a better basic wardrobe.

With the cost of clothing becoming a substantial investment, clothes should have the ability to care for themselves. Unfortunately we read the labels and do all the caretaking.

Laundering and dry-cleaning is but the first overture in the continuing concert on caring for clothes, so save all applause for the grand finale which is a program about proper care, upkeep, and maintenance of clothes as they enter the closet, hang in the closet, and leave the closet.

Maintenance of clothes goes beyond mere wash-and-wear care. It involves control of the clothes and the closet after the clothes have been put in order. It involves order with a minimal expenditure of time and toil. If there is no system for maintaining clothes, the closet becomes a victim of neglect. You'll end up spending much time hanging, sorting, stacking, and ironing, whereas the adherence to a few standard operational procedures in the beginning will save you much trouble later on.

Standard operational procedures

1. Remove belts from the belt loops of slacks, skirts, and dresses because belts stretch the garment out of shape, especially big-buckled belts. Either place the belt on the hanger with the garment (although they'll dangle and intrude below) or use a belt rack.

2. When hanging slacks, match the inside seam to the outside seam at the bottom edge. Hold it here and the crease-line is automatically defined. Buttoning or zipping slacks, disaligns the crease, so simply follow the crease line up to the waistband, gently mold the zipper and placket into this natural continuation of the crease to retain the slacks' shape. Fold the slacks near their middle and insert them through a hanger so the fold is centered on the hangers.

3. For blouses, shirts, and dresses, fasten the top button, perhaps the top two, or best of all, every other one, all the way down the garment. If you do so, wrinkles and cock-eyed collars will be a thing of the past. Consistency is the key to upkeep.

4. Care for sweaters, purses, and other accessories are covered in future sections.

5. When putting garments onto hangers, always face both the hanger and the garment in the same direction. Hook the hanger over the rod so that the point of the hanger faces the back wall. Otherwise, the point of the hanger will puncture hands or snag clothing. Be sure the hanger is actually connected with the rod, thereby eliminating piles of clothes or empty hangers from accumulating on the floor. Never rip the garment off and away, leaving the hanger to dangle or angle in odd and dangerous ways. Worse yet, is tearing the garment off forcefully enough to cause the hanger to disengage from the rod. Instead, take the garment off the hanger gently and place the hanger in the Workspace area of the closet (discussed in the next section).

Incorporated into every closet is an area that's left empty for work-in-process, such as outgoing and incoming dry cleaning. Without workspace, you spend time in front of the closet trying to remember what needs to go to the cleaners, whereas when soiled, dry-cleaner-bound garments are hung in the Workspace, errand day is easier. You grab the dry cleaner's dirty duds without giving it a second thought, drop them at the cleaners, and return home with the fresh batch of martinized, deodorized, wire-hung, plastic-encased dry cleaning. They'll hang in the Workspace until you're prepared to insert them properly into the closet system: the plastic is removed and the items are hung by category and color.

We place all the empty hangers in the Workspace each time we wear a garment. The empty hangers are ready and waiting for laundry day to roll around. It's a matter of personal choice as to whether you take the empty hangers to the clean clothes in the laundry area or whether you bring the clean clothes to the hangers. In either instance, they will eventually make their way back to the Workspace where they will hang until they're incorporated back into the system.

Even though Workspace takes some space from the closet, the reality is that clothes aren't being crammed on the rod when they're returned from the cleaners or laundering service. Cramming clothes causes wrinkles and wrinkles cause the cleaners to get more business.

Workspace is expedient in improving most typically meddlesome methods of mending. If an item is missing buttons, has loose threads, or the seam is pulled open, put the damaged garment in workspace where it stays until chore day rolls around. If you have no scheduled day to take care of little odds and ends such as this or if you're a proud procrastinator, you may be less than thrilled to see this garment hanging there day after day, month after month as a constant reminder and probable source of irritation. But this irritation is minor compared to our feelings after we've been fully dressed in a damaged garment for the third time and only then do we remember or notice that it can't be worn.

CHAPTER THREE

CLOTHES CLOSET

HANGERS

- ✔ How to Standardize
- ✔ How to Learn Layering
- ✔ How to Subscribe to Skirts
- ✔ How to Solidify Slacks
- ✔ How to Expedite Extensions

How to Standardize

Providing adequate hanging space was our foremost concern, but it's equally important to realize there are numerous types and styles of hangers to choose from, each one contributing or detracting from the closet's ability to handle clothing properly.

In my formative years, I was repeatedly told, "if you're going to do something, do it right." So it's premature to stop our thought processes without contemplating hanger selection, especially once it's recognized that the clothes hanger is the workhorse of the closet, performing the most vital service of all. We've never had to do without them, since we weren't around when pegs and nails in the wall furnished us our only hanging space. Advancing times brought special places for clothes, like cupboards, armoires, wardrobes, and the closet itself, so a look at the evolution of hangers is long overdue.

There has always been a veil of mystery surrounding the typical wire clothes hangers that leads us to believe sometime dire and dreadful will happen to us if we should ever throw one away! Is it because they're free to good homes or merely because we've amassed such huge quantities of them that we're reluctant to get rid of them?

Wire hangers work superbly well when we've locked our keys in the car, but the ability to twist, bend, and hook objects is not necessarily an attractive feature when we're considering our expensive clothing.

ILLUSTRATION 38

There is also the tremendously annoying habit wire hangers have of procreating without the slightest regard for overpopulating their habitat. Garfield has done extensive research on this phenomenon, as evidenced by the cartoon shown at the beginning of this book.

Switching from wire hangers to any of the many alternatives will add uniformity and attractiveness to the closet. As with all aspects of closet organizing, each individual element is multifaceted, so spending time now is beneficial in the long-run. A choice made in haste can harm rather than help the smooth efficiency of a closet's performance.

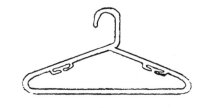

The plastic tubular hanger (illustration 38), is usually chosen to replace the wire hanger, simply because it is readily available and resembles a wire hanger in size and shape. It furnishes only one function: it hangs clothes. Other styles of hangers offer extra features that not only conserve closet space as they hang the clothes, but oftentimes add versatility or satisfy a specific need while serving their fundamental purpose.

The plastic tubular hanger is available in a wide range of colors, although white hangers create a feeling of spaciousness, neatness, and cleanliness. And since most other products are also white, it enhances the overall effect. When these hangers are on sale, 10 for $1.00, the quality is inferior, so expect breaking or bending to occur. Spend a few pennies more for a sturdier hanger.

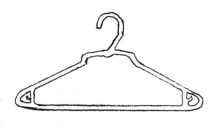

ILLUSTRATION 39

The plastic tubular hangers are available with or without notched shoulders, but of those shown (illustration 39), the first one is a better design since the other two are not only awkward and difficult to access, but the garments fall from the notch at the slightest touch. Choose colors that mix, match, or coordinate with other closet organizing products or with the room's decor for a harmonious appearance. Psychologically, this standardization in hangers, seemingly such a small accomplishment, drastically alters human behavior, motivating us to stop treating our clothes ruthlessly, but with courteous attention instead. Perhaps the fact that we exchanged hard-earned dollars for hangers is sufficient reason to change bad habits into good.

Padded hangers (illustration 40), are more costly than others without providing any multipurpose capabilities. They are sometimes scented, but the aroma soon dissipates. To prolong a lingering essense, spray them with perfume or distribute sachets periodically.

ILLUSTRATION 40

Unless a padded hanger is the sole means of supporting a specific specialty garment, their extreme cost exceeds their worth.

While the discussion is revolving around hangers and their qualifications, it's a good time to interject some thoughts on odd and unusual gimmicks that are advertised as revolutionary aids for arranging a clutterfree closet. Some are truly advantageous and, like illustration 41, create more problems than they solve. Supposedly, this gadget prevents hangers from tangling, but using any hanger other than a wire one will achieve this goal automatically. This entire unit slips over the closet rod

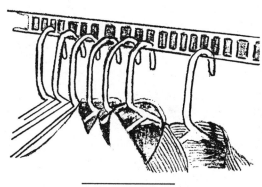

ILLUSTRATION 41

providing individual slots for individual hangers, but a great many of us might need an eye examination before we could find the slots. Having to hunt and peck to hang clothes in the closet isn't exactly in line with organizational genius.

Since few of us, having lived a number of years in blissful ignorance, could have ever forseen the rewards of standardizing the hangers in our closet, we've probably accumulated quite a variety of various, assorted, mismatched, bent, broken, and totally worthless styles and types.

If the hanger being scrutinized is easily and gratefully relegated to the trash heap, then it doesn't need a run down of its merits. But if it could conceiveably contribute a measure of manageability to the clothes in the closet, then it needs to be evaluated.

The following two types of hangers are the only ones we'll review because they are basically the only ones that weren't discussed previously.

1. Men's Contour Suit Hangers: whether they're wood or plastic are perfectly acceptable be cause they serve two functions. They maintain the sportcoat or suitcoat's molded and padded shoulder shape and, since men always wear the matched or coordinated pieces together, it's good to have the slacks on the same hanger as the jacket. Best of all, they are included in the original purchase price of the ensemble.

2. Gold-tone aluminum, rattan, lucite, wooden, and designer hangers add a tremendous cost to the closet's conversion without adding any advantages other than an elegant and classic appearance. The cost puts them out of range as a high-volume closet transformer, but using them exclusively in the coat closet, where there are far fewer garments, a dozen or two, makes for not only an interesting proposition, but an affordable one. These types of hangers are generally much larger, broader, and sturdier than standard hangers, making their entry into a coat closet even more sensible, since coats are the biggest, bulkiest, and heaviest items we own. And last but not least, these hangers are without a doubt the most ravishingly attractive, so why not show them off as each guest arrives?

How to Learn Layering

Attachable hangers are also known as add-ons because they've added a hook in the center of the hanger (illustration 42) which allows each subsequent hanger to hang from the hanger immediately above. The clothes are then aligned vertically in the closet rather than horizontally across the closet rod.

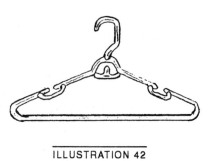

ILLUSTRATION 42

This vertical alignment is known as a layering effect and if little else in the way of order and routine were established in the closet, especially if funds are extremely limited and a massive overhaul is beyond that limit, then this is probably the single most effective organizing technique that can be initiated with a minimal outlay of time, energy, and dollars.

Anywhere from two to eight garments hang in a layer, depending on the garment's length. A shirt, for example, is much shorter than a dress, so more shirts than dresses could hang in a vertical layer.

Nearly everyone's closet is currently laid out in a typically mismanaged fashion.

Their clothes are hanging on the closet rod, yet when the eye looks below the bottom edge of those garments, there's a tremendous amount of space from there to the floor that isn't being used. Layering not only installs much of our clothing into that empty space, but it has taken all of those clothes off the rod.

Assume there's only one rod in the closet, installed at a standard height of 65 inches, valiantly attempting to keep up with your demands. Because layering distributes the clothing vertically, the rod's capacity to hang clothes is virtually doubled, if not tripled.

Illustrations 43 and 44 show the increased capacity of a closet using attachables. Both closets are 84 inches wide, so the top closet, without benefit of the attachable hangers, will hang eighty-four garments, one every inch, whereas the closet below it with add-on hangers, hangs not only the eighty-four garments, but hangs them in three feet of space, which leaves an additional four feet of rod space for hanging more clothes.

With attachable hangers, clothes simply won't wrinkle as readily as they did when they were tightly bunched together along the rod. Follow the category and color-range procedures. When a garment is replaced, it needn't be inserted between garments in a layer. Just hang it at the bottom of the color-ranged row and it will recycle itself.

Attachable hangers are quick and easy to remove from the middle of the layer. None of the clothes above or below are mussed, inconvenienced, or man-handled and none of the layers of clothes on either side need to be shoved aside in order

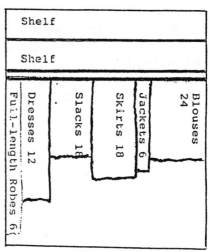

Closet BEFORE attachables

ILLUSTRATION 43

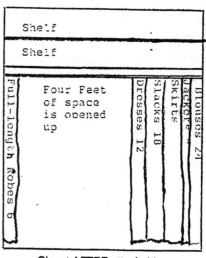

Closet AFTER attachables

ILLUSTRATION 44

for us to touch and take the object we desire.

If layering the entire closet isn't feasible, versatility can still be obtained by occasionally layering a singularly selected smaller category of clothing.

The basic layering principle was derived from this old-fashioned blouse-tree (illustration 45). It's a sound and sensible concept, but the blouse-tree is bothersome and awkward because of it's stiff metal spine which is too inflexible. And the permanently attached hangers are difficult to reach. Many people who purchased blouse-trees discovered their faults and stopped using them.

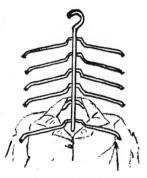

ILLUSTRATION 45

There have been a great many attempts at creating the layering effect and most of them were failures (even if they were successful TV commercials and sounded good in the promotional literature).

In actual fact, recovery of garments once they are positioned in their vertical mode requires the services of a well-trained and muscular weight-lifter, since the entire unit must be hefted up and down and on and off the rod to access the hangers. See illustration 46.

Before even this maneuvering can be accomplished, the clothing on each side of the unit is shoved out of the way, clearing the rod so the unit can monopolize it.

In the never-ending search to finally find the best way to layer, some nameless person invented this gimmick (illustration 47). Instead of having our hangers hanging on the rod, they hang from the hole of this device, which places our hanger a few inches below the existing rod.

ILLUSTRATION 46

This gadget, however, still occupies the same amount of space on the rod as our own hanger did, so what advantage have we gained? Why should we spend any of our funds for this?

Obviously, there's no question that effective

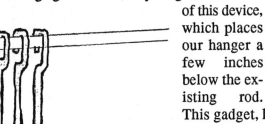

ILLUSTRATION 47

layering uses our limited space wisely. So how do we determine which of the products does it best? Don't hesitate to personally manipulate and envision the products in operation. In this way, their underlying faults and liabilities are discovered before it's too late.

How to Subscribe to Skirts

Using safety pins or straight pins to attach skirts to hangers isn't exactly an enlightened or modern method, nor are the meddlesome metal clips the dry cleaner loves to send home with us.

These clips and pins are rather nasty. They have a terribly short attention span and will leave their assigned positions without any warning, disappear for days on end, and then reappear at the most inopportune times, poised and ready to inflict pain and suffering on an unsuspecting piece of flesh or fabric.

Believing that the pin or clip securely fastens the skirt to the hanger is silly, for pins are in constant motion, skating around the edges of the hanger, shifting the weight of the skirt around as well. The skirt not only wrinkles from this gross mistreatment, but it's often damaged by the sharp little teeth or the pointy pins, as they try to maintain their death grip on the waistband of the skirt.

Equally unbelievable is the method in which the skirt is dropped over a hanger, hem first. The waistband, which winds up around the hanger's neck, flip-flops in wild abandon, while the hip part of the skirt is forced to duplicate the hanger at its widest and most accentuated point, which changes both the skirt's original shape and your own when you wear the skirt.

The skirt's hanger shouldn't have the ability to alter or damage the original style and shape of the skirt. It should control the skirt so as to keep it wrinklefree and unblemished.

Simply flopping a skirt over the rung of a hanger, even if it is in a partially folded state, isn't going to acheive this goal, since hangers will accentuate any wrinkles and creases.

This unusual skirt hanger (illustration 48) multiplies the problem because it holds multiple skirts in an unmannerly way. The skirts are kept in a relatively small space, but it isn't worth the wrinkles we'll get after the waistband has been twice or triple folded before it will fit between the separate slots on the hanger.

Wrinkles are a result of cramming too many clothes together on the rod, hanging clothes

ILLUSTRATION 48

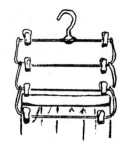

on inappropriate hangers, or hanging them improperly. Obviously, one of the reasons for organizing the closet is to eliminate as many wrinkles as possible. The specialty skirt hangers shown in illustration 49 present the different versions available and explain why some designs are more successful than others.

The first drawing depicts the original attempt at layering skirts, but as with the blouse tree, the structure itself was so rigid that it was difficult to access the skirts. The next stage of its evolution was to simply separate the concept into individual hangers with the add-on hook feature, so that we were then able to handle just one hanger at a time, which simplified the process tremendously. The layering aspect of the hangers stopped the overcrowding of the rod.

Do you really know how to hang a skirt on a hanger properly?

Pull the waistband taut, attach the outermost edges of the waistband to the clips on the outermost edges of the hanger, which stops the skirt from bunching up in the middle. Button and zip the skirt, unless the zipper or the buttons are positioned in unusual or abnormal locations. Always remove detachable belts.

Of the four clip-on styles of skirt hangers, only the last (illustration 50) is made out of lightweight plastic. The others are made of metal.

ILLUSTRATION 49

Clip-style skirt hangers offer the best way to hang strapless dresses, tops, tube tops, and halter tops, also.

Metal hangers not only tangle on the rod, except for those with a larger diameter neck, but they are frequently designed to accomodate both pieces of a suit or ensemble; the blouse or jacket with the skirt hanging from the clips. See illustration 51.

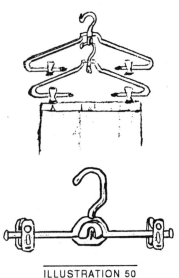

This squanders two inches of the closet's space, since the skirt hangs much lower than it does on the plastic hanger just discussed. By hanging matched sets together, their versatility and wearability is restricted, so it's not a good idea to submit suits to this practice. Hang them as two separate pieces on two separate hangers, each in their own categorized section of the closet.

Clamp hangers (illustrations 52 and 53) are usually constructed with a metal hook, which creates

ILLUSTRATION 50

an added hassle. They often have to be untangled and disengaged from each other before they can be removed from the rod.

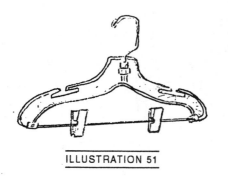

ILLUSTRATION 51

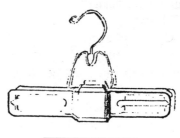

ILLUSTRATION 52

The selection that's ordinarily offered in the stores consists of either a wooden variety, with some being wider and thicker than others, or a molded plastic style, which is usually only available in white. All of the clamp hangers are prone to pressing the waistband of the skirt too tightly, thereby leaving pressure marks that are difficult to steam or press out.

ILLUSTRATION 53

How to Solidify Slacks

Having the proper type of hanger is important for each type of clothing. Although these three slacks hangers are mentioned (illustration 54), they are flawed by inflexibility. The last hanger adapted an ingenious swing-arm that improved accessibility, yet operation of the arms causes poking and probing of the clothes hanging on either side. In each instance, it's difficult to retrieve any given pair of slacks without a great deal of motivated motion, so the hanger usually ends up with only the castaways and rejects.

The better method is to limit the operation to handling one hanger and

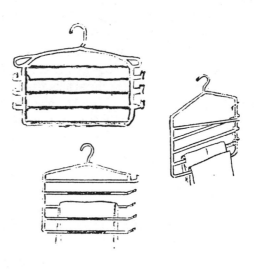

ILLUSTRATION 54

one pair of slacks at a time.

The swing-arm slack hanger did improve the layering concept even though it wasn't the perfect solution for hanging slacks. (See illustration 55.) The arms are incorporated onto a tension pole that is inserted under the closet rod. The pole does manage to work its way loose, however, so that pole and all might someday take an unplanned plunge.

The swing-arm action infringes on the garments that are hanging on the rod nearest this pole and lots of valuable inches are wasted above the top rung and below the bottom arm of the unit. There are certainly some situations where this unit could provide an adequate alternative, such as in a tiny nook or corner that's otherwise providing no service at all.

A great many of the slacks hangers have a tilted tip built-in at their outer end, which is supposedly placed there so we have an incentive to hang our belts and ties on it, putting them right next to the slacks. If we adhered to this practice, our belts and ties would not only interfere with slacks selection and withdrawal, but the dangling ends of the ties and belts would intrude on the items assigned to the space below.

Many of the slacks hangers also feature the rubber grip, which is nothing more than a tube surrounding the rung of the hanger. It supplies a grooved padding to prevent the slacks from slipping off the hanger and alleviates the crease marks that often appear on the knees of folded slacks.

Certainly, the clamp hanger bypasses those problems since the slacks are hung by their cuff, but it exchanges those problems for ones that are far more compromising.

Because the clamp hanger carries garments by the cuff, it uses so much lengthwise space that that area can't be double-rodded.

When slacks are folded over the rung of a hanger, their total length, measured from the top of the rod to the bottom of the hanging slacks, is only 26 inches to 30 inches, whereas the total occupied

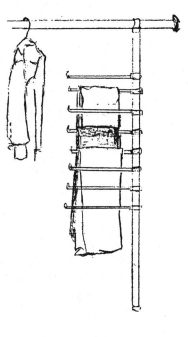

ILLUSTRATION 55

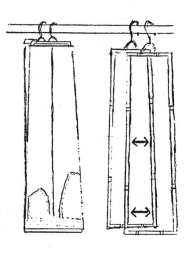

ILLUSTRATION 56

length when they're clamped by the cuff is 45 inches to 48 inches. This is simply unacceptable when we're trying to conserve and design space effectively.

Clamp hangers aren't discriminating. They'll mar the cuff of the pants just as readily as they did the waistband of a skirt, and the cuffs aren't concealable beneath an overhanging shirttail, jacket, or sweater.

The slacks hanger shown in illustration 56 is preposterous. It's meant to hold a pair of slacks as they drip dry, minimizing shrinkage and eliminating all ironing and pressing.

This is all well and good in theory, but stretching a wet item onto a piece of metal and letting nature run its course results in a rust-ridden, tentlike pair of stiff pants. There's a huge degree of effort involved in operating the hanger as well, since the hanging process actually consists of inserting a separate hanger into each pants leg. If the pants legs don't hang evenly, looking like you have elephantiasis is the least of your worries.

Illustration 57 shows a slacks hanger, commonly referred to as an open-end slacks hanger for obvious reasons. This hanger for a number of sound and sensible reasons, packs a mighty wallop in wrestling control of the closet space. First, the slacks slide onto and off of the unencumbered opening of the hanger without the bother of removing the hanger from the rod. The hanger comes with the grips and the neck is bigger and rounder than on almost any other type of hanger, so it never snarls and snags with other hangers on the rod.

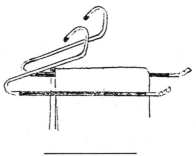

ILLUSTRATION 57

Secondly, and most important of all, its shorter stature (both heightwise and lengthwise it's 3 inches shorter than the height and the length of a standard-sized hanger) grants it abilities that none of the others have, making it unique and highly qualified to render extensive improvements in the closet. Because we do gain inches we never before had at our disposal, we are more likely to create an inspired and innovative closet configuration.

For instance, this hanger enables us to consider installing rods on the side walls of the closet because we don't require as many inches of vertical hanging space. Also, it's much more probable that we could double-rod more of the closet than usual, especially if we were critically short-changed with an existing closet rod than was lower than the normal 65 inches.

The open-end slacks hanger is unquestionably a wise choice in both typical and atypical closets. At a cost of approximately $1.00 each, they're not prohibitively expensive.

When slacks are folded over the rung of a hanger, they are the shortest garments we own, so they can hang in places around the closet where our longer garments can't go.

Specialty slacks racks such as the one shown in illustrations 58 and 59 that folds flush against the wall is sometimes a rare treat installed on a door or unobstructed wall.

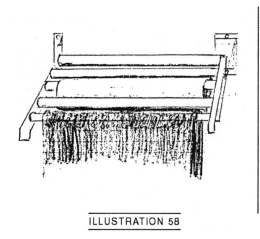

ILLUSTRATION 58

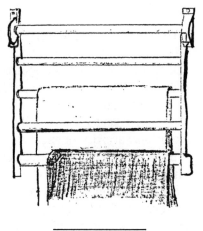

ILLUSTRATION 59

If it's a side wall of the closet that's chosen, the rack is concealed behind the clothes hanging from the rod and it hasn't got the required clearance for the bars to be pulled up into their full operational position. On a door however, if two racks were installed, one above the other, ten pairs of pants would be in perfect position.

ILLUSTRATION 60

Simply rolling a cart (illustration 60) into the closet seems a simple enough solution for servicing slacks, yet there's one disagreeable hitch. If the existing closet rod is too low, there isn't enough room below the bottom edge of the hanging garments for the rack to reside.

Either the rod must be moved higher to accomodate the cart, or the rod above the cart should be limited to slacks only, since they are the shortest garments in the closet and the cart could then stand below them. If we didn't, however, possess a substantial inventory of slacks, enough to fill the rod above and the cart below, we'd be squandering a great deal of space, both on the rod and the cart.

How to Expedite Extensions

The established height of the closet rod either allows for innovative and creative attainment of additional hanging space or it doesn't. There are ways of working around the limitations to acquire much-needed space for hanging our clothes that might or might not require the moving of the rod. You're the only one who can determine if it's necessary in your own situation and that is dependent on a number of variables.

The factors that effect this are: 1) the length of the garments that will hang from the existing rod, 2) the length of the garments that will hang from the newly installed second and lower rod, and 3) the advantage or disadvantage that's supplied by the present height of the existing rod.

The higher the existing closet rod, the more likely it is that jackets, blouses, and other separates can be hung from both the top rod and the bottom rod. The lower the existing closet rod, the less chance there is of hanging anything but slacks at both levels.

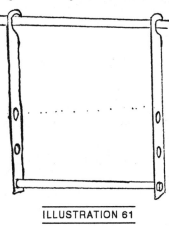

When I mentioned installing a second lower rod, I wasn't meaning to be taken literally, since we can quite handily obtain the benefits of a second rod without touching a single tool. Isn't that the best news you've had in a long time?

This second rod is nothing more than a concoction that hangs from the existing closet rod. It is called an extender rod. It has become very popular and comes in a wide range of styles, colors, and materials.

ILLUSTRATION 61

The extender rod pictured in illustration 61 is usually either wood or plastic, but it offers only three choices of height, which limit its ability to adapt to various closet situations.

The bars on the extender rod shown in illustration 62 come in a choice of colors, but the vinyl straps are always white. The straps are so flimsy they stretch until they eventually break. The positions of the three rods are permanently fixed at heights that seldom lend themselves to the lengths of the garments, so either inches are unused or the bottom edges of the clothes obscure the rod below or drag on the floor.

Versatility should be the key factor in selecting an extender rod. The rod should fit current clothes and conditions but should be adjustable for future changes. It should be adjustable not only to various heights, but the rod should expand to various lengths as well, so it

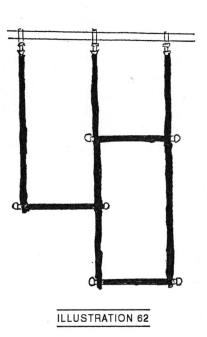

ILLUSTRATION 62

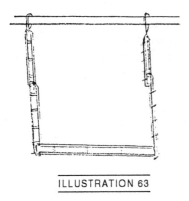

ILLUSTRATION 63

conforms to clothes and closet space.

The extender rod in illustration 63 is constructed in a manner not unlike the way ventilated shelving is constructed. It has three interlocking pieces. Two identical hookpieces fit over the closet rod to become the top sections of the two sides. The third U-shaped piece completes the bottom half of the two sides and includes the extender rod itself.

Each side of the U-shaped piece has a prong so that it can be looped over the slots that are in the two top side pieces, which is the extent of its ability to adjust—only four different height possibilities.

This unit attaches to either a regular closet rod or ventilated shelving and is rather expensive. Most extender rods that aren't adjustable are usually 28 inches wide, whereas those that do adjust can start telescoping from as little as 15 inches wide.

Although the extender rod in illustration 64 is metal and can be adjusted to different heights and lengths, it's not structurally reliable because of the the way the rod is secured to the vertical support poles. After the poles are slid through the precut holes in the horizontal rod, a metal clamp pin clips around the selected notch, preconstructed at various increments on the pole. This pin, however, doesn't have the strength to handle the stress once the clothes are on the rod, leaving the clothes to fall as they may. When the clothes are lopsided on the rod, the pin is often forced off the pole. A variation not illustrated has rope or cord for the side supports with a metal extender bar, but the ropes aren't strong and the knotted ends slip through the holes in the rod. It is a very inexpensive model and perhaps that accounts for its poor behavior.

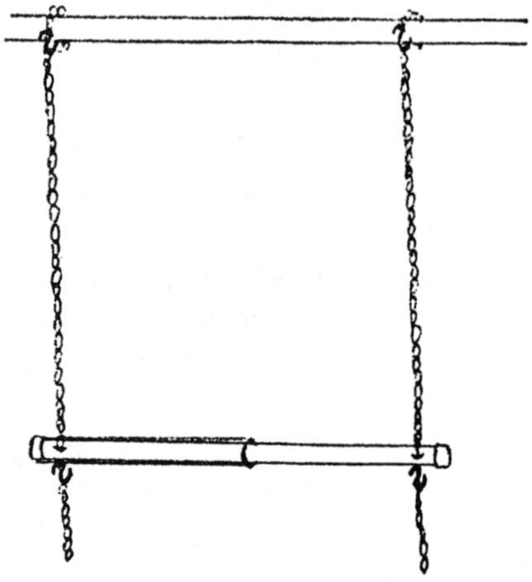

This version (illustration 65) loops a length of chain around the existing rod, which is then secured

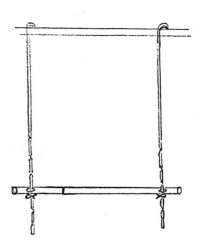

ILLUSTRATION 64

ILLUSTRATION 65

with an S-hook. The chain hangs through the holes on each end of the extender rod and they, too, are secured underneath with an S-hook.

This product is the best all-around extender rod on the market today, even though it's probably among the least expensive. This is due not only to the fact that the chains are strong and reliable, but also because each half-inch link in the chain gives us height adjustability. By simply deciding where to stick the S-hook, you can change the height of the extender rod. The width also adjusts from a compact 15 inches to a fully extended 28 inches.

We can even increase the length of the chain by adding more. None of the other extender rods are able to exceed their maximum 34-inch length. The chain can be lengthened by either joining two pieces with an S-hook or by opening links, adding the new chain, and closing the links back.

This provides us with a much larger range of possibilities, such as placing an extender rod under longer garments like dresses, thereby customizing space in a way that's seldom seen. Or the extender rod could hang from the ceiling for a totally new approach and perspective on space utilization.

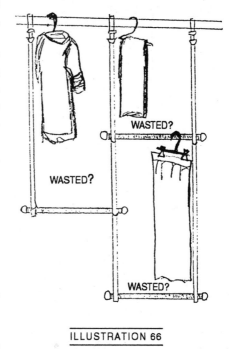

ILLUSTRATION 66

Extender rods are ultimately the easiest way to expand hanging space, but they must be flexible enough to satisfy very personalized predicaments and if they don't have that ability, they'll end up wasting closet space, as is exemplified in illustration 66.

The extender rod shouldn't preplan the space. Based on the lengths of the clothes that will be hung, one category above another, plan the placement of the extender rod for maximum utilization of the space. (See illustration 67.)

There are some unusual alternatives to choose from, in acquiring a small amount of hanging space that require little installation and nothing in the way of rethinking of the space. They are simply contrived conveyors of meager mercies. Any product or approach that can redistribute hanging space, thus easing the rod's burden is the main objective. For instance, the device in illustration 68 attaches to the doorframe to supply a few small rungs for hanging items like jeans, sweats, nightgowns, or items we habitually toss on after our busy and exhausting day. Since it isn't terribly attractive, place on it a group of garments that are similar, rather than a hodge-podge that will cause you to forget what garments are even hanging there.

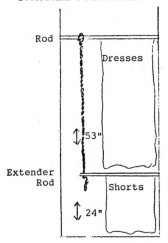

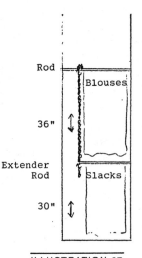

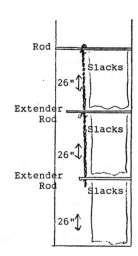

ILLUSTRATION 67

Even a few inches of space can help the closet and your own peace of mind, especially when there's no room for workspace. Like when selected items are being reviewed and considered for vacations, business trips, black-tie affairs, or when it's just plain handy to have a quick picker-upper for the robe in the bathroom.

Illustration 69 shows one such item. It is forged from metal and folds flat against the wall when not in use. The item in illustration 70 attaches to the edge of a shelf and when pulled out to its full length, it holds a half dozen hangers or more. Both aid laundry and ironing areas.

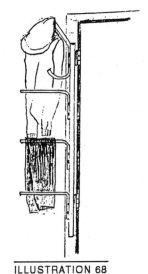

ILLUSTRATION 68

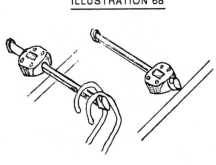

ILLUSTRATION 69

ILLUSTRATION 70

CHAPTER FOUR

THE CLOTHES CLOSET

FOOTWEAR

✔ How to Show Off Shoes

✔ How to Sock Away Shoes

✔ How to Fight Shoes on the Floor

✔ How to Battle Boxes of Shoes

✔ How to Stack Shoes on Shelves

✔ How to Set Shoes Free

✔ How to Bail Out Boots

How to Show Off Shoes

Once the hanging clothes are in place in the closet, most of the space is occupied, leaving only smaller spaces for our remaining possessions, usually sweaters and accessories. It's important then to assign these limited areas wisely because it's through their effective utilization that the closet becomes truly organized, functional, streamlined, and attractive.

The smaller areas recognized immediately, of course, are the shelves above the hanging clothes and the floor space below the hanging clothes, but many other areas exist inside the closet that are frequently overlooked, yet offer extremely suitable space for storing accessories.

For instance, the side walls of the closet, above the door and on each side of the door (lips), and the closet door all provide valuable space.

Where should shoes, ties, sweaters, or belts be placed? Give up? Generally, shoes are the first to go back into the closet.

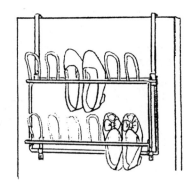

Sweaters and shoes vie for the next biggest portion of the remaining closet space because we've managed to amass a substantial quantity of each, especially in the case of shoes. We usually have a pair to match every outfit we own and pairs, too, to go with outfits we haven't yet purchased.

Second, shoes are easier to store than sweaters because the methods for doing so are often compact, versatile, and innovative, allowing shoes to go places where sweaters cannot. The best example of this is a shoe rack on the inside of the door.

Shoes fit remarkably well in small amounts of space, in places that were lying dormant, in spots incapable of performing any other service for any item of apparel; and at the same time, the shoes can be displayed for enhanced visability and accessibility. On a door, the shoes can be stored without using a single inch of shelf or floor space.

It's important then, that we review the types of doors that permit or prohibit utilization of shoe racks.

Obviously, pocket doors, bifold doors, and draped or curtained closures at the entry to the closet won't support a shoe rack. Louvered and shuttered doors could work if they're at least 24 inches wide or if the shoe rack were a scaled down version having less than the usual 22-inch width. Sliding closet doors can hold shoe racks only when the depth of the closet exceeds approximately 29 inches, otherwise when the rack is installed on the door, the shoes are inaccessible and they brush against the hanging clothes. The best door, even if it's hollow, is a regular, standard, ordinary open-out door.

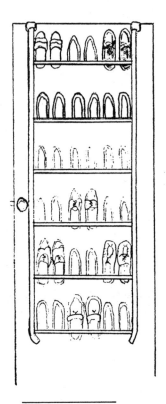

ILLUSTRATION 71

Most all shoe racks available on the market (see illustration 71) adapt to either a door or wall mounting, since the hardware includes the gear to fix it over the upper edge of the door.

In either instance, the amount of space required for the rack to have adequate clearance is a mere five inches. When it's installed on a closet's side wall, however, it really uses only three inches of space because two inches were already being used to support the closet rod on the side wall. Therefore, using those three inches for the shoe rack is a smart move, since we have exchanged only enough space to hang three garments, but gained a storage place for at least six pairs of shoes. Even though clothes do hang alongside the shoe rack, it doesn't effect our ability to reach and see the shoes.

Shoe racks are constructed of aluminum, chrome, or white epoxy coatings over metal, available in sizes to store either six pairs, 12 pairs, 18 pairs, or 21 pairs of shoes. Base your buying decision on both the quantity of shoes to be stored and the size of the space you have to work with. Feel free to match and mix any combination of sizes to customize and satisfy your individual requirements.

NOTE: For appearance's sake, place the sole of the shoe inward so it faces the wall. This keeps the dirtier side away from clothes. The top side of the shoe is then facing outward for easier identification. Some styles of shoes that are slimmer, flatter, or less bulky, like flats and sandals, can be fitted together as a single unit and placed together on one rung of the rack by slipping the toe of one shoe into the toe of the other.

Open-toed sandals don't have an enclosed toe area, so they tend to slide farther and farther down the prong, infringing on the shoe below. To prevent this, simply loop the ankle straps or criss-crossed decorative straps of the sandal over the prong as well. This puts a stop to the slippage problem by controlling how far down the shoe can drop.

Very few shoe racks accomodate the width or length of men's shoes, but a few do, so with a bit of determination, the search will produce the exact shoe rack desired for size, shape, color and weight.

Pictured in illustration 72 is a wonderfully innovative update to the wall and door racks. Because this rack is a narrow strip with only one row of prongs, it's possible to turn a wall or door into a shoe display without wasting any space whatsoever between rows, since these racks can be installed more closely together than the preset and preconceived units previously depicted. This difference in design gives us better control over the area we have to work with.

This flush-to-the-wall shoe rack protrudes from the wall only an inch or two so it can fit into tight places with little clearance required.

Each shoe on this rack is wedged between two of the sup-

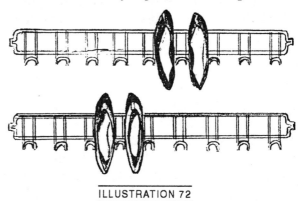

ILLUSTRATION 72

ports. On other racks the toe of the shoe is slipped over a rung.

These wall units are usually available in varying lengths, which enables us to better control their precise configuration, whether we install them side by side in a continuous line or stagger them in alternating positions so they fit the unusual or segmented sections of space we may have to work with. We have less chance of conforming to the wall space with the door or wall rack because the multiple rows are prearranged into a unit that demands a much larger wall.

Most shoe racks are designed with a tilt that is supposedly helpful in displaying the shoes but in reality requires extra inches of closet space.

The two tilted shoe racks shown in illustration 73 can be installed on the wall in a smooth flowing row around the baseboard of the closet or higher or in vertical rows from floor to ceiling. But even when they're positioned as close together as possible, the angle eats inches.

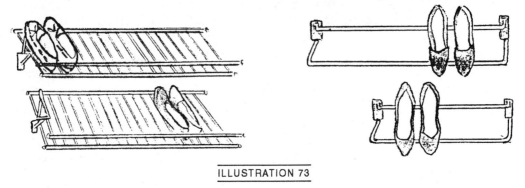

ILLUSTRATION 73

For a clearer understanding of the value of these few inches, illustration 74 shows the number of shoes that can be stored on door or wall racks and on tilted wall units. Both racks are on identical walls.

Three flush-to-the-wall shoe racks are capable of holding 63 pairs of shoes. The racks themselves protrude only five inches from the wall.

The five tilted wall racks are 12 inches deep and can hold only 45 pairs of shoes. That's 18 fewer pairs and that's too many to forfeit given the substantial wall size.

A revolving carousel for shoes! (See illustration 75.) Only a spacious environment like a walk-in closet or a walk-in room could sustain one. A standard closet would need to exchange valuable hanging space, which is an unacceptable trade.

Even if we had a huge closet, this wheel of shoes spins a web of deceit, since there are far too many inches of space wasted between each wheel. If that weren't the case and the wheels were closer together, there would be enough room to have one more wheel inserted. This wheel would hold an additional five pairs of shoes. There is a half-size unit also, which fits under the bottom rod of a double-rodded closet, but again the same space could hold more shoes if it used a different storage method.

How to Sock Away Shoes

Shoe bags would appear to be a worthwhile solution, yet they have many disadvantages when we begin to investigate them.

First of all, in reviewing each of the six sample shoe bags presented, notice how they are all intentionally designed to hang from the closet rod and we know what a disservice this is to the clothes that must hang from the rod. So why take this considerable amount of space away from them?

Some bags are adaptable, however, by circumventing their intended destination. Our first and best option is to place shoe bags on a door or side wall. Obviously, those that don't lie flush won't work.

As with the structured shoe racks in the preceding

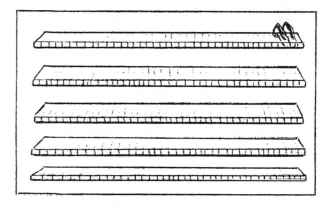

ILLUSTRATION 74

section, open-out doors provide optimum conditions, but sliding, louvered, or shuttered doors can handle shoe bags if the size of both the bag and the door work in unison to supply the necessary visibility and accessibility.

Only the shoe bags in illustrations 76 and 77 meet this criteria. But even so, they don't have the capacity to control nearly the number of shoes that the previously shown structured racks manage in the same amount of space. Another drawback found with these two shoe bags, even the more expensive, sturdier ones, is their tendency to rip and tear when put to routine useage. This tendency more or less limits their use to sandals, slippers, and other lightweight footwear or seldomworn shoes.

Shoe bags that furnish shelves for each pair of shoes in its own compartment are

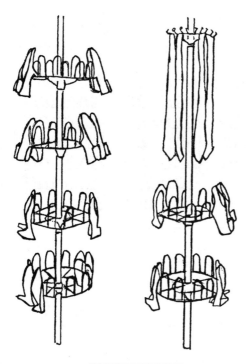

ILLUSTRATION 75

PLASTIC OR VINYL

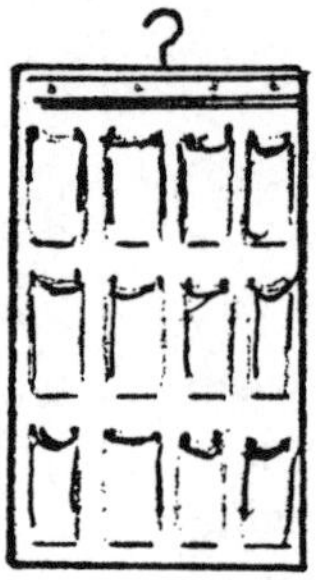

ILLUSTRATION 76

VINYL, PLASTIC, OR CANVAS

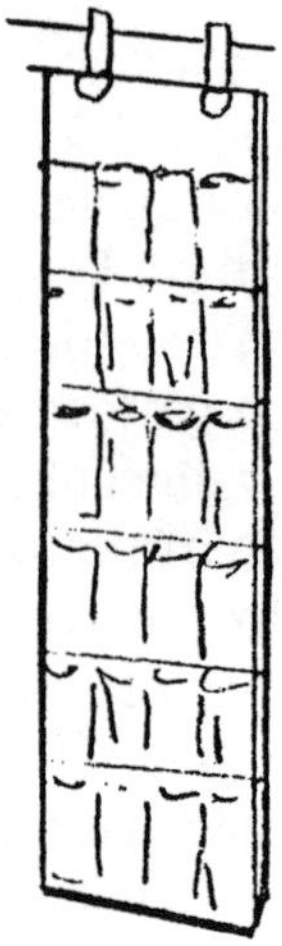

ILLUSTRATION 77

CLEAR VINYL

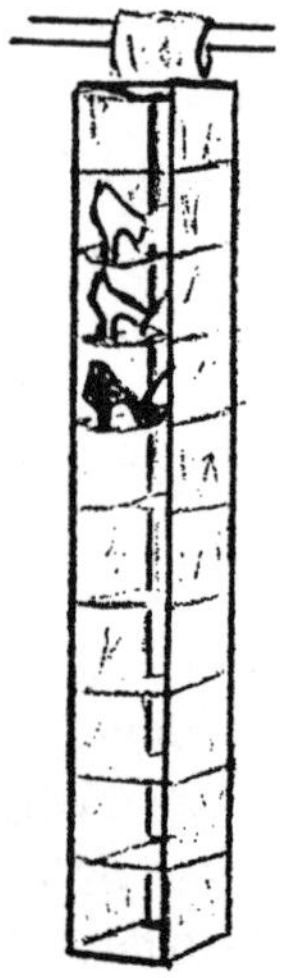

ILLUSTRATION 78

CANVAS

ILLUSTRATION 79

well designed between the shelves themselves, but they demand entirely too much room to accomodate their depth. (See illustrations 78 and 79.) The full length of the shoe, 12 inches or more, juts into the closet when it's positioned on either the door or the wall. Of those 12 inches or more, six or seven of them could be saved using a flat or flush shoe bag.

Shoe bags with shelves eventually sag and sway, allowing the shoes constant contact with the floor below.

Shoe bags with a system of layered pouches divided by a central partition are usually made of transparent vinyl. (See illustrations 80 and 81.) While this feature is beneficial, the arrangement of the pouches on opposite sides of the unit itself is less impressive. When this style of shoe bag is hung from the door or the wall of the closet, one complete side of the bag is rendered inaccessible. Even though the racks usually contain a swivel hook, it's still a struggle to maneuver the bag around to select a pair of shoes from the concealed side.

How to Fight Shoes on the Floor

Stowing shoes on the floor is a dirty proposition even if they're uniformly positioned under the bed, aligned neatly along the side or foot of the bed, or on the floor of the closet. It's impossible to maintain order in those locations considering how often our own feet, the cat or dog's paws, and the vacuum cleaner romp through them and scatter. Even if it weren't such an ordeal to keep them in line, they are unsightly.

All this hassle about picking a place to place our shoes is silly, since the solution is to simply set up a sensible system for storing shoes.

Whether the system selected for storing shoes on the floor is typical and thrifty or elaborate and expensive, like the rolling pine cart drawn in illustration 82 or the free-standing systems in illustration 83, there are factors that help determine what is the best system for you to use.

The vast majority of shoe racks manufactured for floor utilization are designed so that the shoe sits on a tilted angle for better accessibility and visibility. Those two aspects are certainly important, but are not usually worth the inches that are squandered in between the tilted rows.

CLEAR VINYL

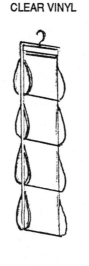

CLEAR VINYL OR OPAQUE CANVAS

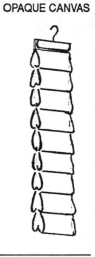

ILLUSTRATION 80 | ILLUSTRATION 81

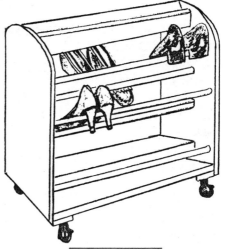

ILLUSTRATION 82

The loss of inches between each tilted row is reason enough to eliminate the types of floor model shoe racks (shown in illustrations 84 and 85) from our list of shoe storage options (or at least consider these methods only after sufficient space has been realized for all

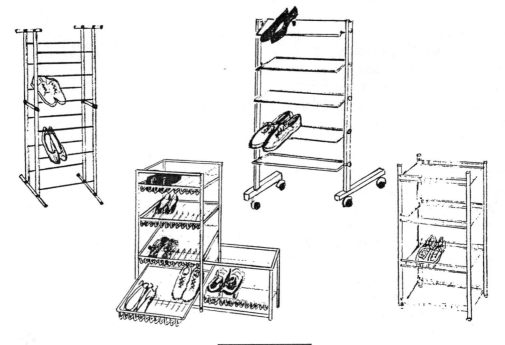

ILLUSTRATION 83

the hanging clothes). Otherwise, placing shoes on the floor on such racks automatically removes all hope of double-rodding the area above the shoe rack, which of course removes a great deal of potentially valuable space away from clothes that could be hanging there.

On the other hand, racks, such as the one in

SELF-SUPPORTING VENTILATED SHOE RACK

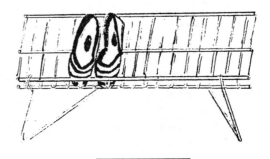

ILLUSTRATION 84

illustration 86, that have structured height or that get their height through their ability to stack are not without merit, if and when the closet has adequate hanging space and still has sufficient vertical wall space left over to accomodate this type of shoe storage system. However, the particular rack(s) chosen should be carefully scrutinized; avoid those that wantonly waste inches between their tiered levels.

Manufacturers must be aware of the importance of shoe storage or there wouldn't be so many types, styles, sizes, and shapes of shoe racks on the market. Manufacturers, however, don't concern themselves with producing products that conserve space. It's our task to evaluate the products to see which ones are truly functional.

EXPANDABLE SHOE RACK

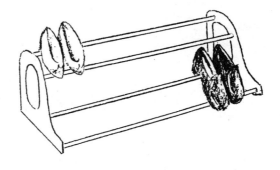

ILLUSTRATION 85

STACKABLE CEDAR SHOE RACK

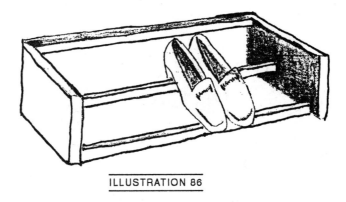

ILLUSTRATION 86

With that goal in mind, the floor shoe racks shown in illustration 87 are tremendous squanderers of space even though they are readily available and economical. Fortunately, the organizing process seeks to achieve far more than merely settling for the quickest, cheapest solution.

The inability to double-rod the closet was mentioned as one of the problems floor racks cause. The racks shown in illustration 88 also add insult to injury.

Once these racks are positioned on the floor, it doesn't take long to realize how awkward and difficult they are to use. The shoes end up lying in heaps near the rack, with only the oldest, least-worn shoes remaining on it, making the rack totally useless.

Other disadvantages are apparent when these racks are compared to wall or door racks. These racks exceed the 5-inch depth wall or door racks take. Compared to storing shoes in shoe boxes, these racks store fewer shoes in the same space.

How to Battle Boxes of Shoes

The method of shoe storage requiring the least amount of space is storing shoes in shoe

15-PAIR RACK
24" W x 24" H x 18" D

9-PAIR RACK
24" W X 12" H x 16" D

ILLUSTRATION 87

9-PAIR RACK
24" W x 12" H x 16" D

8-PAIR RACK
12" W X 24" H X 12" D

ILLUSTRATION 88

boxes. It should be duly noted, however, that how the boxes are stacked or aligned contributes greatly to the success of the system.

Naturally, stacking box upon box upon box to unheard of heights will not only create difficulties in retrieving the boxes near the bottom, but it's also an accident waiting to happen. Therefore, the logical procedure is to limit the number of boxes being stacked. After spending years maneuvering shoe boxes, I've discovered a workable arrangement dictates stacking to a height of only three or four shoe boxes. Setting this limit eases the awkwardness and creates a sensible system that conserves space.

Shown in illustration 89 are various shoe box configurations, a wall shoe rack, and a self-supporting floor model rack specifically designed for shoe boxes. Each example shows twelve pairs of shoes being stored. Notice the amount of space each method takes.

There's no need to discard cardboard shoes boxes since they're free, but purchasing

This isn't a portrait of ideal or effective space management, but rather an illustration of projected possibilities.

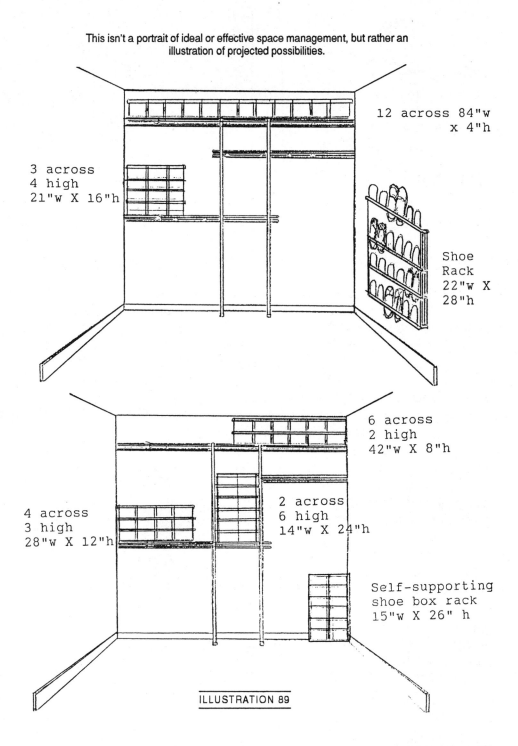

12 across 84"w
x 4"h

3 across
4 high
21"w X 16"h

Shoe
Rack
22"w X
28"h

6 across
2 high
42"w X 8"h

4 across
3 high
28"w X 12"h

2 across
6 high
14"w X 24"h

Self-supporting
shoe box rack
15"w X 26" h

ILLUSTRATION 89

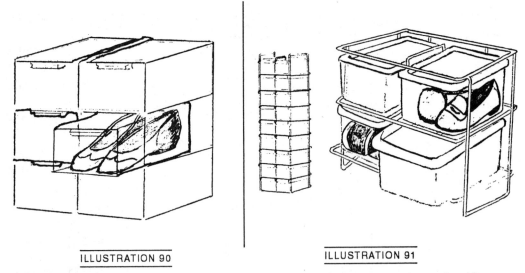

ILLUSTRATION 90   ILLUSTRATION 91

the transparent plastic ones isn't a bad investment since they are attractive and uniform while displaying the shoe within. Cardboard boxes aren't consistent, so unless their lack of uniformity furnishes the ID for the shoe inside, you will need ID tags on the boxes.

Arranging the shoes by color does offset the need for labeling the box by color, but labels are more important for recognizing the style of the shoe in the box. The idea of pulling out one box after another to find the black sandals, the black pumps, the black slings, the black flats, or the black loafers isn't a time-saving proposition.

Most shoes come in boxes that are 4 inches high, 7 inches wide, and 12 inches long (with men's oversized shoes and baby booties the exceptions).

Illustration 90 shows what looks like boxes, but they're actually drawer units designed for stacking. They have protruding nubs that help stabilize the stacking process. Stack them as high as the ceiling as long as there's a stool around to see, reach, open, remove, and replace the shoes without dragging the whole structure down in the process.

Manufactured in a rigid molded plastic, these

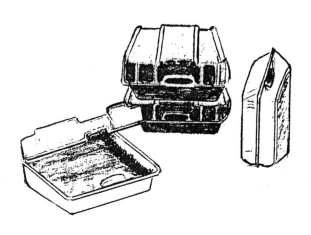

ILLUSTRATION 92

units are easily chipped and broken and except for some of the more expensive ones, the drawers are often extremely difficult to operate.

Illustration 91 shows a particular style of shoe box that is usually made from a material that isn't quite transparent, but is soft and therefore unlikely to chip or break.

The lids vary. Some of them work like the lid on a Tupperware container, while others don't seal at all and simply sit on top.

These are self-supporting, self-contained structures that can be built to various heights and lengths to fit your closet.

I call illustration 92 the out-to-lunch box because it looks like a fast-food container, except that it's larger and more translucent than fast-food containers. Nevertheless this container is more suitable for sandwiches than shoes.

They don't differ from standard shoe boxes when it comes to stacking, although you can stand them on end, so that it's feasible to pull out one at a time.

If this type of shoe box is appealing, it may lessen the attraction when you realize that lots of shoes need lots of boxes, lots of shelf space, and lots of money.

Take 8 to 12 shoe boxes, structure them into a self-contained unit, and we eliminate the need to manipulate individual boxes (see illustration 93). Although the unit uses more space and costs more especially if you're a shoe freak, the horizonal unit readily conforms to the shape of a shelf. The vertical unit occupies floor and wall space and the openings on the front are lift-up panels. Both units are transparent, and they're made from a padded, shiny vinyl material available in assorted colors.

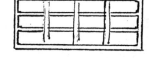

Due to the framework of these units, a great deal of space is lost in their construction—space that could be used for more constructive shoe storage.

How to Stack Shoes on Shelves

We've already discussed stackable, tilted shoe racks. Illustration 94 shows shelves that are flat rather than tilted.

This style of shelf can sit on either the existing closet shelf to divide it into more functional and appropriate sizes for storing shoes or it can create shelves from the floor up, wherever floor space and wall space permit.

The shelves built into closets are unrealistic for storing shoes unless the shoes are in boxes, since only one row of shoes will sit along the entire expanse of the shelf. This leaves at least 6 inches of stagnating space above the row of shoes.

These stack shelves shown in illustration 95 divide height, providing additional shelves for shoes while turning

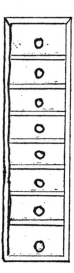

ILLUSTRATION 93

the whole area into a functioning shoe station. The stack shelves should, however never exceed 7 inches in height because anything higher than 7 inches is wasted space. The tallest recorded height for any spiked heel ever made is seven inches.

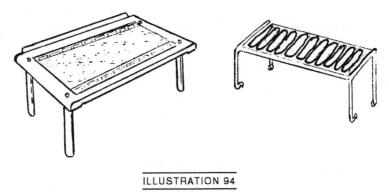

ILLUSTRATION 94

Typically, existing closet shelves measure 12–13 inches from one shelf to another, while the distance from the top shelf to the ceiling is usually 20 inches or so. Needless to say, chopping those inches into 7-inch segments provides multiple shelves for shoes, making far better use of the space. Costs will vary based on the material used in shelf construction.

Modular shelf units are attractive and certainly heavy duty compared to other materials, but a heavy price is paid (both in dol-

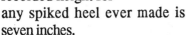

ILLUSTRATION 95

lars and unnecessarily expended inches) due to their manner of construction.

If planned properly, stack shelves are effective not only in the existing closet shelf as depicted in illustration 96, but also on the oftentimes overlooked side wall. Placing shelves on the side wall still allows for double-rodding. The biggest difference between stack shelves and wall or door racks is their depth. The rack is only 5 inches deep and the shelves fluctuate between 9 inches and 12 inches deep.

At this point it would be beneficial to review stack shelves to understand how they affect the number of shoes that can be placed on them.

As an example, modular shelves are 24 inches wide. Shoes average seven inches in width. This 24-inch shelf will accomodate three pairs of shoes with three inches left over. Therefore, when you select a shelf for shoes, measure it and make certain it is a multiple of seven so that you don't waste inches.

As far as height is concerned, modulars shelves are 7½ inches tall. So when two are stacked they take up 15 inches of height. Reason tells us that most shoes aren't seven inches tall, so again we are wasting valuable space.

How to Set Shoes Free

To further aid the process of selecting strategic shoe storage, it's time to explore the prospect of whether shoes should remain on the shelf "au naturel" or be confined to a shoe box or, like illustration 97, tossed anywhere. The subject of whether or not shoes should be stowed in boxes or left to stand on their own two feet is seldom broached, yet definite advantages and disadvantages accompany the modes.

When shoes are left to sit on a shelf, it guarantees eventual clutter and chaos because they're bound to fall over. Worse still is the outcome when shoes are placed on stack shelves that have open holes in the pattern, just perfect for the point of a high heel shoe to poke through.

Another disadvantage in allowing shoes their freedom is that we suffer the consequences in both our failure to obtain a uniform and orderly appearance and the tremendous territory we donate.

This volume of space we grant them can be calculated quite accurately if you've got the guts to view the results. Even with a stack shelf only seven inches high, most shoes will only occupy three inches to five inches of that space. Add together those two inches to four inches for each and every stack shelf employed and the total tally of lost inches might very well cause serious rethinking of the situation.

If the same number of shoes and the same number of stack shelves are employed but the shoes are put in shoe boxes, at least a third more (if not two-thirds more) pairs of shoes can be stored in the same given space. Add to that the fact that the boxed shoes don't even need the stack shelf at all.

Side Wall

ILLUSTRATION 96

ILLUSTRATION 97

For instance, if we placed just one stack shelf measuring twenty-one inches wide by seven inches high on the existing closet shelf, it would hold six pairs of shoes. If the shoes were in boxes, those boxes could be arranged three across and three high (nine pairs of shoes rather than six). In addition, we've saved ourselves the cost of buying the stack shelf.

It seems unbelievable that by adding the extra height, width, and depth of a shoe box around a pair of shoes we could actually utilize less closet space rather than more. But it's true.

Considering all the points presented, the shoe box offers us one of the better systems.

Shoe Storage Summary

There's probably a feeling of wonderment now that you've realized just how many options and ways of storing shoes are feasible, logical, sensible, or at the very least applicable, given your own individual circumstances. Here's a list of items to consider when figuring out the best way to store shoes.

1. Place shoes in an otherwise unproductive or unused area of the closet. Don't ever use hanging space for shoes.

2. Use the least amount of space possible for storing shoes.

3. Allot a little extra room for growth. If all of the shoes won't fit into one assigned place, divide the shoes into smaller categories: casual, sport, dressy, etc., and store each smaller group together for easier selection and less wasted effort.

How to Bail Out Boots

Shoes and boots are classified as footwear, but because they are not similar in size, shape, or height, they don't belong in the same category. Their distinct differences demand different allotments of space and that point is clearly shown in illustration 98.

The placement of this single pair of boots beside shoes eliminated the possibility for installing another shelf. A very negative exchange of space.

Subcategories of boots exist. Ski boots, hiking boots, cross country boots, mountaineers boots, none of which are frequently worn and therefore don't belong in the closet with the boots that are worn consistently.

ILLUSTRATION 98

More often than not, when it comes to boot storage, boots are left standing at the back of the closet, playing peek-a-boo with you and the clothes that hang in front of them, so that everytime the boots are to be worn, the clothes are pushed aside before retreival of the boot is possible. Or the boots stand or fall in great disarray in front of or below the hanging clothes, making it not only difficult to reach the clothes, but also to find a matching pair of boots without doing some digging first. In either case, it's a constant source of irritation. Another commonly practiced method of boot storage is the boot "shaper." Those who employ it are the unknowing victims of both false advertising and heresay because it isn't mandatory, as we've been led to believe, for preserving a boot's quality. (See illustration 99.) Although shapers are wooden, cardboard, styrofoam, plastic, or even inflatable, they're an unwarranted expenditure. Worse yet all are equipped with a hook for hanging from the closet rod, which is by no means a move in the right direction.

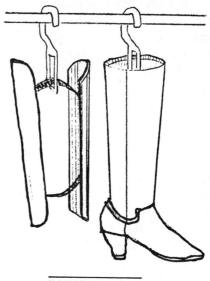

ILLUSTRATION 99

Because of the unsubstantiated belief in shapers, another method of storage has been discounted and overlooked, while being actually one of the more sensible choices. It quite simply allows the boot to follow it's natural inclination to automatically fold or flop over. (See illustration 100.) Even in the case of very expensive boots, it's a perfectly acceptable practice and the shapers can now be eliminated from serious consideration.

There are logical reasons for allowing boots to fold. Foremost among them is the conservation of space. When boots are stored with

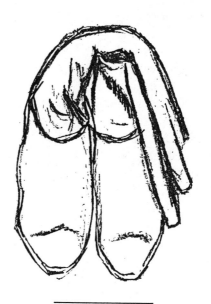

ILLUSTRATION 100

shapers, they need twelve inches to eighteen inches depending on the height, plus four inches for the hook, for a minimum of sixteen inches to twenty-two inches of overall vertical space. When boots are folded over, they take only eight inches. That's a substantial difference, significant enough in fact to drastically hinder or help the closet's overall ability to function effectively. (See illustration 101.)

When boots are left in their boxes, they exhibit the same stacking disadvantages as do shoes, except that they are larger and therefore more awkward and cumbersome to handle, especially when on the top shelf of the closet.

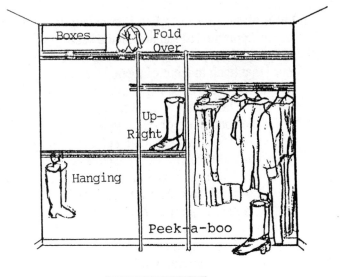

ILLUSTRATION 101

There is another sensible method for storing boots. By engaging the services of either a very inexpensive all-in-one, drip-dry type hook as depicted in illustration 102, or an oversized vinyl-coated paper clip, often seen in office supply stores and mail-order catelogs,

ILLUSTRATION 102

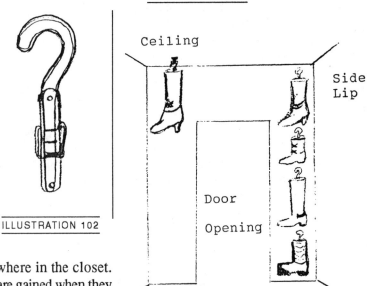

ILLUSTRATION 103

boots can hang anywhere in the closet. The greatest benefits are gained when they are positioned in those areas previously thought to be inoperative. Consider the areas above the door frame, the lip areas on each side of the door frame, the accessible portions of the ceiling or any spot that would permit the depth, height, or width of a boot. The boot-clip itself can hook over fancy nails, cup-hooks, or pegs of any sort.

Six pairs of boots can fit in the lip area down the side of a door frame if the boots aren't overly tall, although only four pairs are shown in illustration 103.

In a standard five-foot wide closet, five pairs of boots can hang *above* the door frame when the toe of the boot is pointing in toward the side walls. When the boot hangs parallel to the side wall, eight pairs of boots can hang above the door frame. The ceiling is usually nonfunctional, but it can supply storage for boots, as long as the boots then aren't interferring with any other closet activity.

CHAPTER FIVE

THE CLOTHES CLOSET

SWEATERS AND KNITS

✔ How to Size Up People and Their Sweaters

✔ How to Defuse Drawers

✔ How to Stop Stacks of Sweaters

✔ How to Beat the Bulk

✔ How to By-Pass the By-Products

How to Size Up People and Their Sweaters

Sweaters are without question the single most difficult, unruly, unmanageable, and disruptive item of clothing. Certainly there are a number of contributing factors we can point to as being directly responsible.

First of all, we seldom own just a few good sweaters. We commonly own a vast collection of dressy, casual, sporty, sequined, appliqued, alma mater, layered over, layered under, and others.

Second, whether these knit garments are extra bulky, oversized, form-fitting, or regulation, they require a large storage area, no matter what mode of storage is used.

Third, if they aren't cared for properly, they tend to retain folds, creases, or wrinkles. Sweaters in some instances are a huge portion of our total wardrobe investment, so they deserve our special and concentrated concern.

The vast majority of people fall within three distinct groups. The first group stuffs their sweaters into dresser drawers, trunks, and other similar containers. Next comes the group who never gave a thought as to handling their knits properly, so they simply hang them in the closet alongside their cotton, silk, and denim garments. The last group, folds their sweaters and stacks, piles, or heaps them onto a closet shelf.

How to Defuse Drawers

Dresser drawers, no matter what style, shape, or size and no matter where they might be positioned, furnish the poorest visibility and accessibility to the sweaters stored inside. (See illustration 104.)

When only the top sweater can be seen and reached, you are forced to rummage to get to the sweater on the bottom of the pile.

Another negative side effect that occurs when sweaters are stored out of sight is that the number of times they're actually worn is greatly reduced, since it's so much easier to just settle for the one that's on top.

When drawers are the only option available for sweater storage, at least roll the sweaters into individual units.

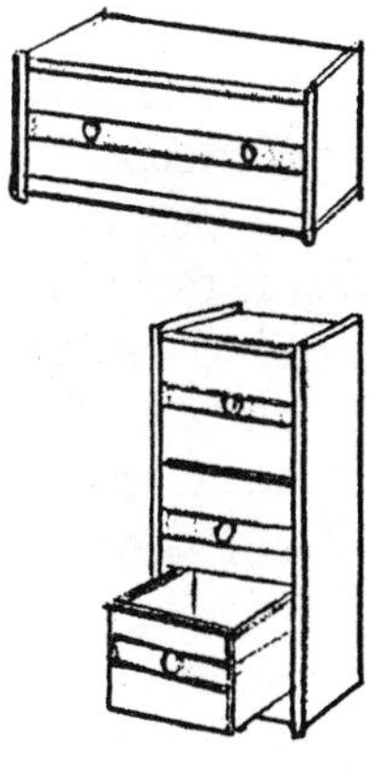

After rolling the sweaters, lay each sweater in the drawer with one edge to the front and the other edge to the back. By placing a rolled sweater on top of the one that is lining the bottom of the drawer, a degree of layering can be achieved, although layering three sweaters is usually the maximum to retain manageability within the drawer.

ILLUSTRATION 104

The primary reasons rolled sweaters will function in drawers when stacks and piles won't is twofold. First, the rolls are easier to handle since they won't fall apart and unroll. More important, by stipulating that each layer from top to bottom will contain only one color, you allow total awareness and recall as to what sweaters are lying just out of sight below the visible one sitting on top.

Following these procedures improves

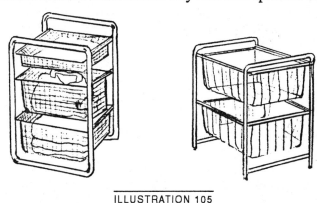

ILLUSTRATION 105

the negatives of storing sweaters in drawers.

A wire basket (illustration 105) is also a drawer of course, and although it's see-through, it's expensive. Wire baskets do not conserve space because the supporting framework is expansive and useless, squandering many inches that might otherwise supply storage. Something else that's seldom realized is how annoying it is when pieces and parts of the sweater poke through the holes and openings of the basket, sometimes damaging the sweater when it inadvertently snags on the basket's runners.

Separate compartments are constructed together (illustration 106), forming a self-contained unit for storing sweaters, each in it's own individual cubicle. The difficulty of searching through an entire stack of sweaters to find the one desired is overcome with this system. The drawbacks are expense and expanse. Numerous sweaters demand numerous units and numerous units demand mucho money and a goodly amount of space.

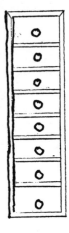

Stacking more than five or six units vertically jeopardizes stability and they may come toppling down, which basically limits them to horizontal placement, with only three or perhaps four in any single stack.

ILLUSTRATION 106

How to Stop Stacks of Sweaters

Some people solve their sweater storage problem by hanging them. (See illustration 107.)

Removing sweaters from the rod, however, makes room for the clothes that can't be stored in any other way. Sweaters not only thrive in a different environment, they won't survive the rod method well.

A specialty hanger like the one shown, lets the arms of the sweater flop around and creates an unnatural and inhuman chest and bust shape when it's folded over the rung. When sweaters are hung like blouses, the shoulders are not only distorted but inches are often added to its length due to gravitational pull.

Is it necessary to reiterate the value of hanging space and why it must be preserved? If we were smart enough to remove sweaters from the rod after learning how damag-

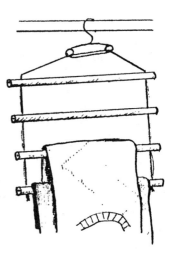

ILLUSTRATION 107

ing it was to them, why in the world would we then hang them back on our closet rod?

Illustration 108 shows sweater bags. Some bags have nothing but a string holding the shelves together and that string breaks easily with the combined weight of the sweaters. Notice how the shelves are sagging in bag #3, typical of most bags, so the sweaters fall out.

VINYL WITH FRONT ZIPPER

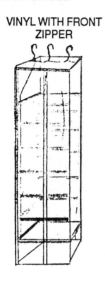

VINYL

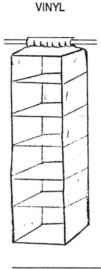

CANVAS

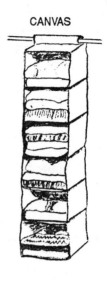

ILLUSTRATION 108

People who fold and stack their sweaters in rows along the shelf of the closet have found to their discomfort that the sweaters don't stay in nice, neat stacks for very long.

To my way of thinking, it's one of the least appealing, least attractive, and least effective options, but in some closets, it's perhaps one of the few op-

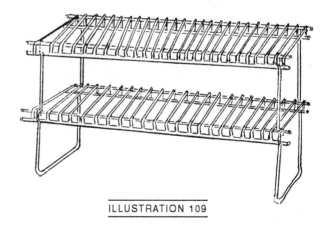

ILLUSTRATION 109

tions available. In that case, dividing the height of the shelf is helpful. Place a portable stack shelf on the existing permanent shelf of the closet to lessen the total number of sweaters arranged in any one stack.

Whether stackable shelves are utilized (illustration 110) or not, a reasonable way to achieve a system that demands less maintenence is to put fewer sweaters in each stack, thereby rendering them less likely to topple, tilt, or fall. Or, roll the sweaters as previously mentioned, laying them on the shelf in a single row. This provides not only visibility, but each individual sweater is retrieved without mussing the others that lie on either side.

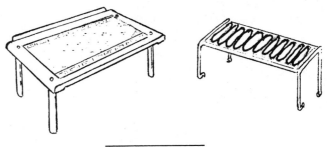

ILLUSTRATION 110

Using ventilated shelf dividers is a good way to improve manageability of sweaters. They offer good strength and durability. The clear, flexible plastic dividers suffer in comparison since the plastic bends out of shape. Either of these products are installed by simply sliding the molded hook located on their bottom edge around the shelf for an instant up-right divider. (See illustrations 111 and 112.)

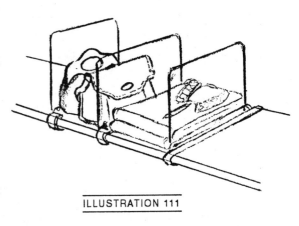

ILLUSTRATION 111

Illustration 113 shows modular shelves. The first one is designed for vertical placement and the second for horizontal. They are too heavy really to be placed on an existing shelf, so the better idea is to use them as an entire wall unit or in a nook or cranny that is otherwise unproductive.

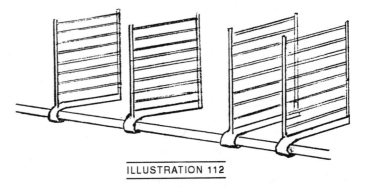

ILLUSTRATION 112

This third picture shows a stackable plastic bin. They can stack to form a self-supporting unit, up an empty wall or along a closet shelf.

Illustration 114 depicts a completely different approach to storing sweaters. In this unit, sweaters are kept separate for better accessibility and the visibility is good because of the dust-protecting, clear front that zips open. Think about whether you will completely open or close the unit each time. Or will the cover fly at half-mast most of the time?

These units are generally made in a padded vinyl material and the shelves aren't usually durable enough to withstand the constant repetition of normal usage, so they self-destruct.

Sweater enthusiasts will find it to be a rather costly endeavor and one that uses every inch of shelf space as well.

Illustration 115 shows three clear vinyl sweater cases stacked one

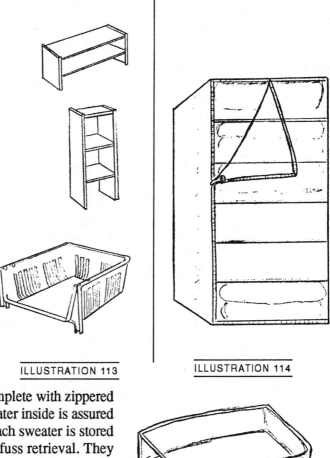

ILLUSTRATION 113

ILLUSTRATION 114

on top of the other, each complete with zippered openings. Access to the sweater inside is assured because of the zipper, and each sweater is stored singularly for no-muss, no-fuss retrieval. They even provide protection against the dust, dirt, and cobwebs of the closet. So why then are these less-than-perfect problem-solvers?

They're just too slippery. Once they've been stacked on the shelf, they never stay. The more they're shuffled for sweater selection, the more often they slip. Once the desired case is finally ob-tained, be it from the shelf, the bottom of the

ILLUSTRATION 115

stack, mid-air as it was falling, or from the accumulated pile on the floor, it has to be un-zipped and the sweater removed. Then you have to decide where to put the empty case. It's an experience we can all do without.

In our continuing search for viable ways to store sweaters, we turn now to the box. Because it worked so well for shoes, why shouldn't it be just as effective for sweaters?

First of all, sweaters bear absolutely no resemblance to shoes. Storing them in boxes is less than satisfactory. It's preferable treatment to store a single pair of shoes per individual box, but this would be an enormous waste of space with sweaters. Yet storing multiple sweaters in one box inhibits not only their accessibility but also their ability to remain neat and orderly within the box. (See illustration 116.)

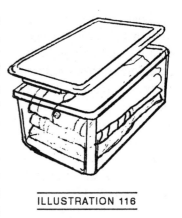

ILLUSTRATION 116

The sweater box method of storage basically functions as a drawer except it adds additional hardships because boxes are more complicated to operate than a simple drawer. Remove the box from its position within the stack by displacing all boxes above the one desired, lift the lid, manipulate the contents to obtain the selected sweater, replace the lid, and maneuver the box back into its position in the stack.

Lining the boxes single file on the closet shelf so that handling is limited to one box at a time is the nearest boxes can come to achieving a degree of success. The good news is that the sweaters are close to the hanging clothes for wearability, and the bad news is how wantonly we misspent the shelf space of the closet.

When all alternatives for sweater storage have been exhausted, a suggestion that could save sanity is to arrange boxes under the bed. Place tee-shirts in one, polos in another, turtlenecks in another, and so forth, labeling the boxes if necessary. Roll each knit item by folding in the arms and sides to the width or length of the box, lay each roll inside the box but don't layer them unless the box is exceptionally deep. Keep the colors in the proper sequence by arranging them from lightest to darkest.

How to Beat the Bulk

We've pretty well covered the traditional treatment of sweaters, yet there exist some innovative, original, and unique solutions that can resolve forever the subject of sweater storage.

Cubbyholes are designed to hang either from a rod (illustration

#1   #2

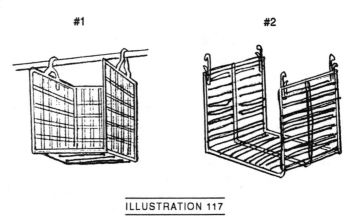

ILLUSTRATION 117

117) or from a ventilated shelf although we'd never allow either of them to take space away from the hanging clothes. Luckily both cubby holes adapt to a wall installation by improvising hardware to achieve this conversion.

Both styles of cubbyholes attach to each other, so one can suspend from another for the entire eight-foot height of a wall, which actually provides eight feet of shelving space since each cubbyhole is 12 inches x 12 inches x 12 inches. They're especially effective when they're installed vertically in the lip area of the closet or horizontally above the the door frame because they create their own useable space from an otherwise empty patch of wall. See illustration 118, which depicts the areas described above and also shows cubbyholes in an inverted position on a top shelf as well as hanging vertically from a shelf.

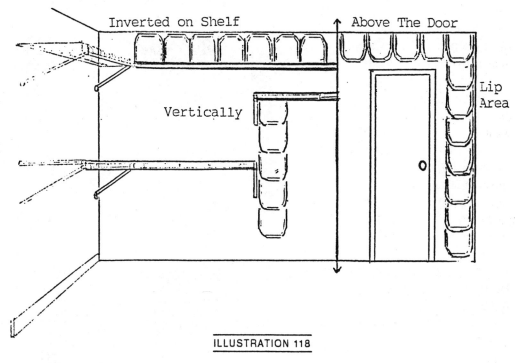

ILLUSTRATION 118

The most amazing, resourceful, and revolutionary idea ever imagined for sweater storage are the Honeycomb cylindrical storage tubes. They actually satisfy and supply the best overall serviceability for sweaters.

Since Honeycomb storage units are a system of individual tubes (see illustration 119), they conform to any space and any sweater inventory, giving it an exactness that all other methods lack. Being portable, they follow flucuating lifestyles from dormitory, first apartment, starter-home to dreamhouse. They're virtually indestructible; therefore, the small and economical investment occurs only once. (See illustration 120.)

By applying velcro strips to their outer contours, they're converted to a free-standing unit that sticks them together anywhere, allowing them to be removed from the closet and placed elsewhere.

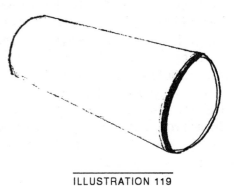

ILLUSTRATION 119

Each sweater has a home in its own individual tube. Only the sweater is removed and the tube always stays in the same place, ready and waiting to welcome the same sweater home each time. This factor alone creates a system that's absolutely maintenance free. It is enhanced and simplified further when the sweaters are categorized by color within the tubes. (See illustration 121.)

When sweaters are readily seen and easily obtained, they're worn frequently, consistently, and with greater enthusiasm. The Honeycomb, therefore, increases the true value of a sweater.

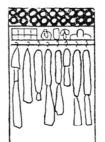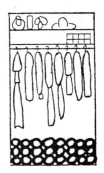

ILLUSTRATION 120

Honeycomb units prevent wrinkling because sweaters aren't burdened by the weight of other sweaters on top of them, the chief cause of wrinkles.

The diameters of the Honeycomb tubes are in increments of four inches, six inches, and eight inches to accomodate the various types of sweaters and knits we generally possess. For instance, a four-inch diameter tube is suitable for lighter bulk knits like turtlenecks, tee-shirts, and polos. The six-inch diameter tube supplies ap-

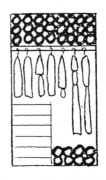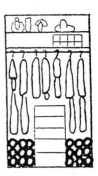

ILLUSTRATION 121

propriate room for our regular, somewhat fitted and proportioned sweaters, and sweats. The eight-inch diameter tube furnishes an increased area for containing the currently fashionable sweaters, sweats, and knit tops that are ultra-long and super-bulky.

The length of the Honeycomb tube can range from 12 inches to 13 inches, but always use the same length. Naturally, the 12-inch length is the precise depth of a typical closet shelf, while a 13-inch tube overhangs the edge, creating a display that emphasizes the custom-designed, built-in look and appearance of the overall system.

To avoid any confusion or misunderstanding as to the proper way to handle the sweaters for correct insertion into the tubes, they are always, always, always rolled into consistently uniform shapes. (See illustration 122.)

HOW TO ROLL A SWEATER

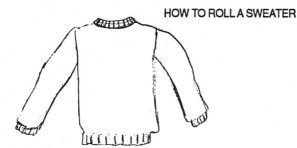 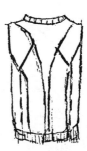

Lay the sweater front side down.

Fold arms over as shown until sweater is 12 inches wide.

Flip up one-third at bottom. Then roll the sweater.

This results in a smoothly rolled unit that fits into the tube with ease.

ILLUSTRATION 122

How to By-Pass the By-Products

It's nearly impossible to picture sweaters in storage without first shivering and shuttering from a mental image of moths and the dreaded damage and holes they represent. But before we can tackle moth prevention, we must first shed some light on the problem and hope it vastly improves the rather bizarre and makeshift attempts people have undertaken in the past. Little can compare to the steadily glowing beam of light achieved by simply attaching a wall or ceiling mounted fixture as shown in illustration 123.

A shortage of electrical outlets in closets is typical of older homes. It's worth contemplating the expense of having an electrician install an outlet or switch in or near the closet, instead of stocking up on flashlights and batteries. Or consider cordless, battery-

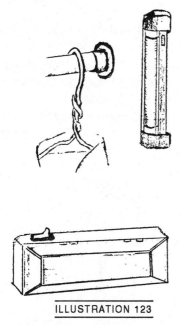

ILLUSTRATION 123

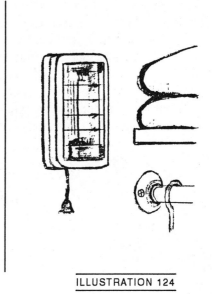

ILLUSTRATION 124

operated portable light fixtures. They cost substantially less than an electrician and they are available in a tremendous array of shapes, sizes, and wattages. (See illustration 124.)

Now that we have light in the closet, we can see whether or not the vermin have invaded our belongings and what damage they have done. Mothballs are nasty, leaving not only residues and stains, but also an unpleasantly lingering odor. We must improve our method of moth prevention.

Cedar eliminates these detestable pests best, and best of all, cedar is sized and shaped to sit beside our wools and sweaters no matter where or how we've stored them. (See illustration 125.)

The cedar pictured in illustration 125 chooses the rod, hanger, or a hook as its place of residency. The marbles, blocks, and boards shown in illustration

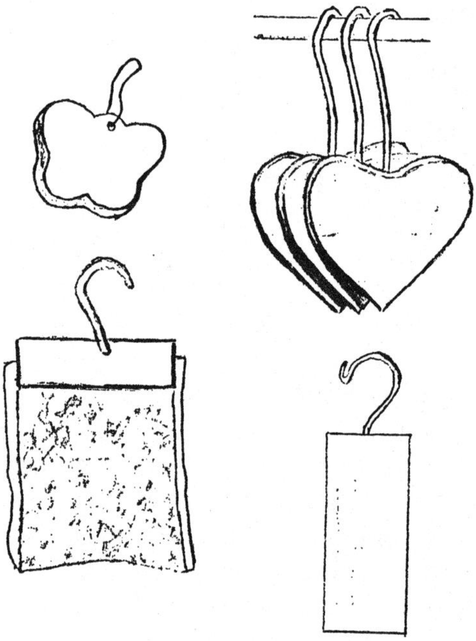

ILLUSTRATION 125

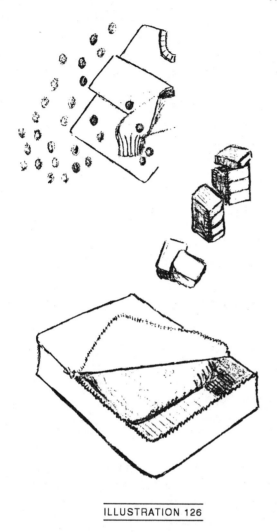

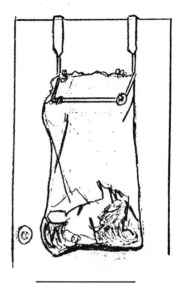

ILLUSTRATION 127

126 can become a lining in a drawer, chest, or box. Place them inside the pockets, creases, or folds of garments or let them rest on closet shelves. Stick-up versions are also available to bring a refreshingly tantalizing aroma to the home and its surroundings.

Dirty clothes should definitely be stowed in a bag, hamper, or elsewhere. They should never mingle with the clean clothes in the closet. (See illustration 127.)

ILLUSTRATION 126

Why look at disgustingly dirty clothes every day? So don't let dirty clothes dominate or dictate the quality control of your closet.

Instead of using regular hampers (which will always look like a dirty clothes hamper) or standard, uninspired, institutional looking laundry baskets (which are seen in everyone's laundry room), start thinking pretty, unusual, or harmonious types of receptacles.

Settle on something, be it a woven-rag, wicker, painted, or plain basket and place it out in the open for all the world, including neighbors and friends, to see and admire. Little will they ever suspect its true purpose when what they see more closely resembles a prized and proudly presented possession. They'll be envious and you'll have a feeling of accomplishment and well-being at your ability to produce a rewarding result instead of a typical household eyesore.

CHAPTER SIX

THE CLOTHES CLOSET

BELTS AND TIES

✔ How to Decide Destinations

✔ How to Regulate and Rule

How to Decide Destinations

Save the space on the rod for the clothes that must hang! When tie and belt racks are specifically designed for placement on the rod, don't buy them no matter how streamlined, advanced, or effortless they appear to be (illustration 128). Battery operated racks that rotate in a circle at the touch of a button and racks that telescope backwards and forwards to deliver the merchandise aren't more desirable just because they're more expensive. Belt and tie racks have managed to gain entry in numerous closets because they came as gifts, thereby making it an act of indecency or ingraditude not to use them.

Many of the tie or belt racks for sale today are equipped with a hook for placement on the rod, but that doesn't mean they all are totally dysfunctional, since quite a number of them can adapt to different modes of operation that are not only effective but also logical and space-saving.

For instance, the lips of the closet, the side walls, or the closet door are perfect places for tie racks because the shape of the space is similar to the shape of ties and belts as they hang. The final judgment rests with determining which of the various racks will make the belts and ties visible and accessible, and which racks will hold the most.

The first set of racks we'll be reviewing has a hook for hanging from a closet rod. We're going to ignore this and install it instead on a wall or door (inside the closet or out).

Guidelines to follow for choosing the rack best suited to our purpose are few and simple. First, consider the first rack that caught your interest and fancy, picture it in its place on the wall or door and if one side of it installs flush and flat to the wall and the other side is equipped with the prongs, slots, hangers, hoops, or loops for holding the ties, odds are it will do the job. The top two racks in illustration 129 come complete with loops that extend from the unit itself. The bottom rack has individual miniature hangers and is ultimately superior because ties are kept separate. The other racks permit multiple ties on one prong.

The racks shown in illustration 130 do most definitely fit flat against the wall

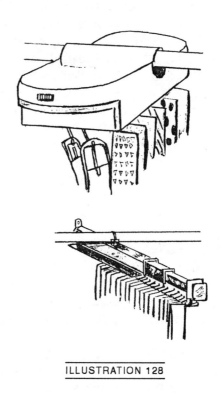

ILLUSTRATION 128

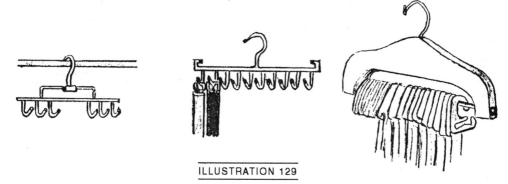

ILLUSTRATION 129

or door, but they don't have protruding prongs, which prevents access to the side against the wall. Another difficulty is the way the ties hang in layers, one overhanging another, making it virtually impossible to extract those that are hanging on the lower levels without disrupting those above.

So far racks have been presented that hold either ties or belts.

Some of the racks are truly multifaceted, able to provide and combine both capabilities into one unit. Others are much less successful.

Belts are distinctly different from ties, so it isn't usually an ideal situation to use a rack that combines both functions. On the belt rings shown in illustration 131, ties would become muddled beyond measure. The rings befuddle belts as well, since the belts huddle together in the center due to the force of gravity. It's impossible to maintain order on a belt ring. You can't categorize by color or type. The open-ended ring in the illustration is vinyl coated and it comes in a variety of colors. The closed ring is acrylic, usually with a six-inch diameter and an electroplated clasp.

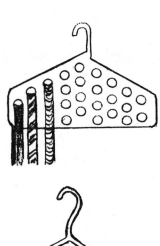

How to Regulate and Rule

Without question, it's far better to place each individual tie and each individual belt on a single peg. Ties are easy since they're all made from the same mold, but belts cause extra considerations since they don't all fasten the same way.

As in any organizing process, it's beneficial to develop standardized procedures so as to make everything routine and so that that routine maintains the orderliness we want to achieve. Belts have certain characteristics that

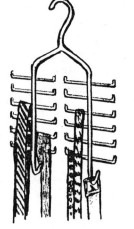

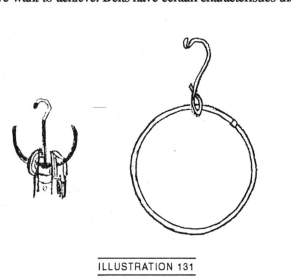

ILLUSTRATION 131

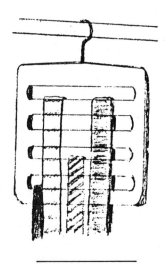

ILLUSTRATION 130

dictate the manner in which they should be hung.

1. Belts that are sashes (having no buckles whatsoever) or that have velcro fasteners, snaps, or trouser hooks should be folded in half then looped over the peg.

2. Belts with extremely little buckles (so small that even the smallest nailhead won't slip through its inner circle), must also be folded in half for hanging.

3. Belts with round gusset holes on one end and a large hook on the other can be hung in one of two ways. If the hole is large enough to fit the peg, hang it on the peg. If not, the hook on the belt must notch itself onto the buckle of a belt that's already hanging on the rack. Remember of course, to observe your color arranging system so that the two belts placed together are the same or similar color.

4. Belts (usually elastic) with a heavy clasp usually qualify for either method #1 or #3 above. Because these styles sometimes have a very large or heavy decoration on the top hook end of the belt, if they'll only hang by being folded in half over the peg, it's important to balance their weight so they won't slowly inch their way down and off the rack.

Look at illustration 132. Is this a good or bad approach to take in affording ties and belts adequate and proper placement, and does it take into account the principles of effective space management? The answer is that this method lacks the means to provide adequate and individualized spacing and it squanders vast portions of the door's space as well. Notice the emptiness above the rack, and then imagine the unused area of the door that would be left below the dangling ends of the ties and belts.

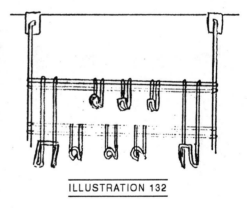

ILLUSTRATION 132

With more than one belt or tie on each hook, Murphy's Law dictates that every time a particular belt or tie is wanted, it will be found not only last, but in the one location most difficult to reach (beneath all the others).

Next we'll look at tie and belt racks designed specifically for installation on walls and doors.

When considering one of these racks, an entirely new source of space becomes available—the back wall of the closet behind the hanging clothes. The racks can't be overly intrusive or protruding or they'll continually tap the shoulders of the clothes.

All-around performance can be enhanced even further if the rod is repositioned farther away from the back wall than the normal distance of approximately twelve inches to allow a extra space behind the clothes for better clearance, accessibility, and visibility. A ventilated shelf-and-rod system, by the way, can't be moved in any way that alters its preconstructed depth of twelve inches.

For a better view of the ties and belts, install the racks as high as possible (or at least level with the rod). You can use nails for hooks instead of buying a rack, but that puts a lot of holes in a wall and it's hard to hammer that many in an even and straight line. Illustration 133 shows several racks you can purchase. The first rack has wooden pegs that alternate to keep the ties on top from bumping into the ties on the bottom. It can be purchased in different sizes.

The second rack is vinyl coated metal. It has a 24-tie capacity with three extra hooks on the structure for belts. The last rack is wooden with an inset center brass panel for 36 ties. The arms fold out and in which is exceptionally helpful for wall useage.

Illustration 134 shows several more racks that are good to use on the inside of an open-

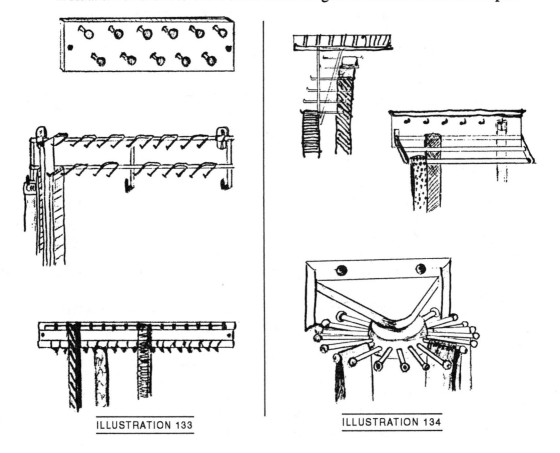

ILLUSTRATION 133   ILLUSTRATION 134

out door (but lips and side walls shouldn't be discounted).

Both the first and second are telescoping units. Lift the arms up for easy access and push them down afterwards.

The third rack is a wooden unit that revolves for better than average convenience, although it requires more space than the others.

Combining more than one rack to accomodate all of your ties and belts is an idea worth investigating. Placing racks either side by side on a door or wall, or installing them in tiers provides precise and consistent accounting of the accessories.

Peg strips as shown in illustration 135 are tailor-made for doing this because they are made in both an eleven-inch and a sixteen-inch length. If you combine one of each on a door, the width of the rack will be nearly identical to the width of a normal door.

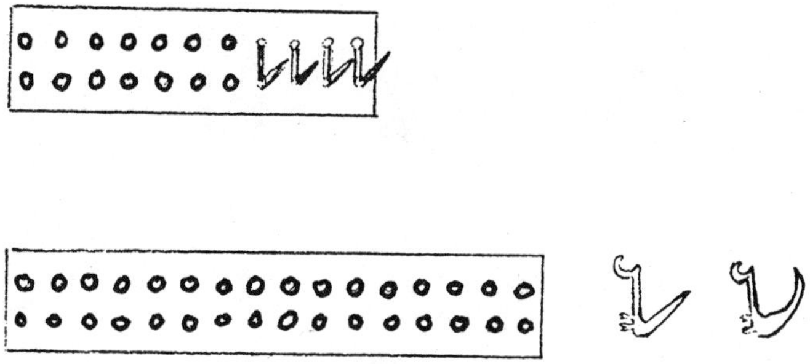

ILLUSTRATION 135

CHAPTER SEVEN

THE CLOTHES CLOSET

HANDBAGS

✔ How to Handle Handbags

How to Handle Handbags

We've been following a sensible progression as we've worked our way through the different categories, having first assigned most of the closet's space to hanging clothes, proceeding to priority placement of shoes and boots, and finally, stowing sweaters. Hence, the larger sections of closet space are mostly filled to capacity, leaving now the smaller, subdivided areas. We are now faced with the hows, wheres, and whys of storing the remaining items as effectively as we can in the areas still left.

With belts and ties squeaking their way into some of these spots, we haven't much room left. In order to restrain handbags and purses from roaming we must deed them to their own plot, complete with fences and corrals.

An overwhelming number of closets have heaps of handbags, piles of purses, bunches of bags, tons of totes, and collections of carriers of all descriptions for carrying our stuff.

Unquestionably, however, heaps and piles will not serve the handbag purpose. Purses are to be placed in an upright, uptight position at all times. It's just a matter of deciding which type of brace will keep them standing straight.

The shelf-dividers pictured in illustration 136 are certainly the easiest, since all they do is slide onto the existing closet shelf. They are quite reasonably priced.

Each divided compartment should contain only one color or one category of handbag (i.e., dressy, sequined, beaded, briefcases, wallets).

When handbags are piled in total disarray, it's a devilish task to tackle them. The simple system of slotting them straight, automatically places the purse in a position of convenience.

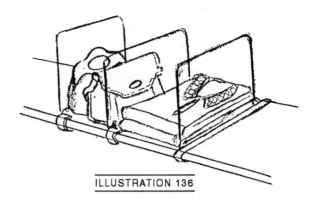

ILLUSTRATION 136

Adhering to this routine incorporates a maintenence program into the system as well. The handbag will always be returned to a specific spot and it will always be found in that same spot.

The container in illustration 137 provides separations for stowing purses, but if it were utilized in the upright position pictured, the cardboard shelves would eventually sag. The container might also be too tall for placement on a shelf, making it difficult to reach the highest purses. The zippered front is located so awkwardly that you have to hold the flap out of the way with your left hand, so your right hand can reach inside.

Turning the unit lengthwise offsets those annoyances, since the flap simply falls down out of the way when it's upzipped, yet it protects against dust only when it is zipped. Operating the unit lengthwise also results in producing another flat surface for storage because the top of the unit becomes an extra shelf and this shelf is especially helpful in handling the briefcases and totes and other large and bulky bags that wouldn't have fit inside the shelves of the unit anyway.

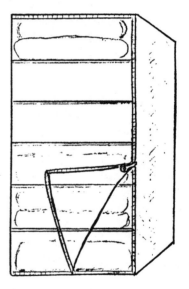

ILLUSTRATION 137

It would seem simple enough to hang handbags on a hook, nail, or peg, yet retreiving the bags isn't simple at all since they fall off the hook and their straps become tangled and intertwined. It seems simple to toss purses in a drawer, but that doesn't furnish a system of neatness, uniformity, accessibility, or visibility.

The ventilated cubbyhole pictured in illustration 138 presents a cubicle for convenient carrybag storage, although mounting it on the bottom of a closet shelf is only advisable after clothes have been consigned their proper hanging place. Then if there is room left over for this contraption, all the better. If the top of the closet shelf has received its full allowance of sweaters, shoes, or whatever and still has room remaining, sit the cubbyholes on the shelf. The top of the cubbyhole then becomes a useable shelf for storing bigger and bulkier handbags, totes, purses, briefcases, and carryalls.

The cubbyhole shown in illustration 138 is constructed of ventilated material and is meant to attach to a ventilated shelf-and-rod system.

Naturally, the cubbyhole performs just as it did for sweaters in all of the less obvious areas of the closet (such as the lip area, above the door frame, or anywhere else). Perhaps it would be advantageous to refresh your memory of cubbyhole contrivances by turning back to the sweater section for more details and descriptions of its feasibilities.

ILLUSTRATION 138

CHAPTER EIGHT

THE CLOTHES CLOSET

SCARVES

✔ How to Scrutinize Scarves

How to Scrutinize Scarves

Scarves are quite similar to ties and belts, so racks for scarves resemble racks for ties, although they are not always interchangeable. Please refer to the section on ties and belts for a detailed description of racks and their merits.

Hanging scarves on racks is the more effective method of storage, just as it was for belts and ties. And just as importantly as it was for ties is the matter of hanging each scarf on its own individual peg. Also, always arrange them by color. It's also helpful when dealing with scarves to subdivide into smaller categories, keeping them together by fabric (like silks, rayons, or cottons) or keeping them together by shape (like squares, triangles or rectangles) because that generally identifies the scarf as being worn in a particular way.

Hanging the scarf is fine, but hanging the rack from the rod is counterproductive. The two racks shown in illustration 139 are theoretically magnificent, but these hangers don't adapt well to wall or door installation because they are too wide. They could however supply scarf storage from the ceiling, as long as the scarves clear other articles in the upper regions of the closet.

The two racks in illustrations 140 and 141 improve our ability to reach, remove, and replace the scarf, even though their two approaches are totally different. The product in il-

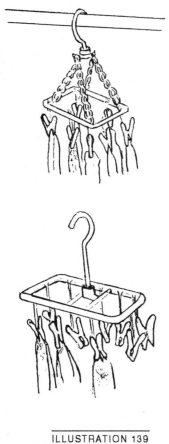

ILLUSTRATION 139

lustration 140 has a top made of clear or slightly tinted acrylic. The rack in illustration 141 is constructed of wood, with a minimum of 50 minature plastic hanger-sleeves for controlling each individual scarf. Fold the scarf lengthwise until it's slim and narrow enough to slot through the opening

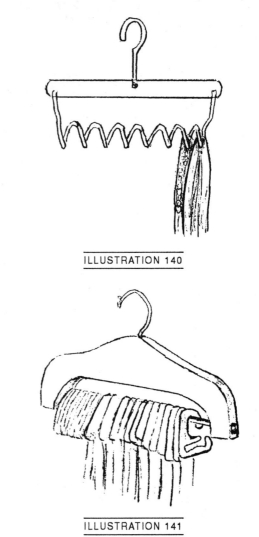

ILLUSTRATION 140

ILLUSTRATION 141

of the mini-hanger, which is then hung on the rack's miniature rod. This system is easy to maneuver when removing and replacing both the scarves and the hangers. Once the scarf is slotted, it doesn't create wrinkles and it can't slip away from the hanger.

The folding technique doesn't apply to heavier, bulkier, shawl-type scarves since they'd never fit the slot. Only when the rack's loop is angled to keep the scarf within the hook's nook, will a heavy scarf stay. If it merely lies across a peg without a partially protected or semi-enclosed means of support, it will escape and any shift in weight will upset its perilous perch. Unequal distribution of weight also affects certain styles of racks. For instance, if the rack in illustration 142 were installed on a door or wall and the scarves were heavier on one end that the other, it would tilt from side to side. Securing the rack to the wall on both ends stops this uneven distribution.

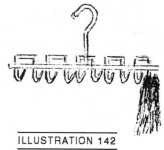

ILLUSTRATION 142

Folding scarves decreases wrinkling too, although it seems the opposite should be true. An artful fold, actually a roll, lets most of the scarf hang free. With nothing pressing against it, it remains wrinkle-free.

Illustration 143 shows a rack that's ideal when scarves are located in the closet near the clothing they're worn with. This arrangement increases the versatility and the frequency they're worn. Just because a scarf was purchased for a particular outfit, doesn't mean it can't be worn with other outfits. Mixing and matching makes a scarf more valuable.

Many beautiful, unique, or specialty drawers exist for scarves, as well as our regular dresser drawers. The difficulty lies in their impracticality for this purpose, since the scarves can't be seen or organized effectively once they're shoved inside. See illustration 144. If scarves have been shoved in one, two, or even three drawers, they are definitely upsetting the balance of power by conspicuously consuming space that could supply services for other garments.

ILLUSTRATION 143

If drawer space is the only space available for storing scarves, keep these few helpful hints in mind. First of all, divide large drawers into smaller sections, so that each section contains either one color or one fabric or shape for easier identification of the scarves (otherwise they'll get lost in the shuffle). Within each section, devise a way to keep scarves separated in rows rather than simply stacking them one on top of another. Try to incorporate a system of individual pigeonholes or compartments, so that each scarf has a home of its own.

As a last resort (in order to keep the scarves in the closet near the action) put scarves in open bins or stackable drawer units, so that the bin can sit on the shelf and be readily handed down to select a scarf. Then the bin can be replaced. Even though the maintenence program for either of these methods is monstrous, at least the scarves are more likely to be worn, making the initital cost more rewarding.

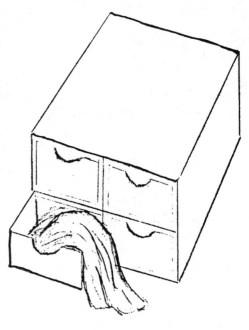

ILLUSTRATION 144

CHAPTER NINE

THE CLOTHES CLOSET

COSTUME JEWELRY

✔ How to Juggle Jewelry

✔ How to Accentuate the Positives

How to Juggle Jewelry

Costume jewelry is commonly consigned to drawers. Needless to say, jewelry has a tremendous tendency to tangle, so when an attempt is made to disengage a single necklace from the mass inside the drawer, it must first be freed from four other necklaces, two bracelets, an odd earring, safety pins, a long lost girl scout badge, and perhaps a well-hidden appliance or two. In the process of disentangling the necklace, you discover its clasp is broken. After all that effort, the necklace can't be worn anyway.

Drawer space can be accomodating and functional for jewelry (although it's not the best option), dividing it into containment areas for each individual kind of jewelry (i.e., earrings, bracelets, brooches, and necklaces).

Start by saving tiny little boxes or purchase drawer organizers from either the housewares section of a department store or office supply and stationery stores. Or go to a store where sewing machines are sold and buy specialty bobbin boxes. They provide a good miniature-sized setting for smaller items of jewelry. Or, when all of the above options don't work, there's always the jewelry box, jewelry case, jewelry pouch, jewelry roll, jewelry bag, or jewelry chest, but they aren't as effective or efficient as the do-it-yourself remedy.

Mass-marketed jewelry boxes are made from preconceived designs that are unalterable, so they don't offer the exact space dimensions our jewelry often requires. Much of it's space is wasted and inoperative and in many of them the jewelry will still tangle. It's far more productive and beneficial to create and devise a personalized, customized storage system.

By all means, use a jewelry box as a jumping off point for designing and combining trays, bins, boxes, and containers for yourself.

Building multiple levels of storage conforms to the height of most drawers. If it's arranged well, the lower layer is never removed; only the trays on top are picked up to see and reach the jewelry on the bottom. For increased effect, keep only one category at each level: earrings and rings on the bottom; necklaces next; pins, brooches, and bracelets on top. (See illustration 145.)

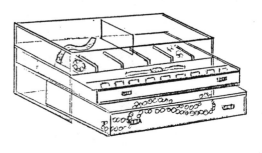

The process can be even further enhanced by dividing each distinct jewelry category into subcategories. When earrings, for example, are classified by material, color, size, how formal they are, and so on, it's much easier to find the exact item desired.

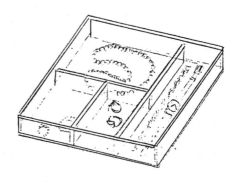

For instance, with the earrings on the bottom level of the drawer, let's say the gold earrings are on the right side, the assorted variety in the middle, and the silver earrings were on the left side of the drawer.

There are easy and inexpensive ways to develop the network of boxes and containers by simply glueing, taping, or velcroing the selected ones together on a piece of durable cardboard or plywood cut to the desired size.

Any or all of the boxes could

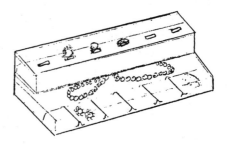

ILLUSTRATION 145

be lined with a soft fabric, which is especially adviseable when the jewelry exceeds dime-store quality. Protecting it speaks volumes about our attitude.

Caring for earrings is a constant concern since they're frequently so small they are easily misplaced or lost and the backs are always long-gone and forgotten. The ingenius book shown in illustration 146 contains page after page for arranging, aligning, and keeping those little rascals in one place. The problem is it's so specialized, it only holds pierced earrings and nothing else. Using the book idea along with racks for hanging necklaces or coupled with drawer space should supply sufficient storage, as long as the entire layout is well formulated in advance to maintain accessibility, visibility, versatilty and convenience.

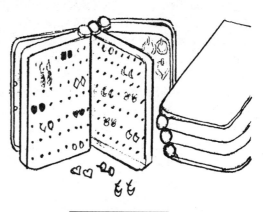

ILLUSTRATION 146

Basically, jewelry boxes are drawers, so unless the drawer space is compartmentalized, the tangles and troubles will persist. Obviously, jewelry containers come in all shapes and sizes, including floor models like the own shown in illustration 147. It does have an advantage, however, in that it supplies a place for necklaces to hang freely, which the majority of jewelry boxes do not provide. To preserve peace of mind and sanity, strive to find ways to hang every item of jewelry that can be hung. The rewards are well worthwhile, since by hanging as much of our jewelry as possible, it puts it in sight, maintains order and fingertip convenience, and saves time by stopping clinging, tangling, snagging, knotting, slipping, and disappearing.

ILLUSTRATION 147

How to Accentuate the Positives

When jewelry boxes don't furnish hooks for hanging, it's time to take matters under your own control. Many racks are specifically designed for hanging jewelry such as the acrylic one in illustration 148 that combines not only hanging capabilities but provides separate bins above for earring. Creating a customized hanging system, however, is utlimately better because it can be designed to meet specific needs and conform to specific spaces. This can be accomplished with peg strips, nails, hooks, or many of the racks arrayed for ties or belts or scarves.

The local hardware or housewares shop also features many racks that are supposed to hold and hang paraphernalia such as kitchen utensils, tools, and the like, but they adapt well to jewelry and are perhaps more acceptable because they are less expensive and present an appearance that is unusual enough and unique enough to be a fanciful or fun alternative.

Illustration 149 shows a very practical necklace and bracelet holder for mounting either in the closet or on a wall. It folds flush against the wall to prevent mishaps.

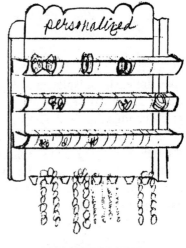

ILLUSTRATION 148

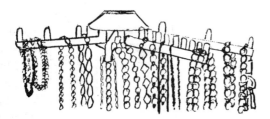

ILLUSTRATION 149

The pronged sections are sufficient and plentiful for keeping items sorted and separated.

Caution is advised when reviewing the various styles of hanging racks because they aren't always the resolvers and solvers they're cracked up to be.

The top rack in illustration 150 proposes to hang necklaces, yet those hanging on top will infringe on those below, making it hard to reach the bottom ones without lifting the tops ones out of the way. And it manages to needlessly waste space between rows. The bottom rack is for both pierced and clipped earrings, but if you use only pierced, a large portion of the space is useless. Using a door or wall for mounting the rack is discouraged if there are alcoves, hallways, bathrooms, bedrooms, dressing rooms, or dressing areas in a more logical or sensible spot.

Perhaps there is a prettier way of presenting these possessions that produces a posi-

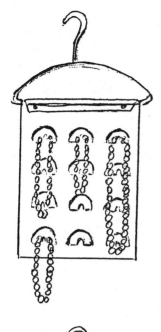

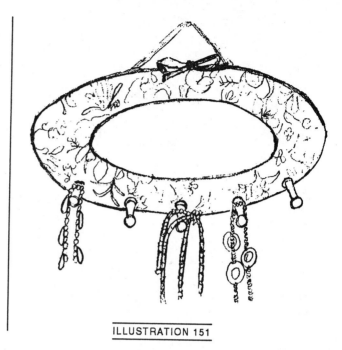

ILLUSTRATION 151

ILLUSTRATION 150

tive response. Using a decorative approach upgrades and brightens our daily lives. Illustration 151 shows a mirror, surrounded by a padded, floral fabric secured by a gross-grain ribbon with staggered wooden pegs to display the pieces of jewelry (although it doesn't offer very many pegs). Add to it other elements that could achieve extra special effects. For instance, create a complete habitat that's for jewelry: the racks, boxes, mirror, and perhaps a dressing table and stool chosen or made because they are delightful, decorative, and personally pleasing and preferred.

Place the jewelry in your customized corner as near together as possible, whether it's hung or confined in boxes. A possible configuration for this project might be a table with shelves installed above it, or simply a system of shelves, with the mirror hung above the shelves. Sitting on the table or shelves would be all the customized containers and boxes that you devised.

One word to the wise about displaying jewelry in an obvious and unguarded manner. It's a wonderful alternative for costume pieces, but the more costly and valuable items would be better left in a vault, rather than out in the open for all the world to see, feel, and touch.

CHAPTER TEN

THE CLOTHES CLOSET

HEADGEAR

✔ How to Distinguish the Differences
✔ How to Cap the Characteristics

How to Distinguish the Differences

Planning sufficient, efficient, accessible, and visible space for hats is relatively simple, provided a few fundamental guidelines are followed. Answer these questions to decide how to store your headgear.

1. Is the headwear worn often or once in awhile?

2. Is it an accumulated collection of show-and-tell hats rather than serviceable headgear?

3. Are the hats similar in size, shape, and style or are they a mixture?

4. Are they worn in the rain, snow, sleet, hail, or sun or only as a decorative touch to an ensemble?

The answers to these questions will drastically affect how you store hats, where you store hats, and whether they should be stored in one place or consigned to separate quarters.

If hats are used regularly, it's only proper we assign them to an area of convenience and visible prominence, as well as arrange them for easy access.

One way to do this is to break the hats into smaller subcategories, which distinguish their differences. Then we can redirect some of them to either a more suitable location away from the majority or supply a separate method of storage for each style.

For instance, outerwear hats belong in or near the coat closet where they're easily obtained while coming and going. Dressy, seductive, and mysterious hats that are worn during evening hours should be in the closet containing the gowns, heels, and beaded bags that are worn for infrequent black-tie events. Only the hats for daytime, anytime activities should stay in the main clothes closet.

Disregarding the in-the-closet methods of hat storage for the time being, we'll consider instead storing them near the closet.

1. Under-the-bed storage containers are available (illustration 152) for hat storage. They come with casters, sliding lids, or zippered tops for access and protection against dustdevils. Costs depend on the quality.

2. Hats can harmonize with the environment in which they are displayed. Instead of tucking them out of sight, display them. One way to do this is to pick out

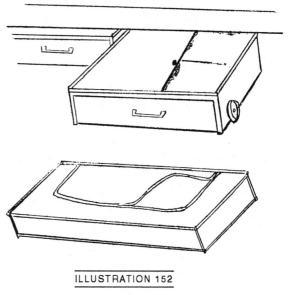

ILLUSTRATION 152

some of the more appealing, unusual, or attractive hats, and place them decoratively around a window, door, mirror, or around the outside of the closet. This approach is successful when ownership is limited to a few exceedingly attractive hats.

3. A display of hats is also possible by placing a tension pole or ceiling-mounted chain in the corner of a room or out in the open as a divider or decorative touch with hats attached attractively. The pole or chain could, of course, complement the color scheme of the room.

4. Another option for storing hats in a decorative display is to hang a basket on

a wall (illustration 153) and flip the hats inside. Or pick an appropriately sized basket (illustration 154) and put in in a prime place on the floor. The word *basket* shouldn't automatically imply a plastic laundry type. Think along the lines of bamboo, rattan, wicker, braided, stenciled, painted, padded, covered, or even brass or wooden chests.

ILLUSTRATION 153

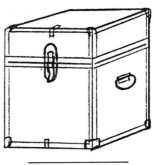

ILLUSTRATION 154

5. Guess what's currently fashionable in containment concepts? Hat boxes and cheese boxes (illustration 155)! Whether tastes run to Amish scenes, floral patterns, or lace-trimmed, purchase a few, stack them artistically and gain not only serviceable storage, but an honorary degree in interior design.

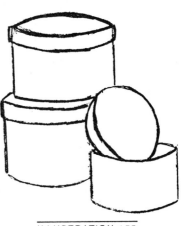

6. Installing a net or a length of coordinating fabric from the ceiling (illustration 156), fashioning it into a pouch, and arranging it in a corner makes the corner into a personal hat rack.

ILLUSTRATION 155

7. Ten to twelve hats fitting any description are in plain view and easy reach when they're tossed on an old-fashioned coat and hat rack like the one in illustration 157. These racks come in a variety of makes and models (such as bentwood or brass and with or without porcelain end-knobs), but they all give a nostalgic feeling.

8. Along the same lines, reminiscent of days gone by, are the free-standing coat racks (illustration 158), also known as coat trees. They need very little floor space, yet they will hold and display numerous hats.

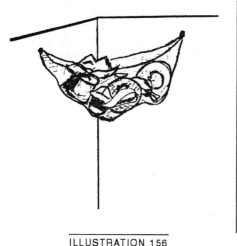

ILLUSTRATION 156

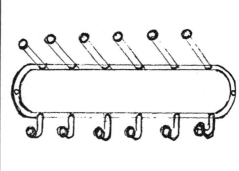

ILLUSTRATION 157

When the only time a certain hat or cap is needed is once a year on Halloween, there's no reason to store it prominently. Hats that are seldom scheduled for an appearance, do not belong in valuable closet space. They belong out of harm's way in the basement, garage, attic, or spare room. We might want to encase the hats stored in these places in plastic to protect against dust and crawly critters.

People have a tendency to stockpile certain pieces of headgear, always anticipating there will come a day when it's exactly what they want and need to cover their head. Remove them from the closet immediately! They belong somewhere else.

How to Cap the Characteristics

We've covered where to store hats in a generalized way. But before the first hat can be placed in the closet, we must decide on its function, shape, size, style, and appearance in order to discover the best way to handle it.

Obviously, with a vast array of hats each bearing little if any resemble to each other, it would be beyond our power to handle them all as identical

ILLUSTRATION 159

ILLUSTRATION 158

pieces of merchandise. To that end, the category of hat is now split into numerous sub-categories, each with its own characteristics.

The cap rack in illustration 159 is incapable of handling most hat styles, so it has limited use installed in a closet or on a wall unless you're one of the new breed of collectors who has acquired hundreds of baseball caps. Numerous nails, pegs, or hooks can accomplish what this rack does if they are installed and aligned properly and if having holes in the wall is allowed. The advantage is that not an inch of space is wasted when each individual peg can be placed exactly where needed in whatever pattern fits your closet or wall. Refer to the drip-dry hook method discussed in the chapter on boots for more detailed instructions. The hat can be stored like a boot.

Finally, we've worked our way into the closet as we look for places to store our hats. It's very possible that there is useable space available here, even though most of our belongings have already been assigned places. Be on the lookout for openings left vacant on top of any of the stackable shelves or cubbyholes we've placed in the closet. (See illustration 160.)

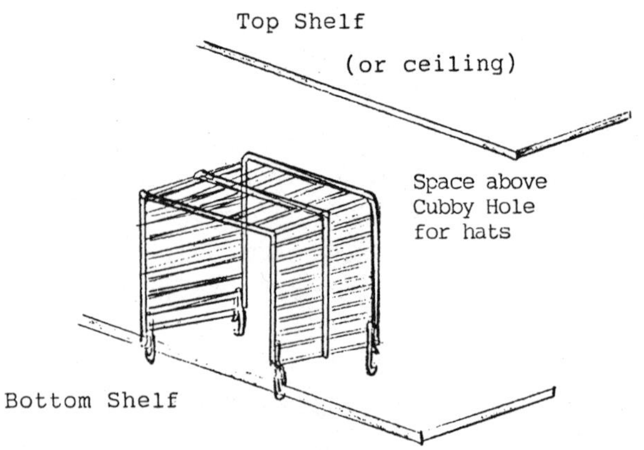

When these few inches can't be squeezed out of the closet's existing arrangement, place the hats in one selected spot on the closet shelf and stack hats together one on top of another.

ILLUSTRATION 160

The cubbyholes may have been installed somewhere other than on the closet shelf. If this is the case, there is still hope of adding hat storage to the cubbyhole's other tasks. (See chapter on handbags.)

Otherwise, we'll have to develop a system of hat storage within the closet that consists of clips and cup-hooks, much like the boots were hung.

Whenever it's possible to do so, hats of similar size should be placed together with one snuggling into the interior of another. The whole bunch can then be clipped together at their brims and hung as one unit or slung over a hook large enough to hold them.

CHAPTER ELEVEN

THE CLOTHES CLOSET

SAMPLE DESIGNS

✔ How to Figure the Facts

✔ Samplings of Standard Size Closets

✔ Working with Walk-in Closets

✔ Offerings on Odd-Shaped Closets

How to Figure the Facts

Examples of closets that have utilized all of the various methods and options explained throughout this book are discussed in this chapter. There are sections on standard closets, walk-in closets, and odd closets.

Each sample design includes a bird's-eye view if necessary. As an aid for assembling your thoughts, a checklist highlights the most important points. Thus, one of the biggest parts of the project will now be behind you, since the physical redesign of the closet is often completed in a few hours.

CHECKLIST
1. Exact closet measurements?
     Did you play with different compositions?
     Did you understand the bird's-eye view?

2. Final inventory list
   Anything unusual to consider and store?

3. The lengths of the garments?

4. How much space is needed for hanging clothes?
   Double-rod?
   Slacks?

5. What types of hanger(s)?

6. What materials will be used for the rods or shelves?
   What can be salvaged?
   Any unusual structural problems?

7. How much space is needed for shelving?
   What goes on the shelves?
   How will the shelf space be divided?
   Organizers needed?
   Step-stool?

8. How will you store the shoes and boots?
   Boxed, loose, racked, or floored?

9. How will you store the sweaters?
   Are they better rolled or folded?
   Will you use a Honeycomb system?
   Lighting?
   Moth proofing?

10. How will you store purses?

11. How will you store ties, belts, scarves, jewelry, and hats.
    What kind(s) of racks and where?

12. How will you use the door?

13. Under-the-bed space?

14. Bedroom, bath, or other wall space needed?

15. Customized products, organizers, or areas of space?

To better see how space is occupied, the sample designs are drawn to scale. The hanging garments on paper occupy the same width as they do in reality. Remember, you have already measured and recorded the lengths of your hanging garments on the inventory chart provided at the end of the first chapter.

As a general rule of thumb, the following list of inches allotted per garment will hang them on the rod in an evenly spaced and orderly manner without crowding or cramming.

1. Most garments are allotted one inch of space.

2. Suits, sportcoats, and blazer or jackets are allowed two inches to three inches each, depending on their bulk and the padding in the shoulders.

The resulting computation for the entire grouping might look something like this:

1. Twelve skirts need twelve inches of space.

2. Three suits need six inches to nine inches of closet rod space.

Keep in mind, however, your other option. If the garments are transferred to an attachable, add-on hanger, the garments can hang in vertical layers. Many are then removed from the rod itself, meaning more garments could hang in the same rod space.

All the while you're seeing the sample designs, it's imperative that you mentally put yourself in the closet and realize exactly how the space inside is being occupied. For instance, if the drawing shows a shoe rack on the left side wall, that rack occupies five inches of space. If you fail to keep tabs on these troublesome details, you'll find yourself trying to use those five inches when they simply aren't available.

The following is an explanation of the dashes, arrows, dots, and symbols that detail and define the designs, including information helpful to understanding the drawings.

1. Ventilated shelf or rod material is portrayed throughout. The separate shelf and separate rod method needs two inches to four inches more vertical space at each rod level, drastically changing the pictured design.

2. A ⫿ at the end of a shelf denotes a brace, meaning that that shelf is free-standing or unsupported by a wall at that end.

3. A ☐ at the end of a shelf is a side anchor, showing it is attached to a wall and uses twelve inches of wall space to do so.

4. The ↑ arrows shown at the ceiling and floor mark the corners where two walls come together.

5. The ↓ arrow with two tails indicates the number of inches between two given places.

Samples of Standard Sized Closets

Standard Closet (42 inches wide)

The first drawing you are about to see is a very typical small standard 42-inch closet. Normally, it has two shelves for a total of 84 inches of shelf space and one 42-inch rod for hanging.

The design in illustration 161 was devised for a client needing more hanging space than shelf space. This design has 66 inches of hanging space and an additional six inches of shelf space as well. However, the shelves aren't needed for shoes and boots. The handbags, belts, and ties were put away from the hanging space on the rod.

By utilizing attachable add-on hangers, the rod space accomodates in excess of 99 garments. This closet if laid out in a typical manner (with the clothes hanging from regular clothes hangers) would have only accomodated 42 hanging garments. Its hanging capacity was more than doubled.

STANDARD CLOSET
42 inches wide

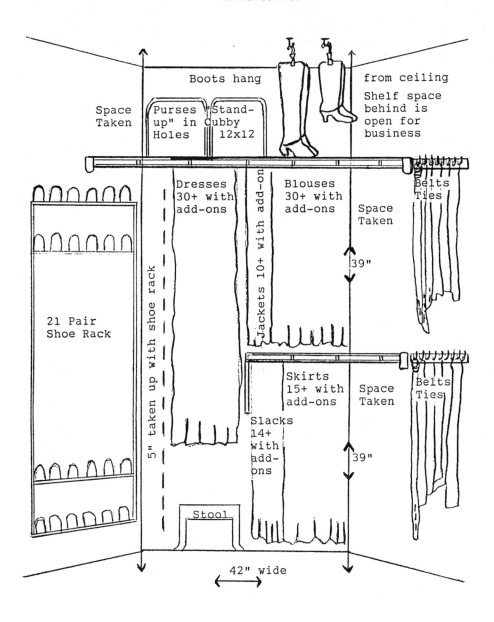

Boots hang from ceiling

Shelf space behind is open for business

Space Taken

Purses "Stand-up" in Holes

Stand-up" Cubby 12x12

Space Taken

Dresses 30+ with add-ons

Blouses 30+ with add-ons

Jackets 10+ with add-on

Belts Ties

Space Taken

39"

21 Pair Shoe Rack

5" taken up with shoe rack

Skirts 15+ with add-ons

Space Taken

Belts Ties

Slacks 14+ with add-ons

39"

Stool

42" wide

ILLUSTRATION 161

Standard Closet (60 inches wide)

This closet needed space for storing a substantial quantity of shoes (48 pairs) and sweaters (35). If your situation is the opposite, shoes could be placed on the top shelf in boxes and sweaters could be placed on the shelves on the left side wall.

If this closet had been arranged in a normal layout, it would have had two shelves totaling 10 feet of shelf space and one five-foot rod. The design shown in illustration 162 gives six feet of hanging space and 15 feet of shelf space. With the 35 sweaters removed from the rod, 35 inches of rod space were gained as well. By using attachable hangers, this closet holds more than 100 hanging garments instead of the 60 that would hang in a typical closet.

The boots were hung from the ceiling above the sliding doors. It's possible to hang six to eight pairs in that space.

Remember that ventilated systems have a two-inch overhanging lip, so when shelves are installed vertically, plan the placement of shoe boxes accordingly. Also, notice how the Honeycomb tubes use 12 inches of wall space on both sides.

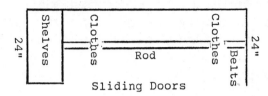

STANDARD CLOSET
60 inches wide

Birdseye View

Sliding Doors

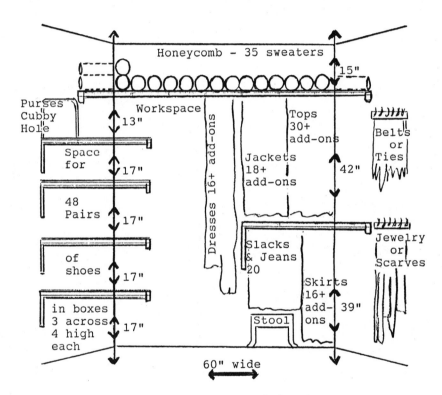

Honeycomb - 35 sweaters

15"

Purses
Cubby
Hole

Workspace

13"

Space
for

17"

48
Pairs

17"

of
shoes

17"

in boxes
3 across
4 high
each

17"

Dresses 16+ add-ons

Tops
30+
add-ons

Jackets
18+
add-ons

42"

Slacks
& Jeans
20

Skirts
16+
add-
ons

39"

Stool

Belts
or
Ties

Jewelry
or
Scarves

60" wide

Boots hanging from ceiling hooks

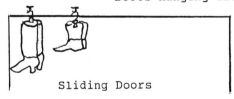

Sliding Doors

ILLUSTRATION 162

Standard Closet (72 inches wide)

Open-end slacks hangers were used in illustration 163. Otherwise the slacks couldn't have been hung in the space provided by the left side wall, since regular hangers demand more space and this client needed space for numerous pairs of slacks.

If this closet had the typical two shelves and one rod, it would have provided six feet of hanging space and 12 feet of shelf space. This design gives 10 feet of rod space and 18 feet of shelf space. A total of 122 garments is accomodated instead of the normal 72.

The boots are sitting on the top shelf of the right side wall and need only eight vertical inches for the flopped position, although this design allowed 13 inches. The rest of the shelves on the wall were for the shoes this client possessed.

STANDARD CLOSET
72 inches wide

Birdseye View

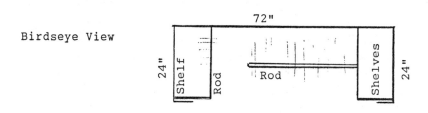

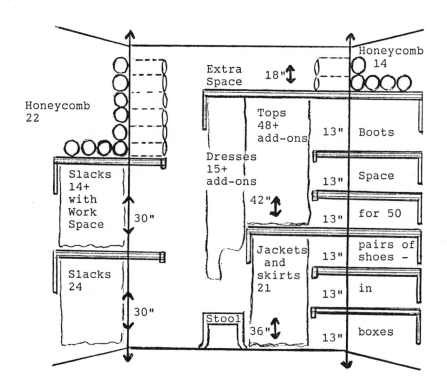

ILLUSTRATION 163

123

Standard Closet (100 inches wide)

The design in illustration 164 was devised to accomodate numerous pairs of shoes (52). If you need far less shoe space, consider a 21-pair shoe rack on the left side wall, which leaves the entire top shelf empty.

This closet in typical fashion would provide a little over eight feet of rod space and a bit over 16 feet of shelf space. This design provides in excess of 12 feet of rod space and just over 15 feet of shelf space.

This closet belonged to a client with an overwhelming number of blouses. Without the attachable hangers the 108 tops wouldn't have fit. This closet now holds 250 garments, double the quantity this closet would typically hold.

Each 12 inch x 12 inch x 12 inch cubbyhole holds on average eight purses or three super-bulky sweaters or up to 15 thin turtlenecks or six regular sweaters or combinations of the above.

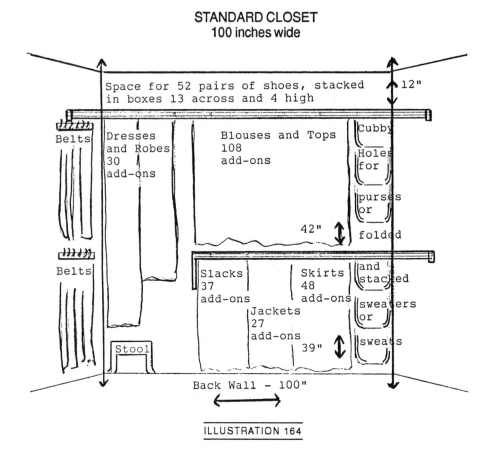

STANDARD CLOSET
100 inches wide

ILLUSTRATION 164

Standard Closet (106 inches wide)

The closet in illustration 165 usually would have two shelves for 18 feet of useable space and one nine-foot rod. This design provides 31 feet of shelf space and 14 feet of rod space.

This client liked to have sweaters in stacks, so we supplied a step stool for reaching the stacks.

This client didn't require an abundance of space for shoes or hanging. By utilizing the stack shelves in the center instead of a shoe rack on one of the side walls, the closet was effectively split into his and her sections, which makes for more harmonious personal relationships.

STANDARD CLOSET
106 inches wide

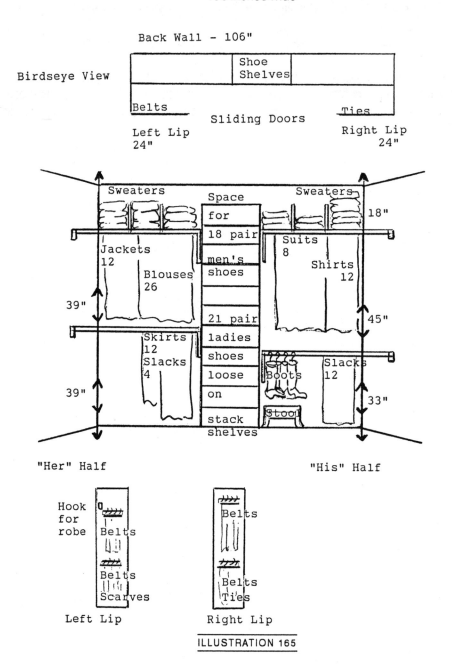

Back Wall – 106"

Birdseye View

| | Shoe Shelves | |

Belts — Sliding Doors — Ties

Left Lip
24"

Right Lip
24"

Sweaters — Space for 18 pair men's shoes — Sweaters — 18"

Jackets 12 — Suits 8

Blouses 26 — Shirts 12

39" — 21 pair ladies shoes — 45"

Skirts 12 — Slacks 12

Slacks 4 — Boots — Slacks 12

39" — loose on stack shelves — Stool — 33"

"Her" Half — "His" Half

Hook for robe — Belts — Belts — Belts — Belts — Scarves — Belts — Ties

Left Lip — Right Lip

ILLUSTRATION 165

Standard Closet (increased depth)

When closets are deeper than normal (more than 24 inches deep) they can be approached differently. The closet in illustration 166, unfortunately, wasn't wide enough to allow hanging on each side wall, but it was certainly advantageous to gain the five feet of hanging space instead of limiting hanging space to only the back wall.

This client owned many shorts, so we were able to triple layer the right side of the closet because the ceiling height of this closet was nine feet and not the usual eight feet.

Typically, this closet would have had two shelves on the back wall for a total of nine feet and one rod only 4½ feet wide. This design decreased shelving to 7½ feet, but furnished 15 feet of hanging space. It wasn't as important to have shelf space, since the shoes fit on a rack on the inside of the door.

STANDARD CLOSET
Increased depth

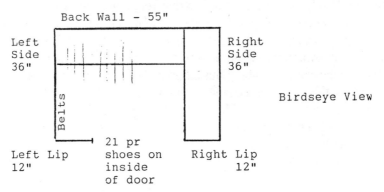

Back Wall - 55"

Left Side 36"

Right Side 36"

Belts

Birdseye View

Left Lip 12"

21 pr shoes on inside of door

Right Lip 12"

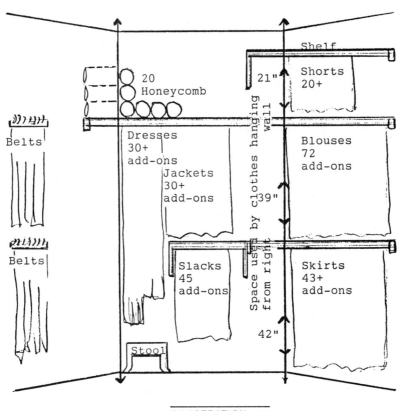

Shelf

20 Honeycomb

21"

Shorts 20+

Belts

Dresses 30+ add-ons

Jackets 30+ add-ons

Space used by clothes hanging wall from right

39"

Blouses 72 add-ons

Belts

Slacks 45 add-ons

Skirts 43+ add-ons

42"

Stool

ILLUSTRATION 166

Working with Walk-in Closets

Walk-in Closet (74 inches wide x 118 inches deep)

With walk-in closets it's extremely important to understand how adjoining walls infringe on each other. Keep in mind also that the ventilated systems make closet corners more productive (although not used in any of these designs).

If this closet were an average walk-in closet, it would provide 19 feet, 8 inches of hanging space from both side walls and a little over 39 feet of shelf space. The design (illustrations 167, 168, and 169) increased the area for hanging to 27 feet and gave nearly 50 feet of shelving.

This client was exceptionally tall, which affected how the space could be distributed, and this closet had an air vent on the right side that lessened the wall's potential usefulness.

The belt racks on the inside of the open-out door were placed side-by-side for maximum space utilization.

WALK-IN CLOSET
74" wide x 118" deep

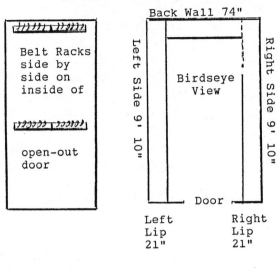

Belt Racks side by side on inside of

open-out door

Back Wall 74"

Left Side 9' 10"

Birdseye View

Right Side 9' 10"

Door

Left Lip 21"

Right Lip 21"

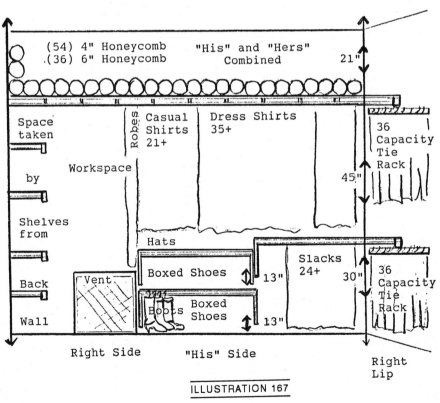

(54) 4" Honeycomb
(36) 6" Honeycomb

"His" and "Hers" Combined

21"

Space taken

by

Shelves from

Back

Wall

Robes

Casual Shirts 21+

Dress Shirts 35+

Workspace

Hats

Boxed Shoes

Vent

Boots Boxed Shoes

13"

13"

Slacks 24+

30"

45"

36 Capacity Tie Rack

36 Capacity Tie Rack

Right Side

"His" Side

Right Lip

ILLUSTRATION 167

WALK-IN CLOSET
74" wide x 118" deep

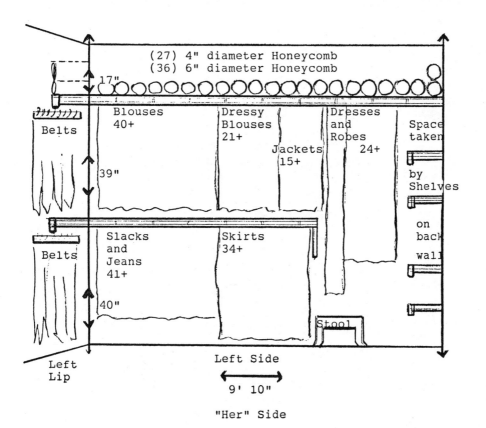

(27) 4" diameter Honeycomb
(36) 6" diameter Honeycomb

17"

Blouses
40+

Dressy
Blouses
21+

Dresses
and
Robes
24+

Jackets
15+

Space
taken

Belts

39"

by
Shelves

on
back
wall

Slacks
and
Jeans
41+

Skirts
34+

Belts

40"

Stool

Left
Lip

Left Side

9' 10"

"Her" Side

ILLUSTRATION 168

WALK-IN CLOSET
74" wide x 118" deep

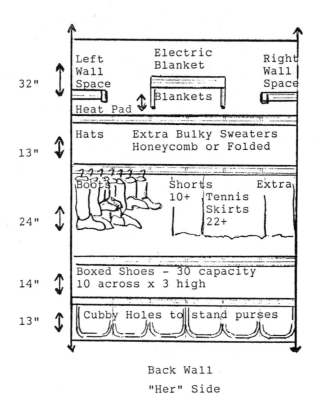

32"   Left Wall Space — Electric Blanket — Right Wall Space / Blankets / Heat Pad

13"   Hats   Extra Bulky Sweaters Honeycomb or Folded

24"   Boots   Shorts 10+   Tennis Skirts 22+   Extra

14"   Boxed Shoes - 30 capacity 10 across x 3 high

13"   Cubby Holes to stand purses

Back Wall
"Her" Side

ILLUSTRATION 169

132

Walk-in Closet (L-shape)

The design in illustrations 170, 171, and 172 gives this closet over 32 feet of hanging space and nearly 96 feet of shelving. Typically it would have had two shelves above a rod on the left side wall, back wall, and right side wall, providing 22 feet of hanging space and a little over 47 feet of shelf space.

WALK-IN CLOSET
L-shape

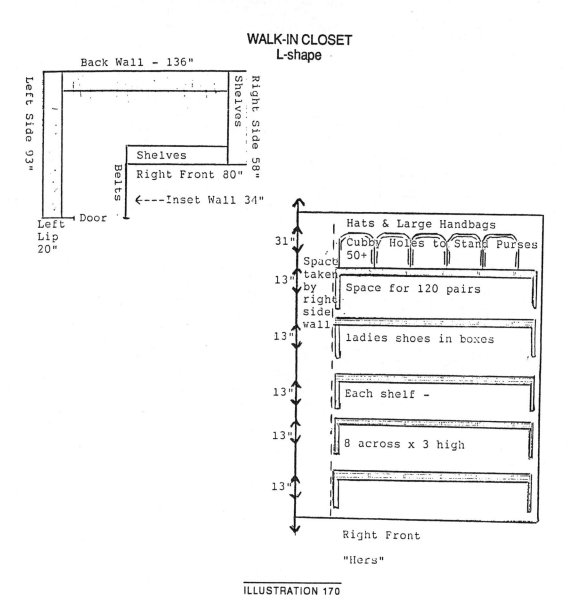

ILLUSTRATION 170

WALK-IN CLOSET
L-shape

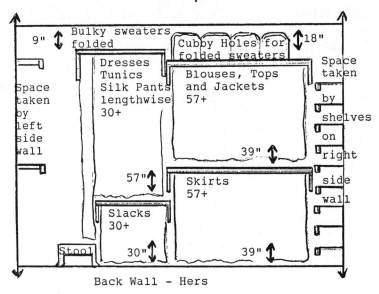

9"   Bulky sweaters folded   Cubby Holes for folded sweaters   18"

Space taken by left side wall

Dresses Tunics Silk Pants lengthwise 30+

Blouses, Tops and Jackets 57+

Space taken by shelves on right side wall

57"

39"

Skirts 57+

Slacks 30+

Stool   30"   39"

Back Wall - Hers

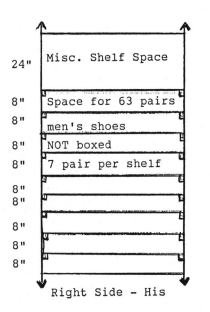

24"   Misc. Shelf Space

8"   Space for 63 pairs
8"   men's shoes
8"   NOT boxed
8"   7 pair per shelf
8"
8"
8"
8"
8"

Right Side - His

ILLUSTRATION 171

WALK-IN CLOSET
L-shape

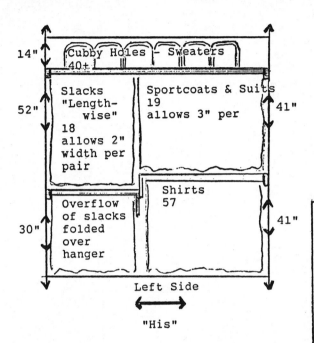

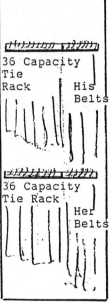

Left Side

"His"

Inset Wall

Combined

"His" & "Hers"

ILLUSTRATION 172

Walk-in Closet (94 inches wide x 60 inches deep)

The design in illustrations 173 and 174 gives 21 feet of hanging space and 27 feet of shelf space. A typical design allows only 18 feet of hanging space and 36 feet of shelf space. Although there's now less shelf space, it was given in exchange for hanging 428 garments (instead of 166).

WALK-IN CLOSET
94" wide x 60" deep

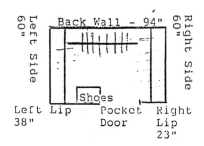

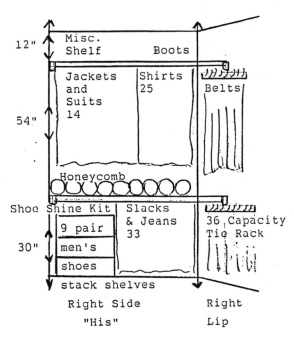

ILLUSTRATION 173

WALK-IN CLOSET
94" wide x 60" deep

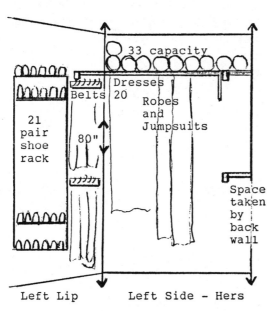

Left Lip   Left Side - Hers

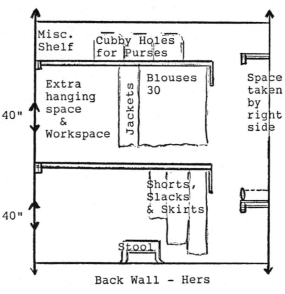

Back Wall - Hers

ILLUSTRATION 174

Walk-in Closet (120 inches wide with different side depths)

The closet shown in illustrations 175, 176, and 177 would traditionally have a single rod with two shelves above, furnishing 19 feet of hanging space and nearly 38 feet of shelf space. This design, however, has given the closet 31 feet for hanging and 41 feet of shelf space plus an additional 50 feet provided by the stack shelves. Many of these stack shelves include drawers for storage within the closet, which was requested by these particular clients, since they didn't want dressers or drawers in the bedroom itself.

It was impossible to utilize the wall behind the open-in door for hanging or shelving, so a mirror was installed there, as well as on the back of the door. This gave the clients a two-way view of themselves.

WALK-IN CLOSET
120" wide with different side depths

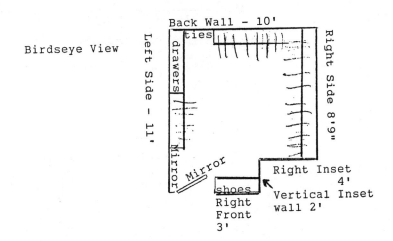

Birdseye View

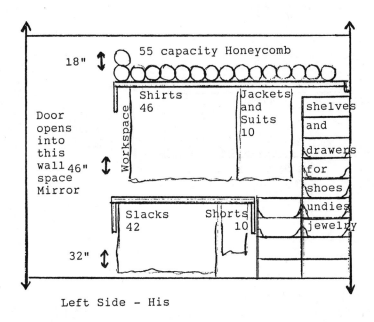

Left Side – His

ILLUSTRATION 175

WALK-IN CLOSET
120" wide with different side depths

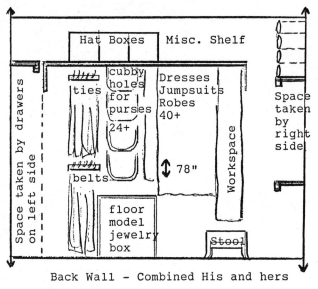

Back Wall - Combined His and hers

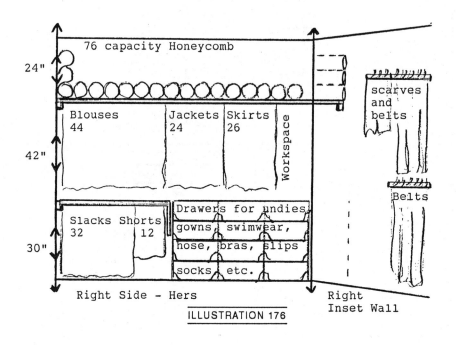

Right Side - Hers

ILLUSTRATION 176

Right
Inset Wall

WALK-IN CLOSET
120" wide with different side depths

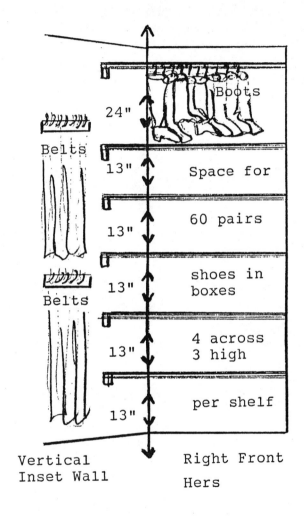

Boots

24"

Belts

13"   Space for

13"   60 pairs

Belts

13"   shoes in
       boxes

13"   4 across
       3 high

13"   per shelf

Vertical   Right Front
Inset Wall
                  Hers

ILLUSTRATION 177

Offerings on Odd Closets

The Odd Closet (144 inches wide x 66 inches deep x 26 inches high)

Odd closets must make every available inch functional as shown in the design in illustrations 178 and 179 where 18 feet of hanging space was obtained instead of the 11 feet that would have been possible had this closet been arranged in a typical manner. With only a regular closet rod it would have had little, if any, shelf space. We managed to provide eight feet of shelving. This wasn't easy considering the maximum height of this closet was only seven feet and the lowest walls, nearly one half of the closet, sloped down to only 26 inches.

THE ODD CLOSET
144" wide x 66" deep x 26" high at back wall

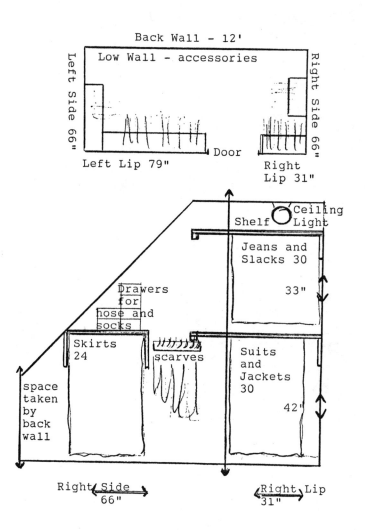

ILLUSTRATION 178

THE ODD CLOSET
144" wide x 66" deep x 26" high at back wall

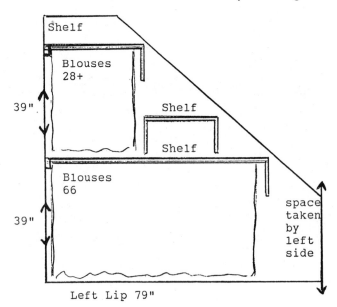

Shelf

Blouses
28+

39"

Shelf

Shelf

Blouses
66

39"

space
taken
by
left
side

Left Lip 79"

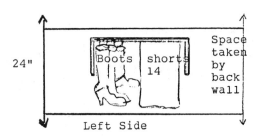

24"

Boots shorts
14

Space
taken
by
back
wall

Left Side

Any combination of shoe racks, shoe shelves, honeycomb
or stack shelves, cubby holes, as needed to accomodate
accessories

Back Wall

ILLUSTRATION 179

The Odd Closet (191 inches wide x 95 inches deep x 30 inches high)

The next closet (illustrations 180, 181, 182, and 183) would normally have a single rod on each side wall for 16 feet of hanging space and no shelf space. This design however, furnishes 43 feet of hanging space and 40 feet of shelf space—an unbelieveable improvement.

The back wall, with a height of only 30 inches, serves best for storing accessories. In order to give it maximum effectiveness, we custom built a portable island with a flat level top that could be used as a work area for folding, rolling, and managing clothing as needed. It sat out a distance from the back wall for easier access and also because this client kept suitcases in the space behind the island, since she traveled a great deal.

NOTE: We put the support braces on the ventilated systems before securing them to the wall, otherwise there wasn't enough clearance to lift the shelf afterwards to install the brace because of the sloped ceiling.

THE ODD CLOSET
191" wide x 95" deep x 30" high

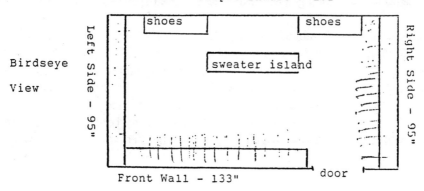

Birdseye

View

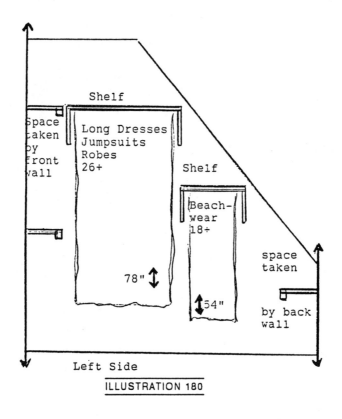

ILLUSTRATION 180

THE ODD CLOSET
191" wide x 95" deep x 30" high

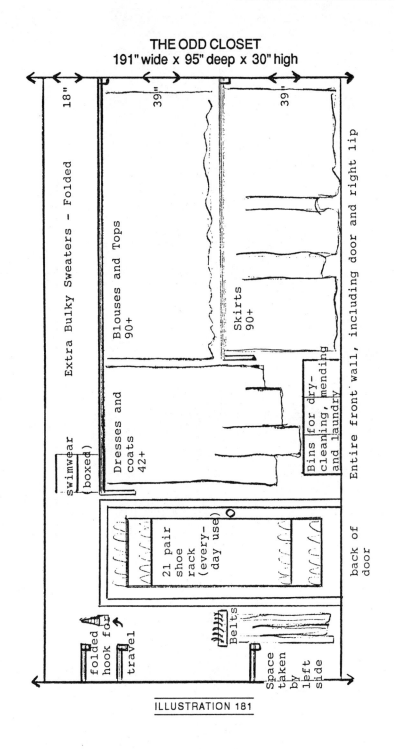

ILLUSTRATION 181

THE ODD CLOSET
191" wide x 95" deep x 30" high

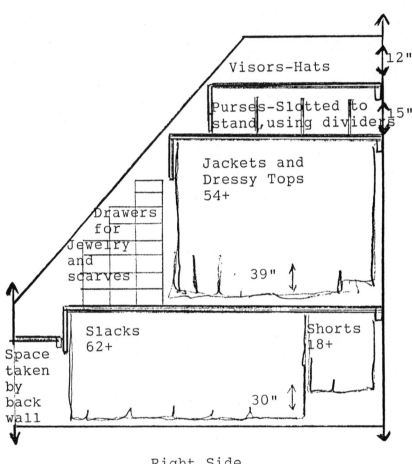

Right Side

ILLUSTRATION 182

THE ODD CLOSET
191" wide x 95" deep x 30" high

Flat Top Surface of Island used for folding/rolling

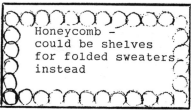

Honeycomb —
could be shelves
for folded sweaters
instead

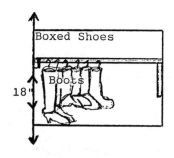

18"

Back Wall —

Back Wall is
30" high

Open area of back
wall behind sweater
island used for
storing luggage

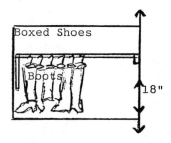

18"

— Back Wall

ILLUSTRATION 183

CHAPTER TWELVE

DRAWERS

✔ How to Seek Solutions

✔ How to Understand Undergarments

✔ How to Utilize Space under the Bed

How to Seek Solutions

A drawer is a drawer, unless it's a bin, but no matter where it's located, there are negative aspects in this type of storage system—like poor accessibility and visibility. However, when drawers or bins are placed inside the closet we have at least eliminated inconvenience from our list of complaints (illustration 184).

When closet space is large enough to permit placing drawers or bins inside or when the closet is designed to specifically include drawers, it does indeed produce significantly improved practicality. Notice on many of the sample designs in the last chapter, drawers were sometimes installed inside the closets, either to keep everyday undergarments near at hand or for grouping items.

It's not to say we would all benefit by or be pleased to have our unmentionables in drawers inside the closet, but the convenience is commendable.

Most of us have become so accustomed to having our drawers or bins far away from the closet that we don't even recognize how inefficient the system is.

Another routine we follow without really questioning it is the view we're presented with each time we open any of our drawers. Mostly, we rummage around as quickly as possible to grasp the first halfway acceptable item we need for the day.

Since we can't stop storing our goods in drawers, our only recourse is to figure out how drawers can work for us, instead of against us.

How to Understand Undergarments

Drawers are the recipients of a vast hodgepodge of personal paraphernalia, some of which is definitely dutiful, some delightful, and some which should be disposed of.

Since sweaters, handbags, scarves, jewelry, belts, ties, and headgear are not stored in drawers that leaves very little to be discussed in this chapter. But the items that do remain are essential and can't be ignored. The first essential that dwells in our drawers are undergarments and the second essential that must be reviewed are the nonessentials.

These are things that aren't meant to adorn, warm, pleasure, prepare, protect, glamorize, or serve the body. They should be removed from your drawers. They belong elsewhere.

The first stage in developing a system of order within the drawer is to separate the categories. Socks need their own drawer. (See illustration 185.) The drawer itself

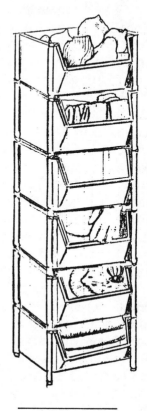

ILLUSTRATION 184

may be divided into compartments by using an acrylic box for socks, or a shoe box will do quite nicely. Or roll the socks into balls. Then they can be easily removed and replaced without mussing up the other pairs of socks.

With all socks visible, the ones with holes or other flaws don't pile up at the bottom

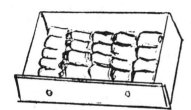

ILLUSTRATION 185

like they do when we store them in stacks. The great thing about socks is that rolling them doesn't wrinkle them.

This drawer in illustration 186 has strips that divided the drawer into sections; however the articles that are in the drawer itself are mismatched and they weren't arranged for consistency even at that. Notice the three compartments that have the socks folded once and laid down lengthwise in their slot. When the socks on the bottom of the stack are the socks we wish to wear, the neat stack isn't going to stay neat. In the far right row the

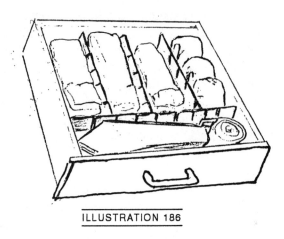

ILLUSTRATION 186

socks are arranged with a folded side pointing upwards, which allows us to see, choose, and pick one pair without messing up the rest. Folding the socks into a bundle also keeps mates together, so we don't go chasing the renegades.

By rolling undergarments, we can lay each group out in a single layer along the bottom of the drawer.

To roll undergarments into a ball, fold over both sides of a pair of panties or men's briefs to a width of about three inches or four inches. Begin at the bottom and roll upward toward the waistband. Place the folded garment in a drawer so the waistband points down and the rolled edge faces up. If the slips, bras, pantyhose, panties, and even nighties in illustration 187 had been rolled, we would see every single item, instead of only the article on top.

Simply dividing the undergarments into categories doesn't turn the drawer into a miracle of management. Obviously

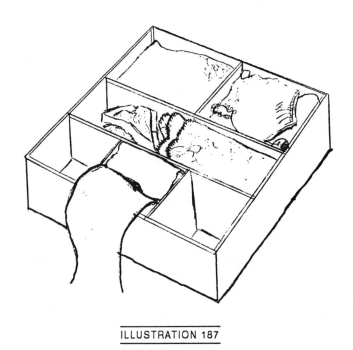

ILLUSTRATION 187

152

a system is required that enables us to see each article in each category.

With a rolled or folded edge is visible, we help meet this criteria, but the crowning glory of a drawer system is achieved when we arrange the articles by color.

For instance, roll all the undies and lay them out single file from the back of the drawer to the front, putting only the colored or print ones in the drawer first. Or you can put all your colored underwear in a shoe box. Then place all the white underwear, beige underwear or nude and flesh-colored underwear on the shoe box lid and set the lid on top of the box. Now, when this drawer is viewed, the items that are worn every day are immediately visible. Simply lift the shoe box lid to obtain the black lace or fire engine red ones for those extra special occasions.

The number of shoe boxes used can be kept to a minimum by leaving space between them (which creates another compartment). Place the first box a distance away from the side of the drawer, so that a compartment is formed there as well. Thus, looking down on the system in the drawer, we'd see the left side of the drawer, an open space, the first shoe box, an open space, the next shoe box, and so on, all the way over to the right side of the drawer.

The lids from the shoe boxes allow us to build a second level in the drawer.

When socks, undershirts, or whatever, are only folded over once and then stacked, they can't help but fall apart. The whole drawer becomes jumbled now and forever after.

How to Utilize Space Under the Bed

Before the advent of under-the-bed storage units, whenever we slid anything under the bed, it was irrecoverable until our next spring cleaning. Or, if it was reclaimed sooner, it couldn't be worn until all the cobwebs and dust had been cleaned off.

If the space under the bed is reachable, there's no good reason not to use it. Common sense should be applied, however. Store things that you don't use every day under the bed.

The space under the bed, would aptly entertain linens, blankets, pillows, sheets, or seasonal or occasional items. Whatever is chosen should always be stowed in a box or bin and never simply stuffed away without a protective covering. The container is mandatory because without it we'd be hard pressed to ever see or reach the merchandise again.

Under-the-bed units are advertised extensively nowadays, which leads one to believe they are worthwhile labor-savers and furnish a way to convert this space into a sensible storage place.

Many of the under-the-bed versions are equipped with casters or wheels for ease in maneuvering them in and out, while the sliding lid on top provides easy entry. Other models, attach to the bed frame to become a pull-out drawer, which works almost as well. (See illustration 188.)

The model in illustration 189 has no support structure, so unless it's completely crammed, it's going to collapse on top of the items it contains.

Think about how under-the-bed space can best serve your needs. Bed linens are feasible because they're seldom changed more than once a week. We generally have an abundant supply of extra blankets, pillows and sheets. So if you've allowed the linen closet to amass extras, the sensible thing to do is to place the under-the-bed unit under the bed in the spare bedroom.

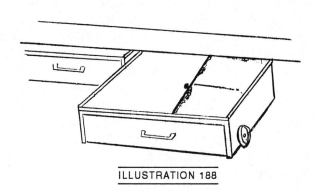

ILLUSTRATION 188

Under-the-bed space is a likely place for seasonal items, such as swim suits, cover-ups, and beach towels, or long johns, ski bibs, and winter apparel.

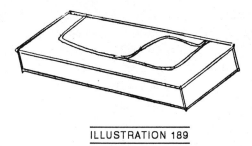

ILLUSTRATION 189

THE LINEN CLOSET

✔ How to Tolerate Toiletries

✔ How to Billet Blankets and Pillows

How to Tolerate Toiletries

Linen closets are seldom the singular storage entity their name implies, since they frequently serve as a storage facility for a hodgepodge of other articles.

First and foremost among these other items are toiletries, tissues, cleaning supplies, and medicines.

Imagine the possibilities if these miscellaneous items were removed, so that the shelves inside the linen closet itself were used for only laundered products and linens.

Moving the toiletries, medications, cosmetics, and cleaning compounds to a rack on the inside of the linen closet door actually kills two birds with one stone. The shelves of the closet are not only opened up, but also the miscellaneous items are managed much better on the smaller shelves of the door rack.

Illustration 190 shows a feasible way to break down the products by shelf.

As with all things that look too good to be true, there is one pitfall with this system. The shelves of the door rack have slotted bottoms, which allow tiny items to drop through the slots.

This isn't an insurmountable problem. One solution is very simple. Buy door racks that have the smallest slots or incorporate drawer dividers onto the shelves.

This calls for measuring the width of the rack (most are either 12 inches or 18 inches wide) and then deciding whether one long divider is appropriate or if two or three shorter ones will suit the items better.

Drawer dividers aren't the only way to separate items. For instance, make-up and cosmetics stored in a clear vinyl carrying case could be retrieved from the rack, carried to the bathroom, used and returned.

Mostly though, the mouthwash, toothpaste, tissues, and other products on this rack are surplus. Cleaning supplies, however, are most convenient when they're placed in their own personal carry-all that sits on the floor of the linen closet. When it is cleaning day we pick it up, attend to our chores, and return it. (See illustration 191.)

By establishing a system for categorizing products, we clearly see and recognize just what we have on hand. It's fine to buy in volume, especially when something's on sale and we can't pass it up. If we place all four bottles of hair spray on the same shelf, it is difficult to use more than one at the same time. Put the newest purchase at the back of the line, so that each time you reach for a replacement, you will automatically grasp the oldest item.

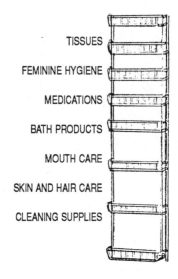

TISSUES

FEMININE HYGIENE

MEDICATIONS

BATH PRODUCTS

MOUTH CARE

SKIN AND HAIR CARE

CLEANING SUPPLIES

ILLUSTRATION 190

ILLUSTRATION 191

To organize, consolidate. Pour half full and nearly empty containers of the same product together and discard the empties. Check expiration dates and pitch those that are out of date. Packages that have seen better days can either be repaired or consigned to Ziploc bags or whatever will hold it best.

This process alone probably lightens the load considerably. Now we will organize, align, and arrange 100 items instead of 200 or 300.

If the door rack isn't a viable option for storing toiletries and medicines, cleaning supplies, and other containers, they will have to share the shelf space with the towels, sheets, and blankets. But linens must be kept separate from toiletries.

Again, putting each kind of item into its own compartment is best. Use shoe boxes, bins, boxes, and bags. We may need to use stack shelves on the floor of the linen closet or on the existing shelves to divide the height. (See illustration 192.)

It isn't necessary to build our system up, since we do have the option in the case of toiletries, incidentals, and medications to build our system below the existing shelves in the linen closet. Again, the wire construction of this particular pull-out basket (illustration 193) will let the smaller items fall through. Sample instead a system of under-the-shelf drawers and bins that are solidly constructed. There are many such variations for sale. Some are wood, some are similar to Tupperware plastic, and some are molded plastic that may shatter, split, and crack over time.

How to Billet Blankets and Pillows

Linen closets have the same shelf design as every other closet in the house. Because of the prespecified placement of shelves, the first obstacle we must overcome is the excessive height between shelves. If we stack the linens to the height we see before us in a closet, our stack would be so big, it would never stay neat and tidy.

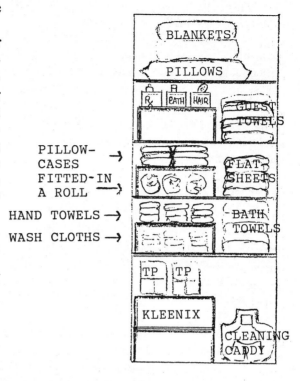

PILLOW-
CASES →
FITTED-IN
A ROLL →

HAND TOWELS →

WASH CLOTHS →

ILLUSTRATION 192

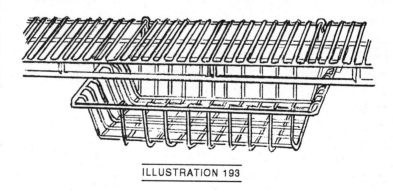

ILLUSTRATION 193

Reproportioning the height is job #1. This is achieved with stack shelves. Dividing the space not only puts a limit on how many towels or sheets we can stack in any one pile, but it helps us to keep categories in separate niches. The result is more stacks, with less in each stack, so we can identify each at a glance, rather than rummaging through to see what's there.

Many types of stack shelves also have a built-in drawer, which increases the linen closet's potential to handle both linens and the toiletries at the same time. (See illustration 194.) The linens would be stacked on the top of the shelf, while the toiletries are put in the drawer below. Wire bins and baskets that attach to the existing shelf will also separate the shelf space.

The floor is a vast space that is generally squandered because we either put the laundry basket here or because we pile in all our rejects.

Inside the linen closet there is generally another large area of unused space. This is the space from the top of the top shelf to the ceiling. It's quite understandable why it's not used. Who can reach that high? Even if we thought far enough ahead to bring along the step stool, we still can't maneuver bulky bundles onto the top shelf.

To use this space, try rolling blankets and quilts so that they form a smaller bundle that can fit on the shelf front to back.

Designers and builders for no good reason build linen closets 16 inches deep instead of 12 inches like other closets. The four inches is virtually useless because we can't see or reach it. We end up losing whatever makes its way back there. There is nothing we own that is so big it can't be quartered in 12 inches of space.

And then of course, we come to the age old dilemma, what do we do when there isn't a linen closet at all?

This instant five-shelf, free-standing unit (illustration 195) could be just the solution for storing blankets and bed linens, towels and bath sheets. The problem lies in where to place it.

Decorative containers like baskets, chests, trunks, or imaginatively contrived shelves, quilt stands, ladders, and the like seem to be a fashionable and appealing approach to take in finding a place for storing these pieces.

The linen closet usually shares space with the vacuum cleaner and its attachments, the ironing board, the iron, and all the starches and sprays that go with it. (See pantry and laundry room sections.)

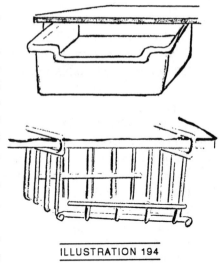

ILLUSTRATION 194

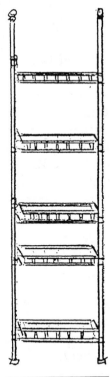

ILLUSTRATION 195

THE COAT CLOSET

✔ How to Negotiate the Negatives

✔ How to Manipulate Mittens and Muffs

✔ How to Forecast More Favorably

How to Negotiate the Negatives

The coat closet is ordinarily a disaster area, with umbrellas, boots, gloves, wool caps, and scarves mingled with coats, jackets, shawls, and windbreakers. We also usually view the coat closet as a wonderful catch-all for stuff like table leafs, picnic baskets, vacuum cleaners, TV trays, board games, and wedding gifts that we don't know where else to put.

Amazingly, the coat closet is one of the easiest closets in the house to revamp. The problem is that the typical coat closet isn't functional for the garments it is asked to contain.

Most of the space is wasted because the longer overcoats and trench coats are treated the same as the shorter coats and casual jackets.

The negatives therefore consist of the following: too little hanging space and what there is, isn't conducive to the varying lengths of the coats, the gloves and umbrellas haven't been assigned to any particular place, and the odds and ends have taken control.

Taking one obstacle at a time, we'll look at hanging space first. The height of the existing rod is our prime consideration. Is it high enough to allow us to double-rod the lower section of the closet? If it is, are we going to install a new rod that spans the full width or will we choose to use an extender rod to acquire our extra hanging space. This choice is not only based on the number of coats and their lengths, but the amount of money and energy you wish to expend on the project.

For samples of the styles and types of extender rods available, see the section on these innovative inventions at the end of chapter 3.

Illustration 196 depicts three ventilated shelf/rods being utilized with the top one moved to a higher position to make room for the shelf that hangs boots and holds umbrellas and hats. The shorter coats on the second, lower rod were removed from the top rod, opening it up for a more evenly spaced arrangement of the remaining coats at the higher level. Notice, that not one of the outerwear accessories is permitted on the top shelf.

The top shelf is totally useless in a coat closet, since nothing can be stored that high and still be readily accessible. Certainly not hats, gloves, umbrellas, or scraves, since they're lost at that altitude.

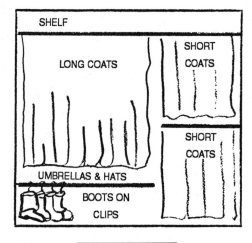

ILLUSTRATION 196

As the illustration shows, the coats are not just a single group but two distinct and very different types. One coat classification consists of longer and bulkier outerwear. The other is comprised of shorter, stubbier, streamlined garments.

The third and lowest rod is optional. There are a great many methods for managing muffs and mittens that are far more advantageous than a shelf system. Although hanging the boots and keeping them off the floor is a major victory in itself, especially if a mat, throw rug, or towel is put on the floor to catch the drips, melting slush, and mud.

The coat closet is perhaps the only closet in the house that is permitted to contain items other than the ones it was specifically designed for. The outlandish objects and outdated items may find their place on the top shelf of this closet. Things that don't defy description should be placed together in a logical location, leaving only rare, unusual, and unique items permission to occupy this ledge. Choose articles that are never needed, seldom seen, and are usually wiped from our memories. Never attempt to maneuver extremely heavy objects onto this shelf. They will crash, club, or cleave our craniums some day.

How to Manipulate Mittens and Muffs

There's no way to survive the cold and wet of winter without having the benefit of a mitten pouch in the coat closet. Yes, it's actually nothing more than an old-fashioned, clear vinyl shoe bag (illustration 197), but what a startling difference it makes. Hang it from the rod, hang it on the side wall, hang it on the inside of the door, but hang it! If the spot selected isn't the rod, simply insert a screw-eye, cup hook, or nail in the desired position and hang the mitten pouch where it's most accessible. Visibility isn't a problem no matter where it might be because it's transparent.

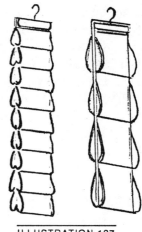

ILLUSTRATION 197

With anywhere from eight to 18 mitten pouches, depending on the style of the shoe bag, there's sufficient slots for every outerwear accessory we possess, including dressier gloves and woolen scarves.

Even though this system for storing matching sets is particualarly effective, it's a wonderful delight for children to manage all on their own.

The best benefit is when we arrive home after a hectic day. We easily slide our coat onto its hanger and smoothly ease it into the coat closet that's now orderly and neat. We peel our fingers from our favorite gloves, look toward the mitten pouch, and push the gloves gently into its opening. And there they will be found tomorrow morning and the morning after and the morning after that.

Heaven only knows why we'd wish to pursue the matter of mittens further, but getting the opportunity to play devil's advocate is fun.

The rack sitting on the shelf (illustration 198) is actually a drying apparatus for gloves and mittens. It's not good for storage, although that's not to say it wouldn't furnish adequate airing in the mud room or garage. But in the coat closet it'd not only dampen everyone's spirits, but it would squander the shelf space. However, woolens are often in a clammy condition, so it's not an entirely bad idea to dry them out before reusing them.

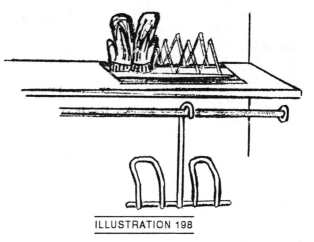

ILLUSTRATION 198

A rack that hangs from the rod is actually a drying apparatus for boots, although it can serve for drip-drying gloves, mittens, mufflers, scarves, caps, and hats as well. Unless it is utilized on a rod specifically designed for boots at the lowest level of the closet, it occupies too much space.

When seeking instant gratification, merely maneuver a drawer unit onto the floor of the coat closet. The drawer could be a handy place for dumping gloves, but be prepared to rummage around to find a matched set unless a system for keeping the pairs together is devised. (See illustration 199.)

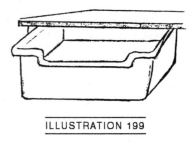

ILLUSTRATION 199

How to Forecast More Favorably

The coat closet is located near the living room, and many people exit the house through the garage, so why do we keep our constant companions, the ones that see us through all kinds of stormy weather, in a place so far removed from the action?

It makes sense to clean out coats in the closet, the ones we frequently wear, and relocate them nearer the garage. This not only accomplishes the obvious, but it also leaves some space in the coat closet for guest's coats.

What happens if we live in a house that doesn't even have a coat closet? We must devise an alternative place for our coats.

We must seek an off-the-wall solution or one that will floor everyone with its creativity. A coat rack on the floor, a coat rack on the wall, or a coat rack we've hand-crafted or purchased is what we seek. By installing a decorative screen around it, we can seal it off to lessen the likelihood of offending anyone.

Decorative screens are available everywhere, in every size, color, material, fabric, and price. The model in illustration 200 has a brass-plated frame. It can be personalized with your own choice of fabric, color, and texture.

In the event we are hanging both our own coats and friends' coats and relatives' coats, it is in our own best interest to investigate the type of hanger we should use.

Examine the range of hangers, like gold-tone aluminum, lucite, wooden, or rattan hangers. They not only enhance overall appearance, but because they are larger, broader, and bigger than regular hangers, they serve coats better. These lovely hangers earn our respect and are worth the investment, although they don't come cheap.

ILLUSTRATION 200

Approaching the problem of hanging coats without using hangers, we could explore using this wooden box (illustration 201). Pine or oak, veneered, stained, or whatever doesn't matter. It hangs on the wall with hooks for our coats or umbrellas.

This box has a lid that conceals a compartment for stowing hats, woolens, scarves, and gloves (but the mates are guaranteed to be missing in no time). Add to that disadvantage, the frightening prospect of hanging the box in a high position. If you hang it too high you'll be relying on nothing but touch to find your way through the contents to find the matching pairs.

This rack (illustration 202) is for coats only and perhaps a hat, cap, scarf, or two, but it lacks the ability to handle hand warmers or mittens. If

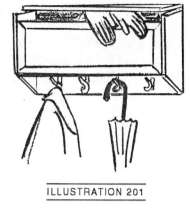

ILLUSTRATION 201

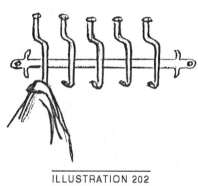

ILLUSTRATION 202

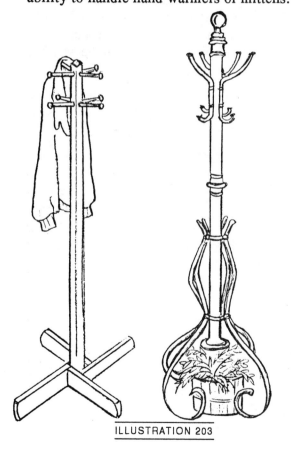

ILLUSTRATION 203

we're selecting this to supply additional space for hanging coats nearer the garage or to accomodate excess coats, then it's just a jim-dandy rejuvenator. But how will the other accessories find fulfillment?

It's a good idea to put up a coat rack or peg strip for children to have a handy and convenient place of their own, perhaps in or near the kitchen, garage door, or back door. This is an exceptionally good idea if their wet and crusty snowsuits are currently residing right next to your mink jackets or other expensive dress coats in the main coat closet.

If we were to choose a free-standing coat rack (illustration 203) rather than a wall model, we'd still be faced with stowing the accessories.

We can readily remedy the umbrella problem by putting an umbrella stand close to the coats and the exterior door. Yet sorry to say, this seldom serves every style of umbrella. The shorter, smaller, compact variety that don't have a hooked handle disappear inside most of the predesigned vases and stands. This means we're back to improvising our own from copper kettles, wire wastebaskets, portly pots, oversized baskets, and jugs we may have on hand.

ILLUSTRATION 204

Umbrellas aren't necessarily restricted to rolling about on a shelf, rolling around on the floor, or standing upright in a corner.

Any sort of clamp mechanism or a nail, hook, or extended arm will serve to hang the handle of an umbrella flush to the wall or the door. See illustrations 204 and 205. Place the racks on the wall in a way that uses the least amount of space.

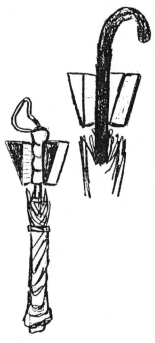

ILLUSTRATION 205

CHAPTER FIFTEEN

THE BATHROOM

✔ How to Cope with Cabinets

✔ How to Stall Showers and Tubs

✔ How to Trap Tissues and Towels

✔ How to Scrub the Brushes

✔ How to Doctor the Medicine Chest

✔ How to Read the Riot Act

How to Cope with Cabinets

The cabinet under the bathroom sink is generally just as bad, if not worse, than the cabinet under the kitchen sink.

Most people have consciously chosen to resolve their difficulties with this part of their home by either slamming the door or by limiting the confrontations. It's upsetting when the items at the front edge of the cabinet fall out or when something is actually needed from the back. And what do we store in the very back of the cabinet? Only the worthless, useless stuff. It wouldn't be in the back of the cabinet in the first place if we ever needed it.

We really shouldn't start each day tracking down our makeup, razor, or the spare tube of toothpaste. How can we keep track of so many small and seemingly incidental toiletries?

We need to establish not only a system of order, but one of priority and prominence as well. With the cabinet being the largest single storage space in the entire bathroom, we'll make it our first target.

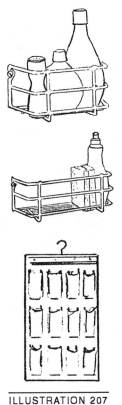

As it sits now, the cabinet is just a big cavernous mouth, so no wonder everything gets lost inside. Simply inserting a stack shelf or two would furnish a separate shelf for each kind of item, while elevating the items to a position of visibility and accessibility. Putting a stack shelf at the back of the cabinet makes every item on it and every item in front of it easily accessible.

ILLUSTRATION 206

The insides of the cabinet doors are the handiest places of all, so why not give them a purpose by giving them a storage rack? If the rack allows many of the smaller articles to slip through, an ordinary shoe bag delivers a wonderful way to stash hair brushes, barrettes, nail polishes, and other assorted or categorized toiletries (illustration 207). Cut it down to size if it's too large or hang it on the back of the bathroom door.

ILLUSTRATION 207

A specialty rack for hair products, especially the blow dryer, is not a bad idea. Many of these racks are too bulky for the inside of the doors. Measure closely before buying one (illustration 208).

Use any of the above ideas inside the cabinet and on the doors to obtain the type and amount of storage you need. Keep an open mind! Frequently, a nail or cuphook on the dividing strut between the doors can produce a perfect place to hang a hair dryer, curling iron, or anything with a built-in loop that allows it to be hung.

ILLUSTRATION 208

Some people don't even have a cabinet, just a sink with some pipes, plumbing and valves looking atrociously ugly underneath.

Putting a skirt around the sink bowl or splash edge (illustration 209) isn't done merely for appearance's sake. It also gives us quite a bit of concealed storage space. Mercifully, no one but family usually has the nerve to lift the skirt, but just in case the minister's wife gets curious, let's organize underneath anyway.

The articles placed here should be accessible, but never visible. We don't want items that peek out or create bulges in the fabric. Stack shelves work wonders in managing the materials that have been wandering around the bathroom. But measure the heights of both the sink and the shelf unit to make sure they're compatible.

If for some reason, it's impossible to find a storage unit to squeeze under the sink, we could at least organize a single category, like makeup, by placing the assorted tubes, brushes, bottles, and jars in into a single structure (illustration 210).

ILLUSTRATION 209

Consigning cosmetics to a single container is one of the better ways to control them, no matter what spot they occupy in the house.

The pack-rat people may have outgrown the cabinet and no amount of organizing can make everything they've acquired fit inside. This means we need to look at additional types of storage that can be incorporated into the bathroom (illustration 211), which is actually asking for quite a lot, since most bathrooms have little room to spare.

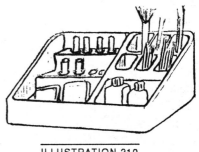

ILLUSTRATION 210

Some space can be found between the toilet and the sink or the toilet and the tub to slip in a small shelf system (illustration 212). This white wrought iron display case is not only small, but the shelves are adjustable and removeable for cleaning ease.

If it's supremely important that additional shelving find its way into the bathroom, then a serious search will produce the space desired. A familiar fixture (illustration 213), is the self-supporting structure that sits over the toilet. In recent years, the quality, character, and poise of these structures has dramatically improved.

How to Stall Showers and Tubs

For some reason, people are hesitant to install permanent shelves in the bathroom. This is understandable if ceramic tiles completely cover the walls from floor to ceiling, but when they don't a shelf can add not only storage space but it can also be a thing of beauty.

There are too many styles of shelves to list and describe individually. The shelf in il-

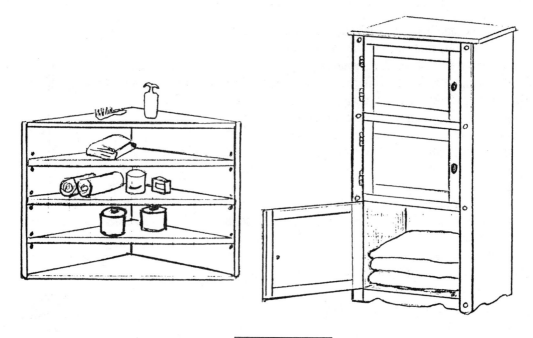

ILLUSTRATION 211

lustration 214 can be installed up or down for versatility and for enhancing a typical wall.

Whether the shelves are inside the shower or outside, extra shelves can hold for our convenience bath accessories (illustration 215).

A molded plastic tray, equipped with a ventilated shelf bottom and sunction cup support is everyone's idea of heaven here on earth. It doesn't require that we drill holes or affix it to the ceramic tiles in any permanent way.

There are variations on the suction-cup shelf, some of which come complete with mirrors and hooks for hanging washcloths and razors, but beware its tendency to fall off the wall.

ILLUSTRATION 212

ILLUSTRATION 213

Much of the time we spend in the bathroom is devoted to showering or bathing. We often juggle the soap, shampoo, conditioner, and wash cloth in one hand while we try to shave with the other. Wouldn't it be handy if we had a place to put our things? See illustration 216 for a couple of promising solutions to this problem.

Naturally, the niches that nestle over the shower-head supply their services at a suitable level for showering, yet they're too far away to reach when bathing.

The corner shelves in illustration 217 can be installed at any height. They're purchased individually. The tension pole system of shelves and towel bars is also available in a shorter version, enabling it to extend from the rim of the tub to the ceiling.

Although these methods of storage in illustration 218 depict rubber duckies and boats, the over-the-top-of-the-tub racks could just as easily bear mirrors, shaving cream, or soap.

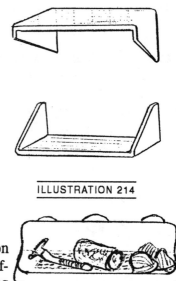

ILLUSTRATION 214

ILLUSTRATION 215

The best method for managing the materials we keep inside the shower is with a shower curtain liner that has numerous pockets, pouches, and loops stitched into its fabric. The assortment of sizes, shapes, and services it gives us, allows us the freedom to utilize it in whatever capacity we want.

Coupled with the shower curtain liner is, of course, a beautifully tailored outer curtain, strictly there for decorative purposes, while the liner receives all the soap scum and mildew.

Even when both the drapes are actually working in unison,

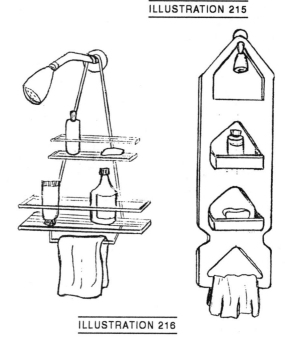

ILLUSTRATION 216

they perform poorly at preventing water from getting onto the floor. Either of these two guard devices will help (illustration 219). One stops the leaks along the side and bottom;

the other keeps the curtain closed tightly against the side wall.

How to Trap Tissues and Towels

Using the last piece of toilet tissue is distressing. Worse yet is knowing that the new roll is beyond our reach. What should we do?

No doubt about it, the spare rolls of toilet paper should never be farther than an arm's length away.

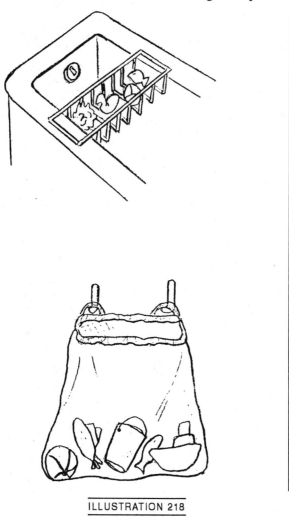

ILLUSTRATION 218

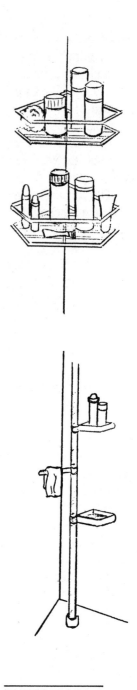

ILLUSTRATION 217

This dispenser (illustration 220) not only delivers our paperwork in a timely fashion, but it stocks the excess in an area that seldom is effectively used.

This industrious dowel (illustration 221) is a dual-delivery device, since it not only offers us our choice of perforated paper products, but allows us to catch up on our reading at the same time.

While a burnished brass stand (illustration 221) can't begin to compete with the multifaceted features of the dowel

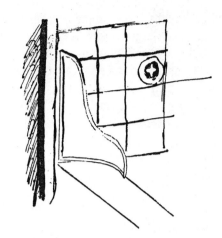

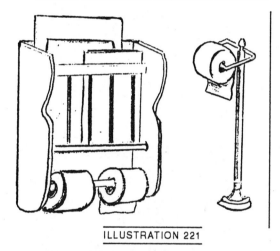

ILLUSTRATION 221

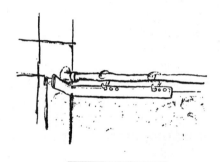

ILLUSTRATION 219

rack above, it does stand attentive and ready to deliver at nearly eye level. Some baths are minus a toilet tissue dispenser entirely in which case this is handy.

Turn tissue storage into a tempting proposition by storing a roll or two in a tightly woven basket atop the toilet tank.

Any covering that conceals the rolls true identity is a mask of merit (illustrations 222 and 223).

Lurking deep within our human nature is a desire to display every halfway decent towel we own. Why hide them in a linen closet when we can pretend we enjoy seeing them every day?

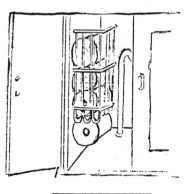

ILLUSTRATION 220

The only problem is that we eventually run afoul of the law of limitations, which states that there is a limit to the number of towel bars and racks any one bathroom may hold.

There's no reason the three-tiered towel rack (illustration 224), couldn't and shouldn't serve as a display rack as well as a utility stand for tending towels between launderings. It demands quite a bit of floor space, so approach it with caution when considering it.

On the other hand, if we've been truly victimized by insufficient space for hanging our towels, it's time we took matters into our own hands. No one ever said it would be easy to do, but no one ever said it couldn't be creative, colorful, or innovative either. This native Indian or rustic looking ladder-type rack is an inspiration (illustration 225). It occupies very little space, yet it's quite distinctive.

Along the more classic and traditional lines are the typical T-bar towel racks and the towel trees (illustration 226). The T-bar takes the tiniest amount of space, so even if the bathroom is small the T-bar can usually fit.

The towel tree tends to tilt when it's tampered with too much or when the weight is unevenly distributed.

When push comes to shove, we'll accept whatever towel rack we can get, if the alternative is nothing. This over-the-door rack (illustration 227) is by no means the most attractive or appealing place for

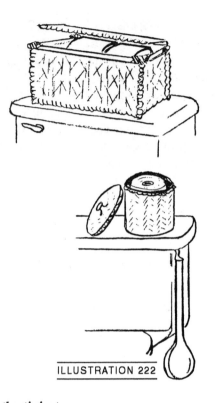

ILLUSTRATION 222

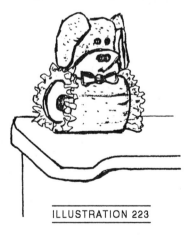

ILLUSTRATION 223

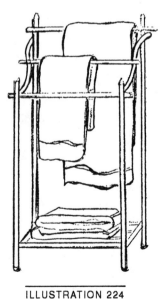

ILLUSTRATION 224

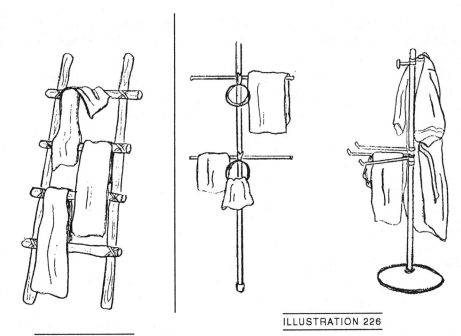

ILLUSTRATION 225

ILLUSTRATION 226

our towels because it can obstruct the door when it's fully opened. Yet odds are we'd close the door behind us upon entering the bathroom, and then grab the towel off the back of the door quite easily.

Obviously, a tension pole that spans the shower stall doesn't look very much like a towel bar (illustration 228) because of the clothes hanging on it, but it could be converted

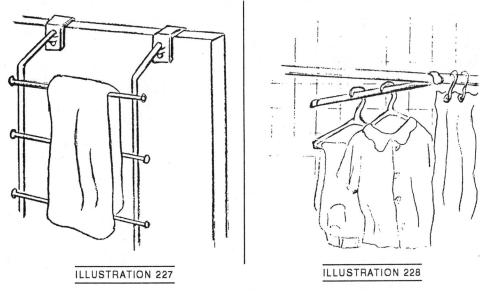

ILLUSTRATION 227

ILLUSTRATION 228

173

if we made it. If it were located at a height and position that didn't cause considerable brain damage to any unsuspecting person who wanted to take a shower, then it could become a viable place to hang drying clothes.

Certainly, some of these options are for extreme circumstances and situations, which I hope few of us will encounter.

What's the best way to go about drying articles of clothing in the bathroom?

Any awkward, tiresome, or bulky clotheslines, clips, and other apparatuses will quickly cause us to lose our temper. Keeping that in mind, strive for a system that's compact but capable of carrying the kinds of clothing we'd typically hand wash and toss over the rod. As an example, this very tiny retractable clothesline (illustration 229) supplies 48 feet of drying space for hosiery, unmentionables, lingerie, and other fine washables.

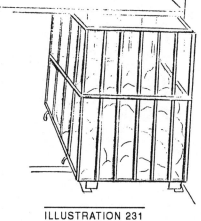

ILLUSTRATION 229

This ventilated hanging wire basket (illustration 230) is too ugly to be positioned in a place of prominence, but it can be used to store a few spare towels in case we use more than anticipated. It can save a trip to the linen closet.

If the space the hamper occupies in the bathroom is replaced with a delightfully different device that not only provides a place for storage, but a place for prettier articles as well, then the bathroom becomes a better place to visit or spend some time in.

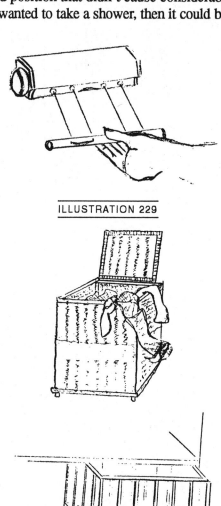

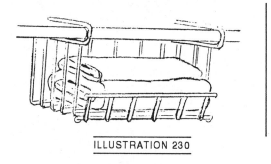

ILLUSTRATION 230

ILLUSTRATION 231

The hamper (illustration 231) could be moved under the sink, since we aren't particularly fond of seeing or smelling it anyway. The towels, bubble baths, dusting powders, and other in-the-cabinet companions that are above average or handsome in appearance can be relocated to the site vacated by the hamper.

How to Scrub the Brushes

No matter how much we'd wish to avoid this subject completely, we can't. Toilet bowl cleaning is a too-frequent fact of life. Like it or not, we're trapped in the same room with this horrible contraption. These two types of toilet bowl brushes (illustration 232) are quite popular, even though they make no attempt to camouflage their true identity. For our own sensibilities it is hereby suggested that all future brushes be conceived in either beauty or placed in a secluded spot.

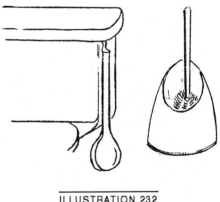

ILLUSTRATION 232

The top of the sink is seldom spacious enough for all the gear we give it. Cups, toothbrushes, cavity fighter, and mouthwash offer us a very confusing array of items to look at first thing in the morning. And that's not all we keep on the sink top, since we couldn't contemplate a day without bars of soap, soap dispensers, soap dishes, dental floss, and cotton balls.

A storage rack on the wall would work wonders (illustration 233) to eliminate some of this confusion.

While we're examining our obsession with stockpiles of bathroom supplies, let's pay particular attention to the abundance of soap slivers we seem to be especially fond of stashing everywhere. Apparently, there are a number of reasons for this behavior, but only two solutions for eliminating it. We hang on to the bits and pieces because we believe there may be another Great Depression. But common sense and conscious choice sug-

ILLUSTRATION 233

ILLUSTRATION 234

gest we get rid of the little shavings or sock them away in a self-contained sponge where they can at least work themselves into a good lather (illustration 234).

When we need to see what we're doing, what we need is a handy mirror. Sitting something else on the sink would be dangerous, especially a breakable mirror. We'd be wise to select a mirror that requires neither the sink top, the toilet tank top, nor our hands.

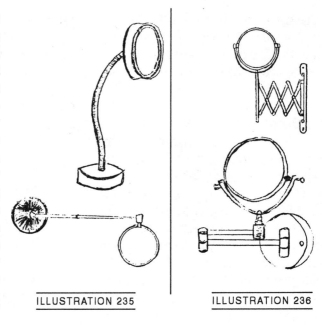

ILLUSTRATION 235

ILLUSTRATION 236

If ceramic tile walls are still a factor, the mirror in illustration 235 is a stick-on job that swivels 360°. It extends to 28 inches and flips from regular to magnified viewing. It sticks on a table top, another mirror, or the glass doors of the shower stall at a moment's notice.

The two mirrors in illustration 236 are very similar in that they must be installed permanently on the wall. They both have a magnifying mirror as well as a regular one. They extend outward when we need to examine our faces or hair up close, and they can be pushed nearly flush against the wall after we're done.

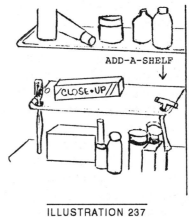

ILLUSTRATION 237

The top mirror extends 22 inches versus the 17 inches of the second, more expensive swivel-arm mirror. The chrome-finish top mirror pivots in two places for multi-position adjustment. The bottom brass model swivels and tilts and comes with two brass screws.

How to Doctor the Medicine Chest

The medicine chest is almost always a problem. Assigning each shelf a specific duty and role is half the battle. *Only* prescription medicines on one shelf, *only* over-the-counter remedies on another shelf, and *only* toiletries and grooming aids on another, and so on.

A large portion of space is wasted because the distance between shelves is so great. Many items are left wandering around, hiding behind anything bigger than they are and wedging themselves in the crevices of the shelf.

We can offset these liabilities and actually turn them into assets.

One way we can control small, assorted containers is to arrange them in a straight, uninterrrupted line on an individual shelf, based on their characteristics. Since the shelves in a normal medicine chest are installed too far apart, we should add more shelves. There are foot-long, stick-on shelves that have holes on each end for hanging razors and toothbrushes, that will split the space evenly. See illustration 237. Appealing as this may sound, it isn't the best solution because items are still able to get lost.

The materials in a medicine chest need constant supervision. Keep categories in their own separate container, compartment, or bowl. A special acrylic jar for both the cot-

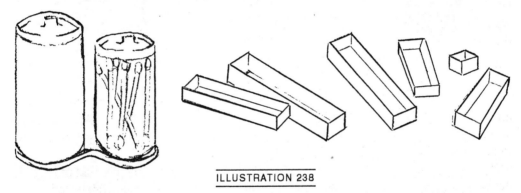

ILLUSTRATION 238

ton balls and swabs or a series of drawer dividers that fit nicely on the shelf (illustration 238) work well.

The drawer dividers are inexpensive, yet they let us easily organize an entire category. By implementing a system of dividers, we don't have to worry about what happens once they are in their compartment. They can pretty well do as they choose and it doesn't upset or endanger the system. We merely grab the whole drawer, remove it from the shelf, rummage through it to secure the tablet, capsule, nail file, bottle, or comb we want, and then place the entire bin back on the shelf.

It might be wise to identify the dividers with concise, legible labels. An all-inclusive list isn't necessary. Simply denote the contents with a major heading like *Hair, Teeth, Prescriptions, Nail Care, Colognes, Tonics, Shaving, Personal.*

How to Read the Riot Act

We'd be hard-pressed to deduce why we store so many newspapers, magazines, cook-

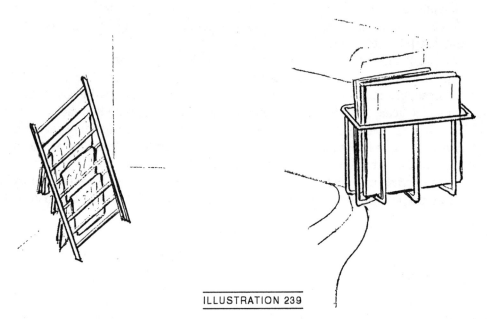

ILLUSTRATION 239

books, crossword puzzles, and novelettes in the water closet, but we do. And there they stay, scattered on the floor, stuffed down the side of the john, or temporarily spread on the toilet tank, soon to slither to the floor.

Although these two racks (illustration 239) keep the literature neat and orderly, the room looks messy, especially when the magazines are dogeared, damp, or stained.

A container, like a basket or chest with a lid, is preferable to parading the pages.

CHAPTER SIXTEEN

THE KID'S KEEPERS

✔ How to Motivate Munchkins and Moms

✔ How to Liberate Little Lost Lambs

✔ How to Activate Assigned Placement

✔ How to Plan for Play

✔ How to Simplify Small Stuff

How to Motivate Munchkins and Moms

Believe it or not, children aren't born disorganized, sloppy, messy, and rebellious about keeping a neat and tidy environment. They learn messiness from us.

Children develop a life-long positive attitude when they're asked to pick up their personal possessions, so long as they know exactly where they should put them once they've picked them up. Preschools and nursery schools, promote the picking-up process as a part of the daily routine.

We need to have reasonable expectations for our children. We need to understand their motivations and capabilities.

Our responsibility is to provide them with the simplest and easiest routines and methods for storing their clothing, playthings, puzzles, and equipment. At the same time, we must make sure we position everything they are to use within easy reach or we'll have frustrated kids instead of ones that are proud of themselves for a job well done.

For the moment, forget the fact we're teaching our children basic values that they'll carry into their adult lives and the sense of accomplishment and pride they attain. The far greater reward is that when our children can find what they want when they want it and then put it away where it belongs, we've gained more time for ourselves!

How to Liberate Little Lost Lambs

Why won't our wee little loveable lambs hang their tops, shorts, pants, and dresses back in the closet? They can't reach either the hanger or the rod!

Assuming we have no closet to recondition and reproportion for the child, let's look at the possibility of a whole new structure taking up residency in the room, in the form of this pictured petite armoire (illustration 240). It provides a low rod and shelves as well, so short folks can easily use it.

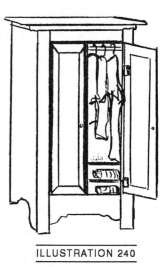

The closet rod has to be lowered for a child to use it, and since we have no doubt the kid's going to continue to grow, the logical resolution would be to install an adjustable rod, changing its height to correspond to the child's height.

ILLUSTRATION 240

Ventilated systems have one variation that supports itself on adjustable brackets and tracks, eliminating the need to play carpenter periodically, drilling new holes and reinstalling the hardware in a new position (illustration 241).

The extender rod (illustration 242) is just super for a kid's closet. It, too, grows in accordance with the changes our children undergo, making it flexible and versatile.

By using an extender rod, the child is automatically given a system for hanging clothes. Each section is designated for a specific type of garment. For instance, pants on

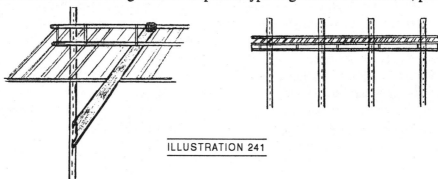

ILLUSTRATION 241

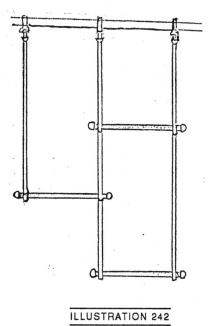

ILLUSTRATION 242

ILLUSTRATION 243

the bottom right with the tops above, and dresses or overalls in the longer section on the left.

If we have a truly tiny tot and even this is too high, is the tot too small, shaky, and insecure to be safely stood on a stool?

Maybe the closet in the child's room is a combination closet, with adult clothes on the top and the child's clothes on the bottom. Try giving him his own miniature, instant closet, complete with shoe rack, hanging area, and shelf section (illustration 243). It's so simple and self-supporting we can shove it into the closet and we're done.

This is rather a nice touch because it is not only accessible and visible for a child's limited capabilities, but it provides a preassigned configuration for the child to follow. Beware the ventilated top shelf though and never allow little pieces like crayons, puzzle pieces, toy soldiers, or midget baby dolls to perch there, or they will end up on the floor.

The free-standing unit isn't especially space conscious. In this case, that might be a pardonable sin, since our primary objective isn't using the least amount of space, but rather putting the space where it's accessible.

Add an extra special touch to the hanging game we intend to play with our children, since it's guaranteed to please them immensely and inspire their cooperation. Take the kids along and let them choose child-size tubular plastic hangers at the store. The hangers are easy for little hands to handle because they are sturdier and fatter than wire ones and the kids like them enough to treat them with respect.

Any process that divides the space inside the closet into smaller sections that are more visible and accessible to children has increased the chances of success. But it is important that each compartment be assigned a specific and specialized role in the child's routine.

Simply providing an empty, open space and then telling the child his toy trucks are supposed to always go in that space isn't quite as refined as the system should be. In order to make each separate section of space a completely distinct and separate system, it'll take a bit of forethought, observation, and analysis.

For instance, if the plan is to stack a whole bunch of garments in a single stack, inevitably the child will want the garment on the bottom of the pile and the system isn't a functioning, workable idea at all. We'd be wiser to slot individual garments into individual containers, such as the Honeycomb cylinders.

Refer to the section on sweaters and knits for details on this system of tubes. Place tubes where the child can reach them (illustration 244) and the child will select socks from the tube that contains socks and will return jammies each morning to the tube for nighties and pj's.

 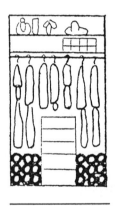 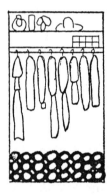

ILLUSTRATION 244

Yes, it's true. Each tube, cubbyhole, cloth cubicle, tray, shelf, box, or drawer will never stay perfectly perfect with little hands moving through them daily, but controlled messes are easier to sort through than complete chaos.

None of the previous products, tubes, cubbyholes, or hanging shelves depicted in illustration 245 are intended for use with itsy-bitsy items like crayons and such.

Help the child to manage the dresser drawers by modifying the layout of the garments inside.

This is merely a matter of inserting dividers into the drawers, so that each compartment contains a single kind of item. This can be achieved with shoe boxes or any other container or divider.

When there isn't a pile of clothes in a drawer, but rather a T-shirt rolled into a compact unit, next to a rolled polo shirt, next to a rolled jersey, the child can choose the top he wishes without ravaging the contents of the entire drawer. He could actually remove the whole box and take his time making up his mind. It's easier to put a box back than trying to close the drawer around escaping pants legs and dangling sleeves.

Perhaps you prefer that the child wear certain two-piece combinations consistently, in which case the outfits can be kept together in a box. The boxes may become a bit untidy in due course, but the child will never again open all five drawers, make a mess in each one while looking for his socks, since he now knows his socks are located in the bottom drawer, only the bottom drawer, and no other.

Drawer systems aren't limited to dresser drawers, since we're ready, willing, and able to drag in extra ones any time we choose to. The openness of the

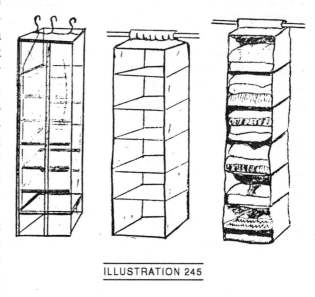

ILLUSTRATION 245

wire baskets (illustration 246) limits their use to clothes. Other items fall out.

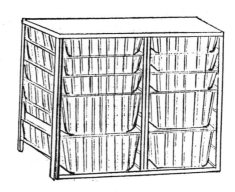

ILLUSTRATION 246

How to Activate Assigned Placement

Whether the kids are with closet or without, they frequently do well if they also have another place for flinging their most prized and everyday companions. By setting up a system as simple as a coat tree (illustration 247), the children can sling their school bag, letter sweater, baseball glove, soccer shoes, pretend purse, real purse, cap, or Cinderella crown on its arms. Our arms are freed from the chore of plucking items off the floor. Some coat trees are equipped with a storage box at the base for items that are difficult or impossible to hang.

The storage bins, baskets, trays, shelves, cubbyholes, cubicles, compartments, pegs, or racks may not win any Scout awards for cleanliness, but at least they've become a routine disposal unit for the stuff that was otherwise being left around the house, on the floor, bed, hallway, and stairs (illustration 248).

The back-of-the-door racks are flexible enough to adapt to changing activities the child is bound to experience. Starting out as a tiny tot, they work well for shoes and stuffed animals. As time goes by, they provide excellent storage for baseball caps and gloves, soccer shoes and hair ribbons.

The idea of allowing dirty clothes to stagnate in the same room where we spend a great deal of our time doesn't exactly tantalize our sensibilities. Yet, the dirty duds laundry hoop (illustration 249) on the back of the door is a vast improvement over a teenager's typical tendency to toss them on the floor.

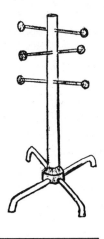

ILLUSTRATION 247

How to Plan for Play

This baseball rack (illustration 250) is definitely a specialty item, but if the Little League champ of the world lives under your roof, it's a valuable item to have on hand, since it suits his interests and therefore its chances of being used are highly probable.

On the other hand, not all of the toys and games our children possess are recognized for their sustained popularity, regularity. Which leads us to realize children actually pos-

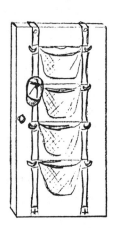

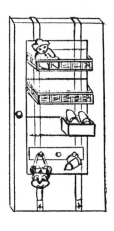

ILLUSTRATION 248

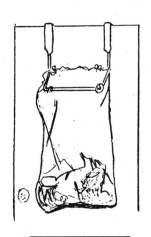

ILLUSTRATION 249

sess two distinct groups of playthings: those they perpetually play with and those they periodically piddle with.

For instance, every child the world over has acquired a massive and overwhelming collection of stuffed animals, cartoon characters, Disney delights, heroes and villain, but how often do they use them?

Even if they do use them occasionally, children only have two hands, and their beds, windowsills and table tops will only support so many squeezably soft sculptures. Allow a selected few to remain, but banish the bulk of them to a carefully contrived containment center that's off the beaten track (illustration 251).

Either of the methods in the illustration present the playthings for visual enjoyment, yet harbor them in safely suspended animation. A simple net strung between the walls in a corner or a vertical pole can be used to store little-used items.

The biggest benefit of all, however, besides being able to run the vacuum over the floor now that is isn't any obstacle

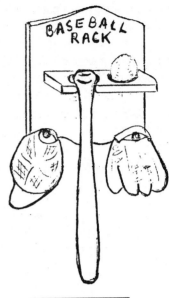

ILLUSTRATION 250

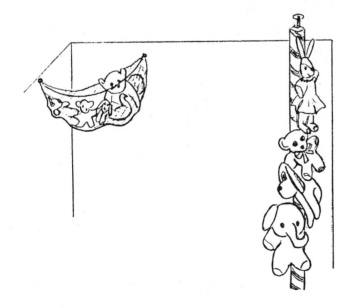

ILLUSTRATION 251

course, is we'll stop hearing, "Mom, where's . . . ?" If you want the child to be able to reach the toys, don't put them next to the ceiling, unless the child has permission to build a ladder from knick-knacks he's perilously perched together.

We needn't buy a net or pole, since we can handily string our own wire or cord anywhere we want and use clothespins or clips to pinch the critters in place. We've taken a chaotic condition and turned it into a marvel of management, while adding delightfully decorative detail to the room.

We can approach the stuffed playthings from a different perspective entirely. Installing a system of shelves (illustration 252) solves the storage problem, but it offers a bit more freedom in the choice of sites.

The shelves shown are lucite, which allows them to blend with any color scheme,

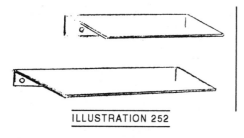

ILLUSTRATION 252

ILLUSTRATION 253

but because they are transparent, they basically disappear entirely.

Stuffed animals are usually purchased with the motto "the bigger, the better" in mind. That's why a relatively large area is needed to keep them in confinement. There are other types of toys that are almost as bulky, and they, too, need a spacious storage container.

The most common of all containers for toys is the toy box, with a hinged lid that lifts up for entry (illustration 253). Caution is advised for two reasons. First, children frequently forget the lid's in an upright position and it falls on fingers, arms, or foreheads.

ILLUSTRATION 254

Second, the traditional toy chest isn't the greatest AllAmerican invention it's cracked up to be.

In fact, it's not any better than either of these hamper or basket styles of storage (illustration 254), but it sure sells for a heftier price. The child is certainly able to open any of them. Yet he must tip them over and pour everything out if he has any hope of finding tiny items inside. That's the reason, plain and simple, why this type of large storage container must be the receptacle for the bigger toys and never itsy-bitsy pieces. Itsy-bitsy pieces need more specialized storage.

If the mesh or net type bag is interesting and appealing, don't purchase one or two overly large ones, rather reduce the size and buy a large quantity of them (illustration 255). Put the individual bags on pegs or hooks. By furnishing more bags, especially a different color for each group of toys, the child can recognize the contents by the color of the bag, enabling him to choose one bag at a time, rather than emptying out a huge bag that contains all of his toys.

Although wire containers are available everywhere, it's a big mistake to use them even for big toys. The tips, ends, loops, hooks, snaps, and any uneven surface on a toy will snag outrageously and often.

Other large receptacles for large toys are colorful trash cans with lids (illustration 256). They must always have lids, and the child can establish her own color-coded system.

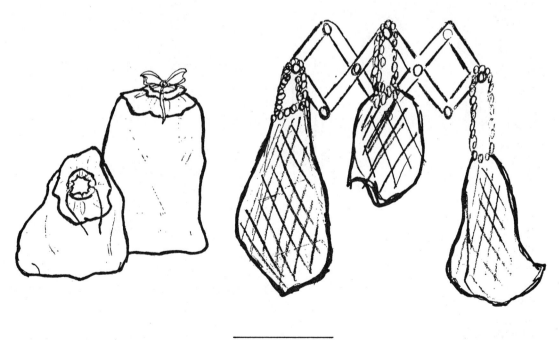

ILLUSTRATION 255

How to Simplify Small Stuff

When we start our crusade to gather up all the tiny toys, small play things, puzzle pieces, board-game cards, miniature baby dolls, we'd be wise to establish a system for storing them that the kid can use or we'll be back time and time again.

Try to match the size of the container to the size of the items. For instance, colored pencils, chalk, crayons, markers, and the like would be very accessible in a Tupperware-type container (illustration 257) that had a lid. Because it's transparent, the kid can see what's inside. If the box isn't transparent and the child can't yet read, place a picture on the outside of the box so the child can identify the contents. It may be a good idea to include the coloring books and scratch pads along with the markers. Then the child can pull out one box when he wants to color instead of searching to find both the books and the markers at the same time.

Besides fitting the size of the container to the size of the

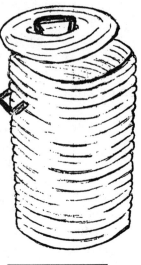

ILLUSTRATION 256

ILLUSTRATION 257

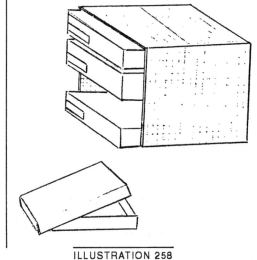

ILLUSTRATION 258

small stuff, it's important not to stack the containers if it can be avoided. When the child is confronted with a stack of games, inevitably she'll want the one on the bottom. Game boxes often leave much to be desired, so you might want to tape them up even when they've just come in the door from the store to stop the spills and rips and all the tiny pieces from scattering and getting lost.

The box with drawers in illustration 258 is intended for storing keepsakes. It's a wonderful idea. A system of drawers work quite well, too, for stowing separate categories of small materials, like paper dolls or animals, crafts, jewelry, or baseball cards.

Illustration 259 shows a piece of fabric with pockets snapped over the edge of a baby's crib. Adapt the idea for bigger kids. It won't hold their barbells, but located next to a bed or desk gives ideal storage for paperwork.

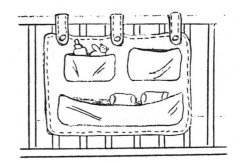

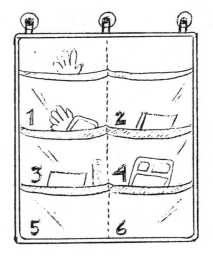

ILLUSTRATION 259

CHAPTER SEVENTEEN

WORK AND PLAY PLACES AND SPACES

✔ How to Orchestrate an Office

✔ How to Save Stubs and Stabalize Storage

✔ How to Coordinate Crafts

✔ How to Manage Magazines and Books

✔ How to Anticipate Audio and Video

✔ How to Be a Bonafide Couch Potato

How to Orchestrate an Office

Few of us are lucky enough to have a spare place that we can convert into a place of relaxation, a place for keeping the household records and finances, a place to operate a side venture, a place for doing handiwork or crafts, or even a place for catching up on paperwork, audits, and reports associated with the business that is the source of our entire annual income.

Whatever the case may be, we often find ourselves trying to fit a desk, computer, comfortable chair, file cabinets, shelving and bookcases, photocopy machine, typewriter, reference books, journals, video and audiocassettes, sewing machines, patterns, fabric, spools of thread, knitting needles, art supplies, and a drafting table into the teeniest nooks of whichever room will accommodate our hobby, profession, or aspirations.

In order to realize a place for our work or play, we must convert the space as effectively as possible and utilize it to the best of our ability.

Whether we simply need a flat level surface and a chair or whether we qualify as an established business operating out of our home, we need to arrange a system for storing our records and valuable papers.

The sensible thing to consider is to remove our paperwork to a location where they aren't pawed through by everyone in the family as they scurry about through the house.

If we have absolutely no hope of a real-life desk and we face a dead end when we seek a spot for a bookcase or storage cabinet, then this situation

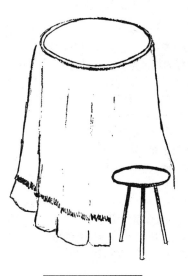

ILLUSTRATION 260

could be resolved by simply setting up a functioning desk that doubles as a decorative table top (illustration 260). Make sure sufficient space underneath can keep one year's tax records or correspondence tucked out of sight. It would be wise, however, to incorporate a stack of labeled boxes or a small system of pull-out drawers that are marked for easy identification. Otherwise, the typical In and Out bins seen in most offices would suffice, since they can be stacked up in the space between the legs of the table.

Illustration 261 pictures some differing versions of the In and Out bins. The In and Out stackable trays create difficulties in maintaining distinctions, whereas the vertical file for folders sorts separate files for retrieval and easy recognition.

The box at the right of illustration 262 has two pull-out drawers for storing cancelled checks. It can also be used as a reference file for index cards, but it isn't the right

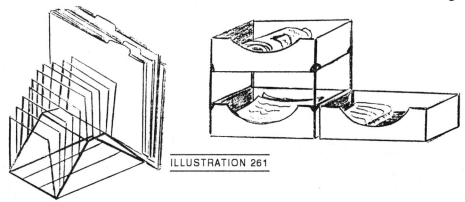

ILLUSTRATION 261

size for storing paper or documents.

The box on the left is a storage system that provides six individual boxes for magazines, tax forms, or insurance policies. Because they are then packed together in the larger surrounding cardboard box, it's a one-stop procedure for removing or replacing the contents of the separate file boxes.

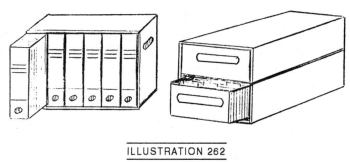

ILLUSTRATION 262

This ladder style desk and bookcase (illustration 263) is a cantilever design that provides plentiful desk space with three shelves above. Personally, if I were able to finagle three feet of wall space and install something that was nearly as tall as the ceiling, far more productive options are available. They are not only smaller but offer cabinet style storage for concealment. Paperwork and similar sorts of materials are seldom if ever capable of staying neat, tidy, and orderly for long, which makes them rather undesireable for exhibition on open shelves.

This home office unit (illustration 264) could be combined to occupy very little wall or floor space, but what a world of difference as far as the amount of storage space it offers. Plus it is designed to accomodate the typical types of articles encountered in an office environment.

ILLUSTRATION 263

The loose papers, letters, and receipts can be concealed in the drawers while binders, books, and manuals would flatter the shelf space, either in the open or behind the cabinet doors. The desk area itself is large enough for elbow-room or for typewriters and computers.

192

The expense involved in purchasing such a complete unit could prohibit it from moving into your home, but the concept is obtainable for less cost.

The file cabinet (illustration 265) is self-assembled, made of particle board with a laminated finish. It's very strong and durable. By resting a board on either two of the file cabinets or on wire baskets, drawer units, or stackable modular shelves, a ready-made desk, complete with storage facilities is furnished at minimum cost.

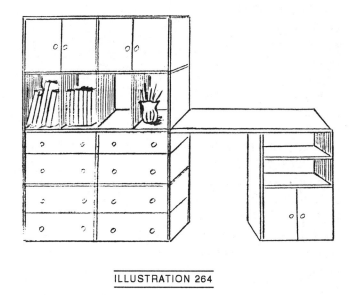

ILLUSTRATION 264

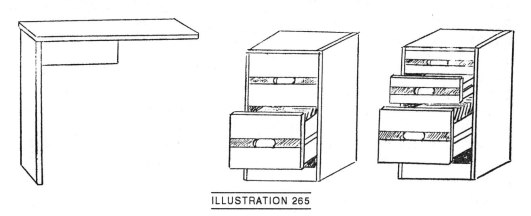

ILLUSTRATION 265

This rolling cart with five drawers (illustration 266) offers ample drawer space for separating correspondence or artwork and supplies. The hanging file cart could supplement an established work center or it may be the whole show, but it carries a full load of important papers, warranties, deeds, insurance policies, and such in a relatively small space. Since both units are portable, they can be moved when not in service.

Anything that offers a safe and responsive pigeonhole, slot, bin, basket, drawer, box,

193

shelf, or niche for our occupational or personal papers, mail, magazines, or postcards, offers a definite advantage (illustration 267).

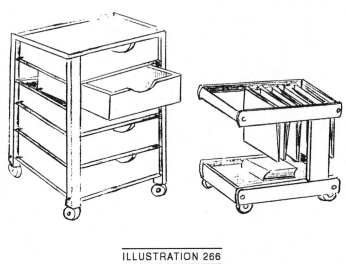

Take for instance, a systematic arrangement of baskets on the wall near the desk for in-coming and out-going mail. It is by no means ideal, but it sure beats the stacks we have assembled on the floor by the front door, on the refrigerator, on the car's dashboard, and next to the bed.

ILLUSTRATION 266

Certainly, a system of woven baskets, functional as they might be will never survive the onslought of anything heavier than a mail order catalog. So what should we do if we maintain quite a stock of manuals, reference books, and binders?

ILLUSTRATION 267

The V-shaped book racks pictured in illustration 268 are unique and ingenious. They can handle quite a number of books, quite a lot of weight, and they are sold individually. The primary reason why they rank higher than a bookcase is because they demand less space. Also, the books can be consigned to an individual V-rack by classification, rather than racked in a row along an entire shelf.

How to Remember Where and When

Cameras strung around our necks, lenses in our pockets, film canisters everywhere, and it's time to take to the road, the backyard barbeque, or Sally's graduation.

Why is it we're excited about snapping shots, we can't wait till they're developed, we show them to everyone we know, yet we lose heart and become quickly discouraged when it comes time to figure out a method of storage for the photos and negatives?

Mostly we throw photos in an old cardboard box without having bothered to date them or identify them. They become a sad and forgotten part of our past rather than a romp down memory lane.

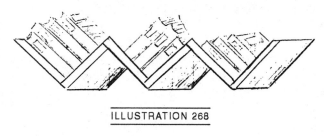

ILLUSTRATION 268

Slotting the slides into the family album is not the chore it's cracked up to be as long as the album is kept simple and selective. Either mark the date and identity on the back of the photo or slide a slip of paper into the slot with the slide. Do it as soon as the shots have been developed. Make it a habit, and the habit will reward you next time the urge strikes to reminisce.

Allow a lot of room for growth in the album itself or by buying a number of albums. The album in illustration 269 is huge and therefore handy for a one-stop shot of the shots for the last 10 years.

My photos are combined with memorabilia in a scrapbook. Photographs do tell a story, yet ticket stubs, corsages, baby's

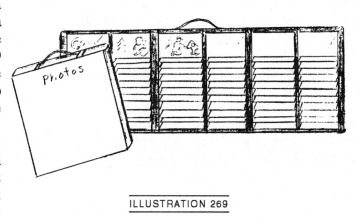

ILLUSTRATION 269

bracelets, candles, balloons, greeting cards, and notes from loved ones enhance the story the picture tells.

No one says the scrapbook must be a work of art, since it is primarily a place for putting the events and happenings of our lives together.

Clearly label the years contained in the scrapbook on the front and store them for years of memorable pleasure. If it's a massive amount of material, make an index so that selecting the specific book that contains the specific event is merely a matter of referring to a chart.

Along the same lines, how often do we forget to send greeting cards or at least dial the phone and wish someone happy birthday? Keeping a calendar of important dates and events lets us know in advance the upcoming occasion.

Record the dates and glance through the book once a month or so and begin to feel like you are in control (illustration 270). The book even has pockets for each month, so the greeting cards await only the date and a postage stamp.

Our minds are constantly cluttered with schedules and important things to remember, so it's no wonder we frequently forget. Sometimes the things we forget are incidental and leave no damaging effects, but there are times when our lack of recall can be extremely bad. For instance, if our house burnt down could we compile an exact and precise list of our possessions?

ILLUSTRATION 270

It's doubtful because we see them so routinely, we don't really see them at all. Even if we did remember every article, knick-knack, and drape, could we recite how much it cost and the date it was purchased? Photos of our belongings, the descriptions, details, costs, and dates recorded in this household property inventory book (illustration 271) answers the insurance questions.

We have a key for the door, a key for the video cabinet, a key for the car, a key for the medicine cabinet, a key for each piece of luggage, and a key for the motorhome, get-away cabin, cruiser, shed, Mom's front and back door, and the neighbor's house key.

ILLUSTRATION 271

Some of the keys are in the cookie jar, some in with the underwear or the loose coins on the dresser. And who knows where the rest of them might be, and even if we found them all, do we know which key fits which lock?

Gather them up, figure them out, pitch the worthless ones and consolidate the rest in an organizing pack (illustration 272) and put the pack in a safe place.

How to Coordinate Crafts

When we're in the mood to dabble with our watercolors or stitch a few seams on the costume for the kid's dance recital, we put it off and put it off until the whim passes or until the dance is over and we convinced our kid that she didn't want to dress up like a ballerina anyway.

We hate to start any project when we have to first drag out all the equipment and set it up, knowing all the while we'll have to fold it all up and put it all back again. Who could blame us for losing interest, since it just isn't worth the effort unless we're truly inspired.

ILLUSTRATION 272

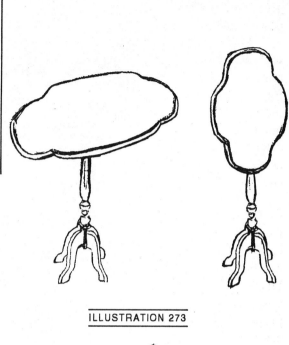

ILLUSTRATION 273

There's really not much point in positioning a portable table top (illustration 273) for our crafts projects, but it sure beats the nothing we now have, since the sewing machine hasn't been removed from its case for two years. Anytime we need to mend the seat of anyone's pants, we cart the damaged merchandise over to Grandma's, where her sewing machine is open for business all the time.

Wouldn't it be wonderful if we could create a crafts center? The hindrance is, of course, finding the necessary space. Measure inches to see just what possibilities exist and go for it.

The sewing center in illustration 274 has a countertop spanning two sets of baskets.

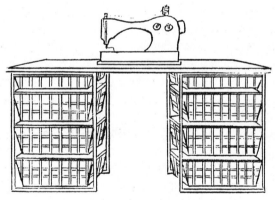

ILLUSTRATION 274

The overall dimension is something that can be controlled, since you pick the size of the support units on each side and the width of the countertop. This approach could operate realistically in as little as 36 inches by 15 inches of space.

A variation on the same theme incorporates a system of shelves and drawers. The table top can be removed or folded up, taking it out of the way when not in use. The crates stack vertically and requires little space, while still supplying drawers and bins as needed (illustration 275).

ILLUSTRATION 275

Spools of threads are usually mangled, mis-managed, and missing when they reside in drawers. Bob-bins, at least, have received the benefit of bobbin bins, a tray specifically made with bobbin storage in mind.

This particular storage rack for thread (illustration 276) loses a lot of valuable space in its design. A minia-ture shelf unit could be made for pennies that would hold twice the number of spools. Having the threads hanging above or to the side of the sewing machine is, however, a tremendous time saver and convenience.

Of all the sewing baskets in the marketplace, this is one of the larger models (illustration 277), although it's basically a mending basket. It doesn't have the capacity to store major sewing projects and crafts.

The accordion-type expansions offer increased visibility and accessibility to the objects inside, which is especially wise when dealing with sharp objects, like needles, pins, and scissors that have a tendency to imbed themselves in something soft (including fingers).

Although knitting needles aren't nearly as lethal as

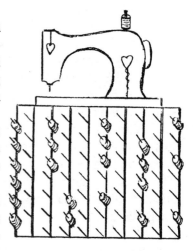

ILLUSTRATION 276

darning needles, they should be approached with caution. Leaving yarn in the open like in illustration 278 exposed to the sunlight to fade is never a good idea.

A container for carrying knits works much more effectively if the various yarns can be separated.

If our favorite hobby puts needles and scissors and other dangerous instruments in our hands, then we need a place to put work in progress.

This ladder quilt rack (illustration 279) serves admirably, since it demands little floor and wall space. It has rawhide straps enabling it to hang from the ceiling in either a vertical or horizontal position.

When our pursuits lead us more into the realm of artistic endeavors, the drafting table is a good way to go (illustration 280). The one shown, however, doesn't supply any drawers for rulers, T-squares, brushes, pens, or the like, nor does it have bins that attach to the sides for holding paints, all of which are handy helpers to have. Cer-

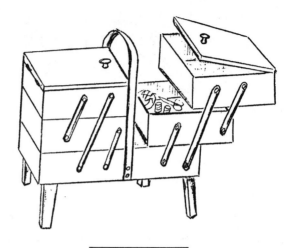

ILLUSTRATION 277

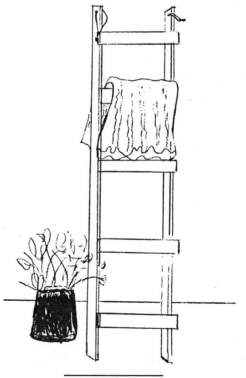

ILLUSTRATION 278

ILLUSTRATION 279

199

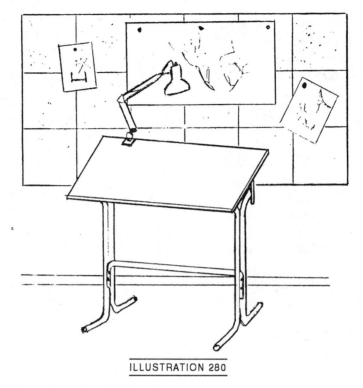

ILLUSTRATION 280

tain styles of more expensive drafting boards do have drawers and bins.

Another way to obtain help around an art or sewing area is to stick up a cork board wall behind or to the side of the table. Not only art work, paintings, and sketches can be hung, but also patterns and even pattern pieces.

Many of us collect one thing or another, be it baseball cards or caps, matchbook covers, wine labels, salt and pepper shakers, thimbles, statues, dolls, or spoons. Whatever the collection may consist of, it was worth our effort and money to acquire it, so it deserves to be exhibited and not left in a corner, a drawer, or a closet.

Any of the aforementioned collectibles have specialty racks for storage, but we'll take a look at only the specialty display for a spoon collection. (See illustration 281.)

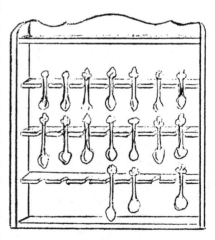

ILLUSTRATION 281

How to Manage Magazines and Books

Where and how do we store magazines and books? We seem to be under the misguided impression that magazines and books must never, under any circumstances, be thrown away.

There should be a method to the storage madness. Stacking magazines in a pile is nothing more than an accident waiting to happen, especially when the stack is placed next to the furnace. There is no way to search the stack for the magazine desired without handling each and every magazine.

It's much better to store magazines in an upright position so that the spine of each is presented for review and selection; however, there are difficulties even with this because as a magazine is removed, the others slump. Replacing the single magazine back into its original upright position is a hassle, even when they've been stood together in a supporting structure like the one depicted in illustration 282.

A rather unique approach that works wonderfully well eliminates the hassle of trying to give a little backbone to a magazine and it allows each of the magazines to be viewed without first having to remove it from the stack. It more or less makes a complete composition from the individual magazines, which also makes it easier to place specific magazines together for instance referral.

ILLUSTRATION 282

These strips are placed in a binder and are inexpensive, far less than the typical upright magazine holders. See illustration 283. If there aren't any extra binders in the house, the expenditure could increase considerably.

Each magazine is slotted onto the opening of the strip, and then the strip is placed in the binder as though it were nothing more than a single sheet of paper. The larger the binder, the more magazines it will hold. Open the binder and leaf through at random or insert tabs for identification.

A conventional approach corrals the magazines in either a floor unit or a wall magazine rack. (See illustration 284.)

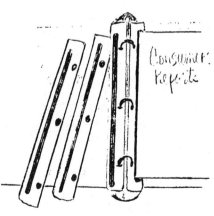

ILLUSTRATION 283

There's no question though that this method will never qualify for the abundant stockpile some of us may possess. Yet it does well for a month's supply of reading material.

There are all sorts of ways to stash magazines (illustration 285). We could put them in baskets, show them off on the coffee table, or lay them next to us in bed. The crisis occurs when we take a tour down memory lane, treating every magazine we ever owned like it was a dear friend or a part of the immediate family.

Without developing a retrieval system, why do we even keep them? It's a saddening sight to see a stack of magazines socked away randomly, inconsistently, and confusingly.

There's no reason to discuss the bookcases that can be found in every discount store, department store, and furniture store worldwide. The selection is large and prices vary greatly.

ILLUSTRATION 284

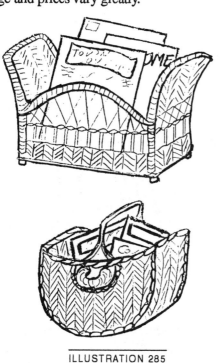

ILLUSTRATION 285

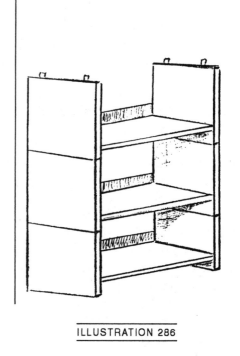

ILLUSTRATION 286

This particular bookshelf (illustration 286) is worthy of mention simply because it comes as a kit to be assembled. It costs much less than most others of the same quality.

How to Be a Bonafide Couch Potato

Where do we put audio and video components? Below the TV or on top of the TV isn't good, since the VCR already inhabits one of those spots. The other contains remote controls for both the TV and VCR. Perhaps the TV and VCR reside in comfort on a console or entertainment center, which provides slots, grooves, niches, pull-outs, and swivel stands for not only the TV and VCR, but all of the sound equipment as well.

We couldn't enjoy any of our video pleasures if we didn't have the TV screen in a prime position. Illustration 287 shows one novel method of keeping the TV handy yet out of the way at the same time.

This product in illustration 288 allows you to swivel the TV around to any angle. It does cause disputes among the viewers, however. Before you provided this marvelous moveable object, the members of the family seemed content to situate themselves in their favorite spot.

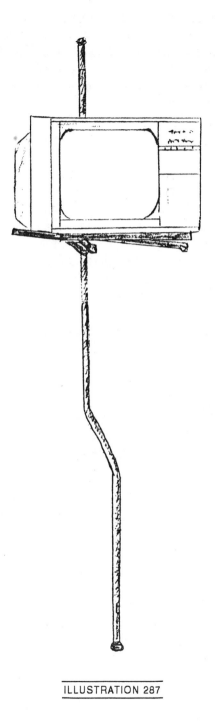

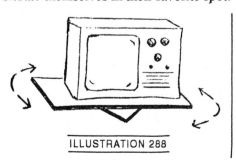

ILLUSTRATION 288

ILLUSTRATION 287

Now they can sit in the exact same spot and argue that they can't see the TV and could it please be swiveled just a inch or two in their direction.

After the TV, the remote controls are an essential element in the couch potato's environment, as are the *TV Guides*, consumer magazines, and movie reviews. In order to keep the controls and necessary data at hand, many devices have been marketed.

The first to come off the drawing board was the pouch that fits over the arm of the couch or recliner (illustration 289). Don't be surprised to find food crumbs or other debris building up inside.

All sorts of organizers are manufactured. Most are meant to rest on top of the TV, coffee

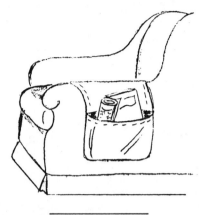

ILLUSTRATION 289

table, or end table nearest the human hand that controls it. Things, however, have gotten a bit out of hand when we're offered an extra set of hands for controlling the controls. Neither of these organizers (illustration 290) could sit out of reach on the TV, since true couch potatoes don't move during viewing hours.

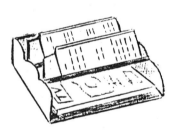

ILLUSTRATION 290

How to Not Experience Audio/Video Difficulties

In our attempt to store our collection of tapes and cassettes, we've probably tried to fit them under the sofa, in the tiny cabinet space in the entertainment center, on every bookcase in the house, or even in packs under the car seat. Yet it's become obvious that we've outgrown most of the typical and traditional ways for storing them.

Before purchasing any unit for their storage, see that it is big enough for the materials on hand. Allow for growth. An expandable storage system is a good idea.

The unit depicted first in illustration 291 is available in sizes to accomodate both audio and videocassettes. It rotates 360°, enabling selection of each tape no matter where it is located.

The second illustration pictures a CD storage rack, but it too is available for audio and videocassettes. It furnishes a lever for standing the discs up so they can't fall over. Both of these storage units are wood, but similar versions come in molded plastics.

This model for videotape storage is available for audiocassettes as well (illustration 292). It has premolded slots inside the drawers for balancing each tape, so that when one is removed the rest won't fall.

This floor model tiltfront unit is probably the most carefree contractor of all. It's extremely streamlined, requiring only the depth of a single video tape. It can be locked, there's no reason to have separate racks for audiocassettes, videos, and CDs since they each have their own tier of storage in this unit.

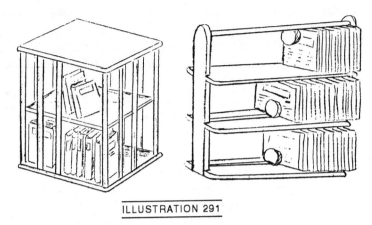

ILLUSTRATION 291

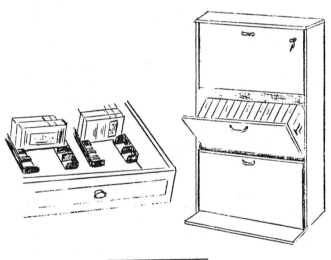

ILLUSTRATION 292

ILLUSTRATION 293

It furnishes enough space for 60 videos, 140 compact discs, or 70 audiocassettes. This unit is also desireable because it keeps the tapes tucked away, free from the dust and cobwebs we constantly battle.

Many storage systems consolidate compact discs, cassettes, and videos together into one unit. This establishes a uniform and standardized appearance.

The rack in illustration 293 is included to store those long-playing record albums we still have.

Arranging videotapes on the back of a door is a viable proposition (illustration 294). The likeliest doors would, of course, be those that are opened infrequently.

The same conditions apply to Rack #1 (illustration 295), a bookcase-type video storage rack, if it were hung on a door. It has the ability, however, to also hang on a wall. Units can be stacked together to build a rack of immense proportions, sufficient to fit any quantity or collection of videos.

Rack #2 could be placed inside a cabinet or on a shelf. The difficulty is in trying to find space in the living room or family room to put it.

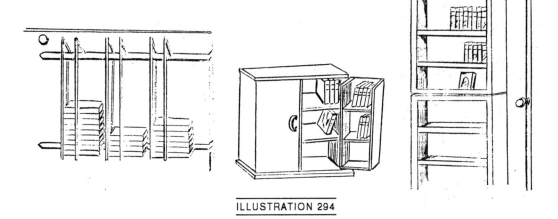

ILLUSTRATION 294

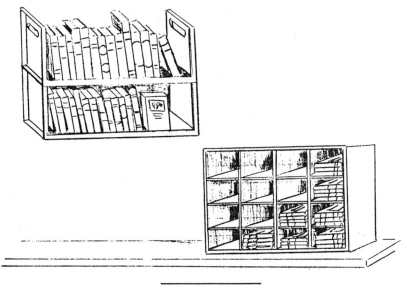

ILLUSTRATION 295

THE KITCHEN

OVERHEAD CABINETS

✔ How to Deal with Dishes

✔ How to Be Nice to Sugar and Spice

✔ How to Control Canned Goods

✔ How to Use the Underside Underneath

How to Deal with Dishes

Dishes generally use a great deal of cabinet space, most of which is misused because of the way we stack them. The shelves inside kitchen cabinets are normally spaced 12 inches apart, yet we use only four inches to eight inches when we stack dishes, bowls, glasses, or cups in a shelf. The inches left vacant and unproductive is shameful. Those same inches could realistically store a complete 12-piece dinnerware set, including serving bowls, platters, and coordinating stemware.

The available shelf space is the single most important factor in planning placement, yet we fail to give it the consideration it deserves.

Determining how dinnerware should be distributed on the shelves is the second component to consider, so that the shelf and the merchandise are working in unison for maximum efficiency, visibility, and convenience.

Obviously, that means dishes must be divided into categories and not lumped together as a single unit.

The only common ground to be found within the category of dishes is that we eat and drink from them. They have few similarities in size and shape, yet we insist on putting bowls with cups and plates with long-stemmed wine glasses. This is an acceptable practice only if each subdivided category is assigned a specific place on the shelf.

One way to set aside shelf space for plates is to divide the space between shelves into more manageable increments (that is, add shelves). This not only increases the number of useable shelves, but can also furnish shelves that diminish in diameter from approximately 12 inches to six inches, which is proportionate to the diameters of the plates, bowls, and saucers. Therefore, an entire set of dishes is accomodated in the same space that would have typically contained merely a stack of dinner plates.

A corner unit as pictured in illustration 296, is beneficial because it utilizes the entire 12-inch height of the cabinet. This unit is an epoxy coated metal and is available either as a solidly constructed unit or one that can be disassembled.

When china is divided into subcategories and then placed into compartments, as is achieved with the corner unit in illustration 297, it's much easier to handle the individual plates, bowls, and saucers.

ILLUSTRATION 296

We also have a tendency to think our plates, bowls, and saucers must be stacked when, obviously, after reviewing illustration 298, that simply isn't true. Placing plates on edge can be effective, although it does demand more shelf space.

First, determine whether the space is big enough to allow the largest dinner plate to stand on edge. If not, perhaps the shelves are adjustable and can be moved to accomodate this type of operation.

If the dishes are arranged on the shelf in this way, will there be sufficient shelf space for all the dishes you possess? It certainly is nice when a single plate can be reached without handling, lifting, and touching all the others!

As with all organizing products however, it's important to understand the principles of space conservation, since many products do more harm than good. Be sure the

ILLUSTRATION 297

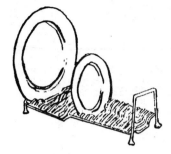
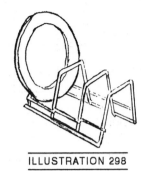

ILLUSTRATION 298

product selected achieves the desired effect and functions better than any of the other products under consideration.

This dish organizer (illustration 299) is very tall and uses more space than is generally available in kitchen cabinets even those equipped with adjustable shelves. Although it is more multipurpose than the previous organizers discussed, it takes more inches than are necessary. The same goal could have been achieved in less space. Second, it seldom meets exact specifications for each need it's attempting to fulfill, so it overcompensates and adds extra inches just in case. If your coffee cups are standard size, this rack wasted enough space to store a second set.

Here again, we have all the pieces of the dinnerware set together on one storage unit (illustration 300). It's just stretched in a horizontal direction rather than a vertical one. And here again, so long as the plates, bowls, and cups fit precisely the preconceived shapes supplied by the rack, it's workable. If not, it's going to be a frustrating attempt to fit a square peg into a round hole.

Another source of irritation inherent with this dish organizing rack is that it's difficult to access the cups hanging at the back of the rack, without gravely endangering the stability of the rack. Forget any and all efforts to hang a mug. It wasn't designed to accomodate mugs.

Although this rack does partially comply with our objective to utilize all of the

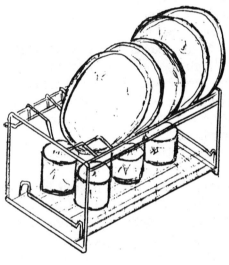

ILLUSTRATION 299

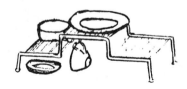

ILLUSTRATION 300

height between shelves, it can be accomplished better with other methods.

Incorporating extra shelf units into the cabinet, divides the height into smaller areas for containing each category for better accessibility and visibility. The heights match more closely the heights of the various pieces of dinnerware (illustration 301). However, these multipurpose modular stack shelves don't provide specialized treatment for each category. Instead it groups all the categories together for an identical presentation.

These modular units are constructed of a high quality, laminated material, making them costly. The same effect can be accomplished with less expensive stack shelves, but stability and durability may be sacrificed.

ILLUSTRATION 301

Examples of different styles and materials used in manufacturing shelf units are shown in illustration 302.

The first is made of molded, high-impact plastic with interwoven strips forming the top surface, so it will not sustain much weight without sagging. The second and third are made of metal overlaid with a vinyl or epoxy coating. While they can carry the weight, their strutted tops don't provide a stable surface, so the dishes are in danger of falling through the cracks.

The best course of action to pursue in maximizing space while keeping dishes handy

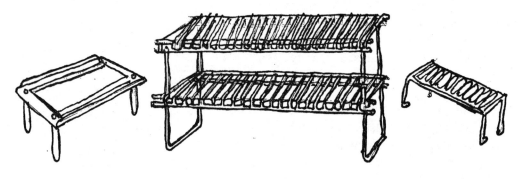

ILLUSTRATION 302

210

and visible is to be creative. By combining specialty products, substituting when needed, and improvising, you can accomplish what you need. Evaluate, picture the product in place, and imagine it in operation to decide its feasibility and merit.

At this point, after perhaps physically moving, changing and rearranging the dishes the realization may have dawned on us that we're never going to get all of our dishes in the cabinet. When there's only so much room, there's only so much room and nothing's going to alter that fact.

If after organizing the cabinet space as effectively as humanly possible, consider a decorative mode whereby the extra set of dishes is put on display in an open area of the kitchen.

This wooden dish rack (illustration 303), tinted a traditional Williamsburg blue, would handle not only the plates but the cups well. The shelf on top where the cups sit could be used instead to keep one glass per family member in plain sight, so that each time they want a drink of water, they'll use the same glass rather than dirtying dozens per day.

A way to generate additional storage space inside a kitchen cabinet is to install one or more of these open-front, under-shelf drawer units (illustration 304). They are also available with fronts that drop down or with permanent fronts that aren't moveable.

Again, this divides the space between the shelves into more manageable units. Each unit has a clearly defined function—one that restricts it into receiving only like and similar objects.

Coffee cups are one of the worst squanderers of space because they are short and small, which in most space-saving situations would be an advantage but not here.

We automatically line them up along a shelf. Certainly, coffee cups must be near enough at hand for groping first thing in the morning, but we should investigate alternative positions for keeping them handy without such a sacrifice of space.

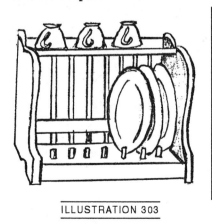

ILLUSTRATION 303

ILLUSTRATION 304

Worse yet, though, is when we line them up in stacks of two or three. Then we're just waiting for an accident to happen. Coffee cups are capable of being stacked and breaking them can be eliminated at the same time by utilizing the twin-cup stacker pictured in illustration 305. It's really quite innovative because it's more multipurpose than it would appear at first. For instance, it contains eight to 12 cups, but it's a marvelous third-hand when it comes time to set the table for guests. Simply lift the entire twin-stack unit out of the cabinet, carry it to the dining room table and deftly remove a cup at a time at each place setting. In the case of informal affairs, the unit, complete with

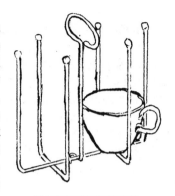

ILLUSTRATION 305

cups, simply sits on the kitchen table for a help-yourself invitation. Another step takes it to the dishwasher for easy restocking of clean cups, and then the unit is replaced in the cabinet. It's much more efficient than carrying one or two cups at a time.

The biggest and most obvious advantage, however, is that those eight to 12 cups are occupying the same space that previously held two to four. This saves a minimum of 16 inches of shelf space.

Unfortunately, it wasn't designed to accommodate large coffee mugs. But mugs aren't as hard to stack as are the fragile china cups that accompany our dinnerware sets. There are other ways to assign cups, not mugs, a permanent place of residence, while keeping the cabinet orderly and systematic (illustration 306). Cup racks that slide out for convenience, not only divides the shelf but keeps any number of cups together in one place.

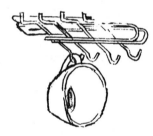

With a cup rack occupying space on the underside of the shelf like the one in illustration 307 that revolves, it's important to know the cup's size and shape. Otherwise it's very likely that the rack won't function smoothly and flawlessly. If the hooks are too close together for the cups, there isn't room for them to hang without making awkward their retrieval.

The main reason and the greatest benefit gained from installing racks on the underside of the shelf is that the merchandise that is then arrayed has been removed from occupying space on the shelf itself.

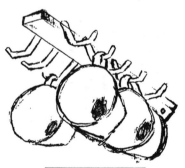

ILLUSTRATION 306

In the typical household, the glasses have been arranged in a nice, neat row on a shelf, and they're maintained in that orderly fashion washing after washing, drink after drink.

All those inches from the top edge of the glass to the bottom of the next shelf are empty and unused.

A way we can prevent this waste of shelf space is through the use of this innovative device (illustration 308), designed specifically for stemware. An identifying name for it would naturally be, a stemware rack. It moves the glasses from the shelf and aligns them upside-down

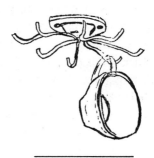

ILLUSTRATION 307

for safekeeping, and leaves the shelf free below it. The same space is now storing twice the number of glasses as it did before. And they are not only positioned by category, but they are certainly more visible and accessible.

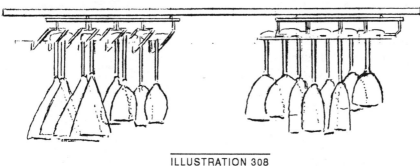

ILLUSTRATION 308

For those glasses without stems and that have flat bottoms, a double layer can be obtained by putting the bottom row of glasses on the shelf with their bases facing up. A second layer of glasses sits on these upturned glasses, base to base.

Each and every nook, cranny, shelf, and open spot in the kitchen should be evaluated for its potential to provide a safe and generous resting ground for any of the kitchen gear we all own.

For instance, the inches below the shelves inside the cabinets, can provide anywhere from two inches to eight inches of space that is otherwise unused.

There are many different types of specialty products on the market that turn this space into a functional area for storing a variety of odd-sized or oversized items.

Illustration 309 shows a sampling of the many designs and styles, some of which simply slide onto the existing shelf. Others must be attached to the bottom of the shelf with screws. They are most effective for controlling oversized or exceptionally large platters, serving pieces, or cutting boards.

Another idea is to put these types of platter racks to good use by allowing them to handle dish towels, woven, plastic, or linen placemats, and napkins. This is especially effective in pantries, where those kinds of articles belong.

Another product that is perfect for these few inches of space below the shelf is known as the paper-plate rack. It's especially helpful if you frequently serve lunch, dinner, breakfast, or a great number of snacks on paper plates.

A similar product is sold for holding an abundant supply of paper napkins (illustration 310). It too attaches to the underside of the shelf, although opening and closing the cabinets each time a paper plate or paper napkin is wanted might prove a bit cumbersome.

In determining placement of these racks then, it's important to consider how, why, when, and where they will function with the highest level of efficiency.

Be wary when purchasing any of the racks or products that are installed on the underside of the cabinet, since they will see the light of day for as long as we're willing to keep them in our sights. If they aren't reasonably attractive, uniformly similar, and their final destination isn't carefully considered, you'll have created clutter.

The dishes were dealt with as a starter because they generally demand the lion's share of the shelf space. However, just because the dishes are discussed first doesn't imply that you should rush forth and begin straightening them before a plan of action has been developed that will resolve each and every element of the kitchen's restructuring.

Before rearranging and revamping the current system for storing dishes, very often much of the other kitchen paraphernalia will be removed and assigned to a new storage site elsewhere in the kitchen. Needless to say, this

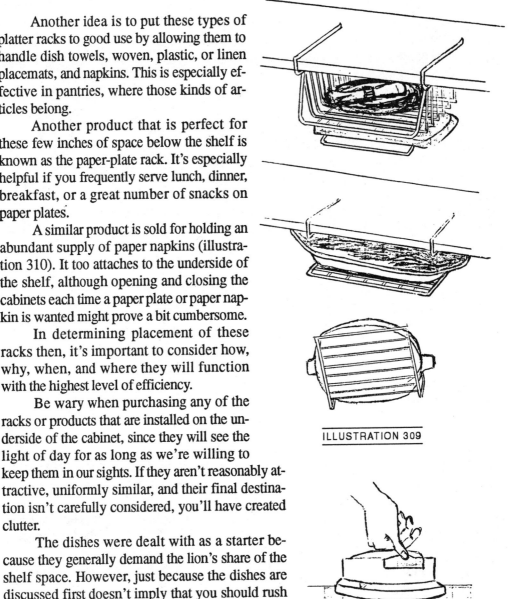

ILLUSTRATION 309

ILLUSTRATION 310

dramatically affects the space that is then available for stowing the dishes.

The bottom line is to create a means of organizing everything in the least amount of space possible, as attractively as possible, and as sensibly as possible.

How to Be Nice to Sugar and Spice

Sugar, flour, salt, baby food, coffee, tea, jelly, pasta, sauces, spices, and seasonings have always been a problem to store.

The first step is to categorize the containers and their contents into distinct classifications.

Overstocking spices is stoppable by devising a system in which any newly purchased replacement is placed directly beside or behind the current one. Spices are most easily kept track of when they are arranged alphabetically.

There are almost as many ways to store spices as there are spices themselves.

The first approach one might pursue in attaining an orderly system to array spices is using shelf units that are expandable. They furnish shelf sizes that more closely match the size of spice jars and tins, and their greatest attribute is that they have staggered steps, so that the varying heights of the spice containers are presented in a pleasantly accessible and visible fashion (illustration 311).

This unit is made of molded plastic. Other units are epoxy or vinyl coated metal, but they do not adjust.

Attaching baskets (illustration 312), whether slide-on or secured with screws, can provide a place for spices, but there are drawbacks to this method. It's hard to reach the items at the back of the basket that is screwed on. And both baskets hinder our ability to alphabetize the contents.

A spice rack is a spice rack is a spice rack until it's time to sit one on a shelf. Doubtlessly, there are certain styles that do sit nicely and unobtrusively, but it's a

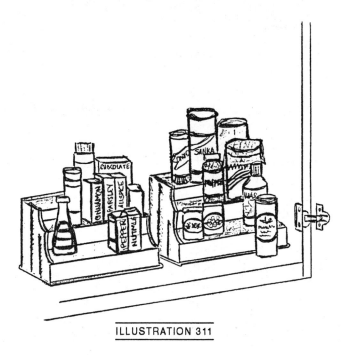

ILLUSTRATION 311

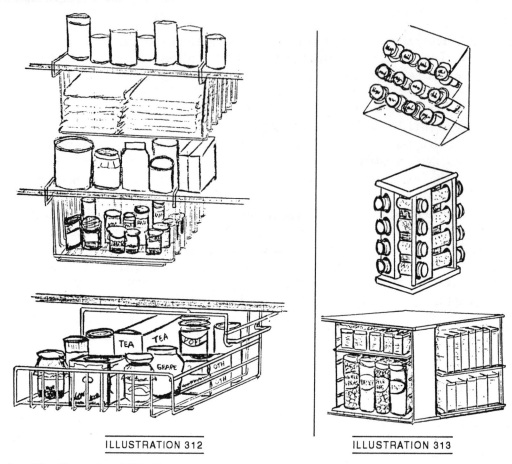

ILLUSTRATION 312   ILLUSTRATION 313

rarity. (See illustration 313.) These racks are inadviseable for use inside a cabinet because they're just too big. But can you count on finding a clear countertop spot for them?

The preceding spice racks are a meager sample of the multitudes of spice racks for sale in marketplaces all over the world. Probably the version seen most frequently is the lazy-susan variety, which is nothing more than a round plate that rotates. Some spice racks are singular, while others are stackable, some are stable and some aren't, some are adjustable, but they are all terrible when it comes to securing any item that is placed behind an item in the front.

Adding a spice drawer to the underside of a cabinet or under a shelf is appealing.

Illustration 314 shows first a drawer that provides progressively higher shelves as they approach the back of the drawer. This allows you to view and reach all of the spices. In the second depicted drawer, the contents are going to be mussed and mangled every time the thyme, vanilla, or white pepper is needed because they are in the rear of the drawer somewhere, alphabetically.

Who would have thought it possible? Putting spices into a kitchen drawer. The reason it's seldom contemplated is because there's seldom an empty drawer available (illustration 315). It's not an altogether bad idea, yet it demands commitment on your part to keep it organized. If you don't, the resulting mess is a major catastrophe, worse than if the spices had been left on a shelf.

Perhaps you'd prefer the attractive but exceedingly costly alternatives shown in illustration 316. At the top is a lucite rack (but again, the jars behind the front row are inaccessible). The oak rack on the bottom rotates for easy reach of all the spices.

The rack in illustration 317 is not only space conscious, but it's just one of a series of matching products for installation under the overhead cabinets in the kitchen. The others (slotted knife storage, bulletin/memo center and cookbook handler) will be reviewed later, so please accept this as a short introduction.

The primary advantage of using this rack and the others like it

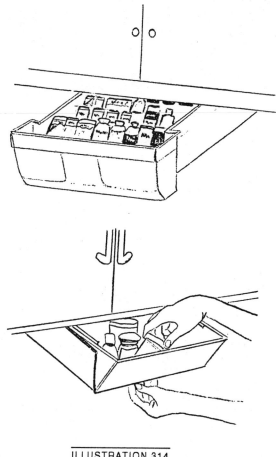

ILLUSTRATION 314

is the uniformity gained for the entire kitchen. However, each piece in itself doesn't necessarily store the kitchen accessory as nicely as another method might.

In the case of this spice rack in particular, what happens to the spices that don't fit the rack? What if they're too big? Or what if you have more than will fit in the rack? Think about it. The best spice racks I have found are ones that are customized for the customer, by the customer.

This transparent storage system (illustration 318) for canister containers is not only easy to install, but it controls a great many other condiments: pastas, coffee, teas, and snacks that commonly cause chaos in the cabinet.

The edge they bring to the elimination of clutter within the cabinet is enhanced even further by the fact they can be truly personalized. By installing as many or as few of the bins as needed, the bulk of the problem has been effectively solved.

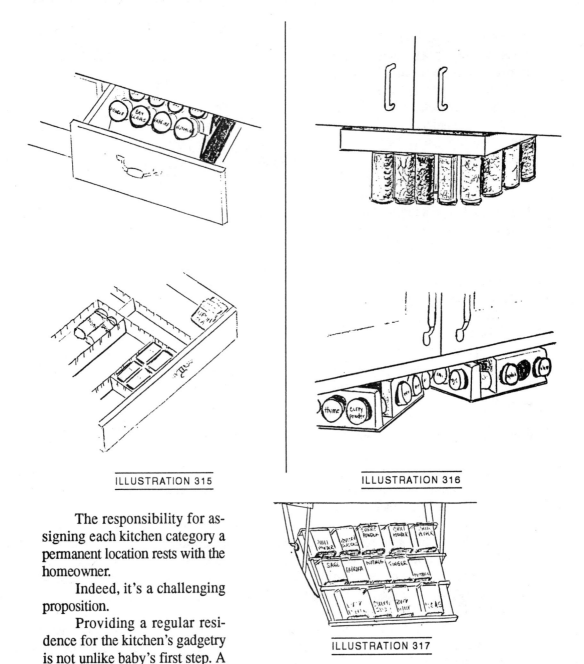

ILLUSTRATION 315

ILLUSTRATION 316

ILLUSTRATION 317

The responsibility for assigning each kitchen category a permanent location rests with the homeowner.

Indeed, it's a challenging proposition.

Providing a regular residence for the kitchen's gadgetry is not unlike baby's first step. A starting point has been established. Now, it's just a matter of moving ahead, one step at a time, progressing from point A to point B.

The principle of assigned placement is an obligation that can't be swept aside.

After first getting a feeling for which locations are most appropriate for which items, determine the method that uses that space best while also displaying the item to its fullest. The greatest rewards often result from discovering a use for a portion of the kitchen or cabinet that was previously unused and unproductive. This stick-on spice rack (illustration 319) is a good example. It is stuck on the inside of a cabinet door as a strip of four or cut into single units, and it's adaptable to any number of spices or to any door. A masterpiece!

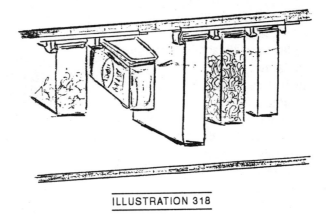

ILLUSTRATION 318

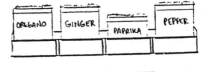

ILLUSTRATION 319

When spices are stored in their original containers, it can sometimes cause problems as we try to fit the various tall, short, round, and rectangular shapes together. But keeping the system going isn't nearly as tedious as keeping matching spice jars filled. Matching spice canisters, like the grid unit in illustration 320 must be filled, refilled, and washed regularly.

This grid spice rack is another product (like the under-the-cabinet, pull-down spice rack) that can offer other services as well. By simply attaching other attachments to the grid as needed (such as a paper towel rack, clock, wax paper holder, memo board, pasta bin, hooks, or a separate shelf) you can make your kitchen more efficient. A detailed description will follow in a forthcoming section.

Refilling each spice container every time it's low is far more time consuming than taking the time initially to think about how to store the spices in the package they came in.

When you have spices stored in matching containers, where are the reserves? Obviously, we have to have some stashed somewhere else in the kitchen.

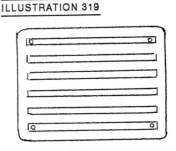

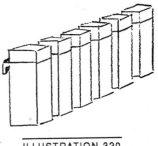

ILLUSTRATION 320

We organize to bring orderliness into our lives and because we want to streamline productivity and lessen our involvement in activities that are needlessly repetitive. Why then would we defeat our own purpose by selecting a system for spice storage that needs not only a back-up system but also constant monitoring?

In the multi-purpose cart in illustration 321, the spices are arrayed on racks, and the unit serves not only as a chopping block, work surface, knife and towel rack, but also as a tiny, self-contained culinary emporium.

The spice rack itself is a product that is readily available in most house-wares departments. It is easily installed on the inside door of the kitchen cabinets or on one of the side or back walls.

ILLUSTRATION 321

The interiors of kitchen cabinets are wonderful resources. The fact that we frequently forget their potential is a grave error.

Case in point. We just finished a discussion of spice racks, but we only mentioned this one function. Spice racks can actually serve many functions. They are extremely useful for holding bottles of medicines and vitamins. Try putting them in linen closets or bathrooms. You can now store row upon row of cod liver oil, calcium, vitamin E, B-12 supplements, headache tablets, cold capsules, and aids for sleeping or staying awake.

The inside of the kitchen cabinet door is an excellent place to store small articles. Take for example illustration

ILLUSTRATION 322

322, showing a transparent vinyl, pocketed sheath. Each pocket holds a packet or envelope, such as seasoning mixes, sauces, flavorings, beverage crystals, soups, gravies, dips, puddings, or dressings. If these easily damaged envelopes were left on a shelf or in a drawer, they nearly always self-destruct or are lost or torn.

Why run the risk of ruining a perfectly good package of dressing mix, and why waste kitchen space for such itsy-bitsy packets? They quite handily fit on the inside of a kitchen cabinet.

This method for storing packages and packets (illustration 323) isn't too efficient. It's likely it could be too deep for the inside of many cabinet doors, which leaves us with the option of racking it up on the wall instead.

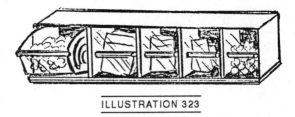

ILLUSTRATION 323

How to Control Canned Goods

Walls are a wonderful way to wage war against cans.

You might wonder how in the world can cans adhere to a wall? Well, turn your attention to illustration 324. It's a single unit with dual-dispensing capabilities. Restocking originates at the top, the cans shoot down the chute, and are halted by the lip at the bottom edge, the location from which they are lifted and removed. What happens when the lunch menu calls for chicken noodle soup, but it's only half way down the chute? The easiest solution is to change your mind and settle for the bean soup on the bottom.

Everyone enjoys a totally unexpected surprise! This innovative gadget (illustration 325) obliges us with many of the criterion we've set out to achieve.

First of all, this can rack places the cans in a location inside the cabinet that is vacant and unproductive. The cans are taken from the shelf space below, which increases the space you have for other items.

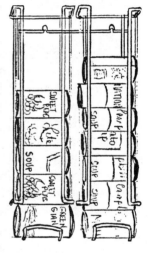

ILLUSTRATION 324

Second, you can attach as many or as few as you like. It permits a margin of customized designing.

The only way this rack could supply superior selection is if each rack held only items that are identical. Otherwise, you'll have to decide whether to settle for the contents of the closest can or remove them all one by one until you reach the one you want.

However, well-stocked

ILLUSTRATION 325

kitchens do commonly keep several of certain items on hand. If this holds true for you, then these racks are good. Imagine one entire racked row of peas, one of tomato soup, one of peach slices, and so on.

The can holder in illustration 326 has three levels, and each level holds three rows of cans. It allows nine kinds of food to be stored. All the items in each row must be the same because it's virtually impossible to reach in to get a grasp on any can in the rear. This is strictly a first come, first served means of dispensing canned goods.

Even without a speciality product to organize cans, cans can be consigned

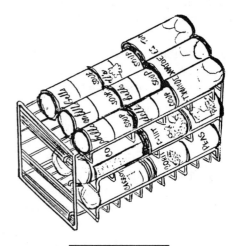

ILLUSTRATION 326

space methodically. Each and every can that is hidden behind the can in front should be there only when it matches the can in front.

If cans are stacked vertically, the cans on the bottom should be the same as the ones that are sitting on top of them. By following this practice, the identity of concealed cans is known.

To simplify the process, suppose there were three major categories of canned goods: soups, vegetables, and fruits. Suppose we had one shelf supplying sufficient storage space for these canned goods. Fruits would go on the far left side of the shelf, soups next, and veggies last. F — S — V, alphabetically.

The fruits are subdivided into kinds and those subdivisions are arranged alphabeti-

ILLUSTRATION 327

ILLUSTRATION 328

cally. Repeat this procedure for the soups and vegetables, and the cans are systematically cared for. It takes little effort to maintain and restock this system. It helps, of course, to divide the cabinet's shelf into smaller sections. This can be accomplished in various ways, such as the basket method (illustration 327) which stops the stacking of cans vertically.

Cans are arranged in a system in which only similar items are placed behind those at the front. The same system applies when modular units or other styles of stack shelves are incorporated into the cabinet. In illustration 328, simply visualize canned goods and boxes of snacks, cereals, crackers, cookies, and so forth in place of the dishes and crockery shown.

Needless to say, fingertip convenience is lost at the higher levels, so only store food items that are seldom eaten in these upper regions. Or make the entire kitchen useable, functional, serviceable, and reachable by having a step stool readily available.

Choose an appropriate step stool based on the space in your kitchen and how high you want to reach. See examples of step stools in illustration 329.

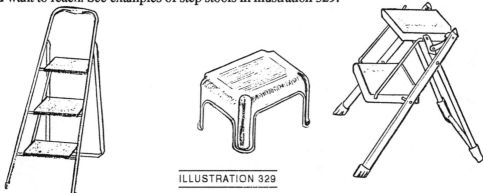

ILLUSTRATION 329

The step stool is a viable solution, yet there is an alternative solution generally viewed as appropriate for only the elderly, arthritic, or disabled.

It is an arm extender (illustration 330). If you don't like climbing on stools, it may be the solution for you.

Removing the canned and boxed products from the cabinet shelves allows us to store our crockery and china in an orderly and pleasant manner. One way to do this is to store the goods in a portable unit (illustration 331). If you don't have space for something like this, then even moving a meager collection of jellies aids the process of organizing the items left inside the kitchen cabinets (illustration 332).

ILLUSTRATION 330

ILLUSTRATION 331

How to Use the Underside Underneath

These three units (illustration 333) show different ways the underside of kitchen cabinets can be made functional. The first drawing depicts a stationary bread box with a drop front. It removes the breads, donuts, biscuits, and dinner rolls from the top of the kitchen counter for increased workspace. The other two drawings show how drawer units are conveniently filled with either silverware or assorted dishcloths and miscellaneous items, all of which have been removed from the kitchen drawers, leaving them ready to store something else.

These pull-down accessories are identical when they are secured in their full, upright position. They supply a specific service when pulled away from the cabinet.

The memo center or mini-office (illustration 334) is equipped with a corkboard, calculator, pads of scratch paper, and paper for grocery lists with separate cubbyholes for pens, pencils, erasers, paper clips, thumbtacks, and other such items.

Storing knives and sharpener in one location, eliminates cut fingers and displays the knives as

ILLUSTRATION 332

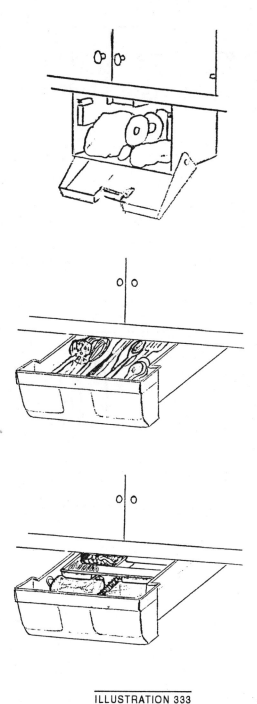

ILLUSTRATION 333

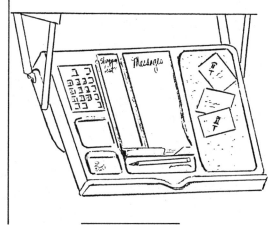

ILLUSTRATION 334

well. If a cookbook demands less of our attention keeping it open and unsplattered, cooking becomes pleasurable (illustration 335).

The reason it's beneficial to convert the underside of kitchen cabinets into storage facilities is twofold.

First, using this space empties out drawers and unclutters counters. Second, these areas under cabinets are expansive and are capable of controlling a great many items. They align these items for better visibility, accessibility, and convenience, all of which are advantages that are frequently missing from traditional kitchens.

There are many products on the market that are helpful in this endeavor (illustration 336). For instance, there are strip

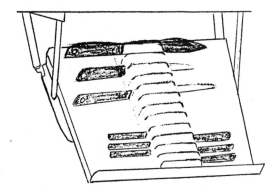 

ILLUSTRATION 335

appliances that can stretch along the entire bottom edge of all the cabinets in the kitchen. They range from coffeemakers to four-slice toasters, from can openers to mini-vacuums, from microwaves to spice racks.

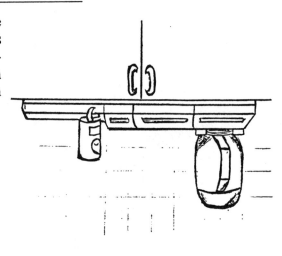

ILLUSTRATION 336

CHAPTER NINETEEN

THE KITCHEN

LOWER CABINETS

✔ How to Position Pots and Pans

✔ How to Win with Wrap Racks

How to Position Pots and Pans

If money's no object, then these roll-out storage units may be just what you need (illustration 337). One is designed specifically for lids, while the other is called a utility tray because of its versatility. Both let air circulate and they are easily installed.

The major disadvantage with the roll-out units is that not all cabinets are the same; therefore, there is often a huge space above the roll-out unit that sits idle. This won't be the case, however, if you install a horizontal shelf dividing the cabinet in half.

A minor disadvantage with these units is the fact that kitchens seldom contain two lower cabinets of the size required for these roll-out trays. Therefore you can only install one.

As in most predesigned products, these units aren't designed to accommodate the size, shape, style, or type of articles we actually own. This ends up costing us space when we attempt to match our possessions to the space the products allot us.

The lids and covers that accompany skillets, pots, and pans, are usually more of a hassle than the pots themselves.

Any lid organizing product that separates and unifies covers and lids is performing a much-needed and valuable service. Isn't it better to grab the one most wanted lid, than to shuffle through an entire stack and finally settle for what's second best. The products in illustration 338 may solve your lid problems forever.

The product in illustration 339 has adjustable braces that slide to any desired width, making it easy to store just about any lid no matter what size. Although it costs more than the others, it's well worth it. It's substantially longer and holds many more items than the others. It's especially suitable for bakeware paraphernalia like muffin pans, molds, cake pans, and cooling racks, plus microwave products for bacon or popcorn and larger articles such as cutting boards, trays, and casserole dishes.

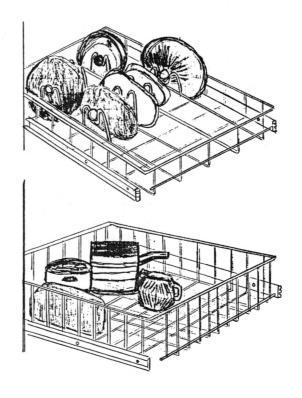

ILLUSTRATION 337

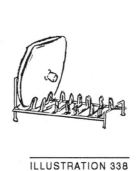
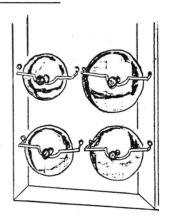

ILLUSTRATION 338

Certainly a product (illustration 340) that has the ability to telescope forward and backward is rather unusual, but there are drawbacks to this product that need mentioning.

First, evaluate your pots and pans to determine whether they have loops or rings at the tips of their handles or they aren't going to hang at all.

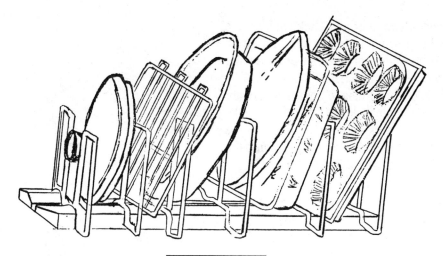

ILLUSTRATION 339

When pots are hanging as they should on this rack, they'll clatter every time the rack's put in motion. But the worst thing about this product is that it occupies an excessive amount of cabinet space compared to other methods.

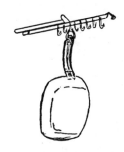

ILLUSTRATION 340

How to Win with Wrap Racks

Wrapracks provide the means for organizing plastic bags, wax paper, sandwich baggies, and the like in an orderly and systematic fashion.

This version (illustration 341) simply sits on a shelf. It can store six boxes at one time. If one rack isn't sufficient for the amount of wrapping products you have, buy two.

This would be a proper time to present a wrap rack that makes sense out of shelves (illustration 342).

It's tremendously versatile because it can be attached to not only the underside of the cabinet shelf (which as we know is usually an unproductive area of the kitchen) but it can also be attached to the inside of a cabinet door.

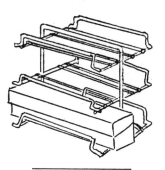

ILLUSTRATION 341

Upgraded, expensive, and expanded models such as this wrap rack in illustration 343 for the wall are fine if there's a handy wall. But remember it isn't logical to walk over

229

and back and over and back each time a sandwich needs to be packed in a lunch pail or the leftovers from dinner need to be stashed in the refrigerator.

It's a good idea to keep Tupperware lids on a cabinet door (illustration 344). The containers themselves should be sorted by size and stacked, one inside the other, in the same cabinet.

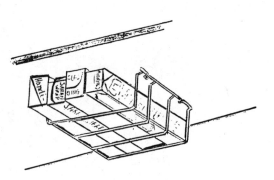

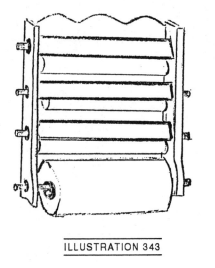

ILLUSTRATION 343

ILLUSTRATION 342

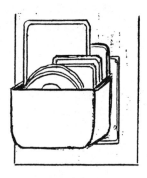

ILLUSTRATION 344

THE KITCHEN

THE KITCHEN SINK

✔ How to Clean up Cleaning Supplies

✔ How to Tend Trash

✔ How to Dangle Dishcloths

How to Clean up Cleaning Supplies

The area below the kitchen sink seems hopeless because it doesn't even have a shelf, and the pipes, disposal, hoses, drains, and even the bottom of the sink itself interfere with organizing it.

Illustration 345 shows two pull-out units. They both increase serviceability but it's important to decide which one fits the space best.

This ingenious gem (illustration 346) is known as a swing shelf since it does indeed swing out and away from the cabinet for maneuverability.

It isn't especially strong or durable, so don't put gallon dispensers on these shelves.

The biggest reason to install this swing shelf over the others is because it does dwell well in a space that is difficult to make functional. So accomplishing even this marginal increase is worth doing.

As always, the inside of the cabinet doors is not only accessible and handy, but it's usually readily available.

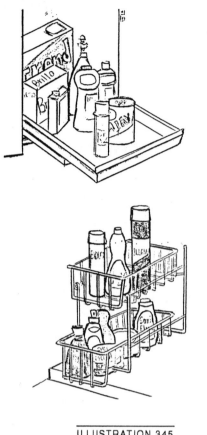

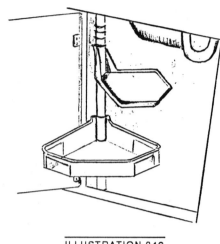

ILLUSTRATION 346

ILLUSTRATION 345

Even though these racks are small (illustration 347), they'll furnish ample room for plenty of detergents, sponges, abrasives, and cleaning powders and sprays.

When many are used, every inch of the door space can become efficient, but don't limit them to simply the door. Because they are small, they adapt well to the little areas at the side of the drainpipe or behind it.

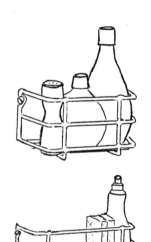

ILLUSTRATION 347

An innovative idea that provides a little extra room is this false front replacement (illustration 348).

It comes in a kit, which contains all that's needed to remove the front panel from the sink. When installed it becomes a tilt-out receptacle for little items like sponges and scouring pads.

ILLUSTRATION 348

How to Tend Trash

Either of these pull-out trash receptacles (illustration 349) fits the space normally found under kitchen sinks. Both use the entire height of this area to operate effectively.

Trash containers that attach to the inside of the cabinet door (illustration 350), save time and energy. The ones that also store spare trash bags save space as well.

If individual taste led you to choose a trash container that doesn't hold the spare bags, it's still possible to have the best of both worlds. Simply install a rack like one of these (illustration 351) on the cabinet door under the sink. Notice, though, that these racks are designed to accomodate paper bags only and not plastic ones.

If thrift is your middle name and you recycle plastic bags, then there is a specialty rack for you. Plastic bags can be crammed into the funnel-shaped opening of the container in illustration 352, and then the bags are pulled out from the hole in the bottom of the rack.

How to Dangle Dishcloths

The obvious place to put dishcloths is as near as possible to the action.

The two pictured towel racks (illustration 353) are quite similar, and they offer

233

fingertip convenience. If dishcloths are stored inside a cabinet, we repeatedly open and close the door and that's exhausting and annoying. Yet if we hang them in the open, the tidy appearance of the kitchen suffers.

We could choose a less elaborate approach and eliminate the need to install a towel bar at all.

This kind of dish towel (illustration

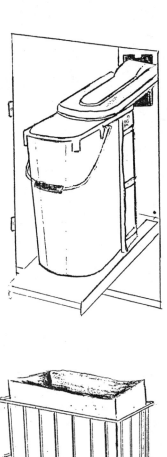

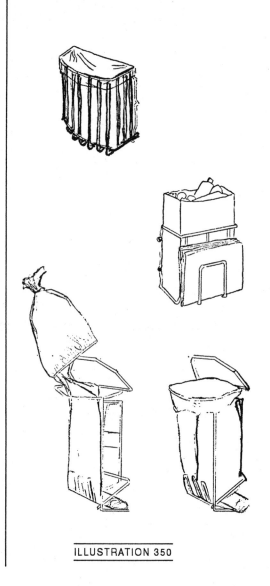

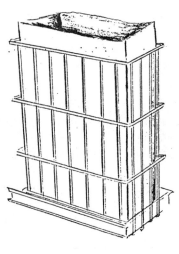

ILLUSTRATION 349

ILLUSTRATION 350

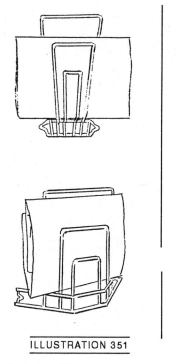

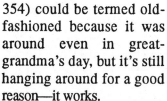

ILLUSTRATION 351

ILLUSTRATION 352

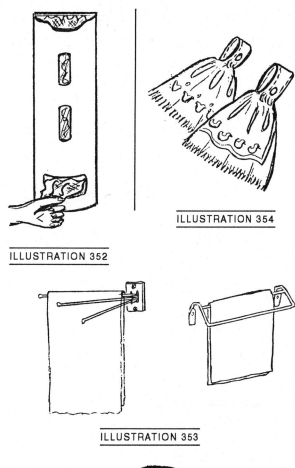

ILLUSTRATION 353

ILLUSTRATION 354

354) could be termed old-fashioned because it was around even in great-grandma's day, but it's still hanging around for a good reason—it works.

An item that is common, familiar, and necessary is the traditional dish drainer. A closer inspection reveals that even it can be improved to occupy less space.

The depicted dish drainer (illustration 355) is well worth the purchase price since it can be folded into a compact unit that closely resembles a briefcase. It then fits in some out-of-the-way place. Other unalterable drainers are unacceptable because they need so much storage space. There are also other variations available that open and shut.

ILLUSTRATION 355

CHAPTER TWENTY-ONE

THE KITCHEN

KITCHEN DRAWERS

✔ How to Separate Silverware

How to Separate Silverware

The ritual we observe for no apparent reason is to simply slide a prearranged, preplanned, and premade silverware tray into our kitchen drawers, thinking we've done the best that can be done.

These predesigned flatware organizers seldom serve our silverware adequately, and they always waste a great deal of drawer space. At the very least, consider this style of premolded tray (illustration 356) because it adds a sliding shelf that sits on top. This tray holds half as much again as the common household variety.

This sliding tray is available in a number of materials, but the more frequently seen ones are high-impact molded plastic (expensive) or the softer plastic and interwoven mesh versions, which are more economical.

It's fine to put sharp, cutting instru-

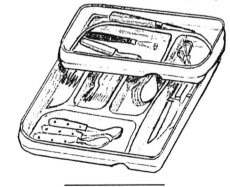

ILLUSTRATION 356

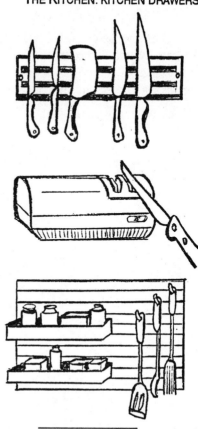

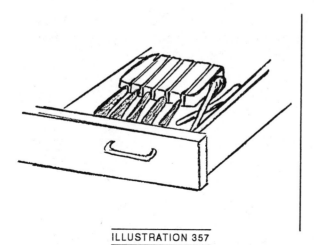

ILLUSTRATION 357

ments in drawers, but it's not OK to put them into the silverware's space, which is exactly what will happen if the knifes aren't stored separately in their own drawer (illustration 357). Don't mix sharp knives and flatware.

The top rack in illustration 358 depicts a wall-mounted magnetic strip that clasps the knives conveniently, visibly, and accessibly. The second rack can be mounted on the wall or it can sit on the counter. It has the added feature of a built-in knife sharpener. The modular grid rack is multi-purpose. These cooking utensils are too large and awkward for successful storage in a drawer.

By using various shapes and sizes of organizing trays as depicted in illustration 359, the drawer realizes its fullest potential. We have the ability to plan not only maximum management of the space, but we can also match a utensil's size and shape to the container's size and shape. We thereby create a system that keeps things organized for a long time.

ILLUSTRATION 358

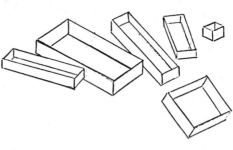

ILLUSTRATION 359

An extra advantage gained through planning a personalized silverware system is that it admits even the largest, bulkiest, broadest, and biggest utensils. This makes each and every day easier when we reach for the items we use regularly.

Perhaps the greatest advantage of all, however, is that they are so versatile. An interlocking system can be used to organize the junk drawer (we all possess at least one). In many cases, we could call all of our drawers junk drawers, and that's exactly why these interlocking systems are so wonderful (illustration 360).

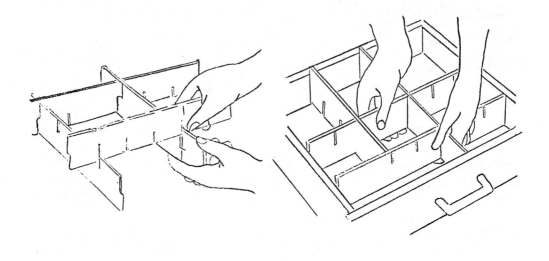

ILLUSTRATION 360

THE KITCHEN

COUNTERTOPS AND FLOORS

✔ How to Create Countertop Space

✔ How to Command Counterspace

✔ How to Fabricate Flat Surfaces

✔ How to Flatter Floors

How to Create Countertop Space

Attaining additional counter space isn't as difficult as one might think. When products such as this wall-mounted, fold-down table or this free-standing shelf (illustration 361) are installed we don't just increase the kitchen's useable space. We also make the counter space more productive.

Opening up space on the countertops in the kitchen is an easier task than one might think. Move the microwave. Now there's a vast expanse of counter space just begging for our attention. Illustration 362 shows a strong-arm rack that mounts the microwave onto any conveniently located wall. The other microwave rack sits on top of the stove, giving a support shelf on which the microwave can perch.

Adding portable countertop space, whether it's something as simple as a table or as complex as a gourmet storage cart, can make life much easier (illustration 363).

There are a number of specialty racks that store all of the blades, tubes, covers, and

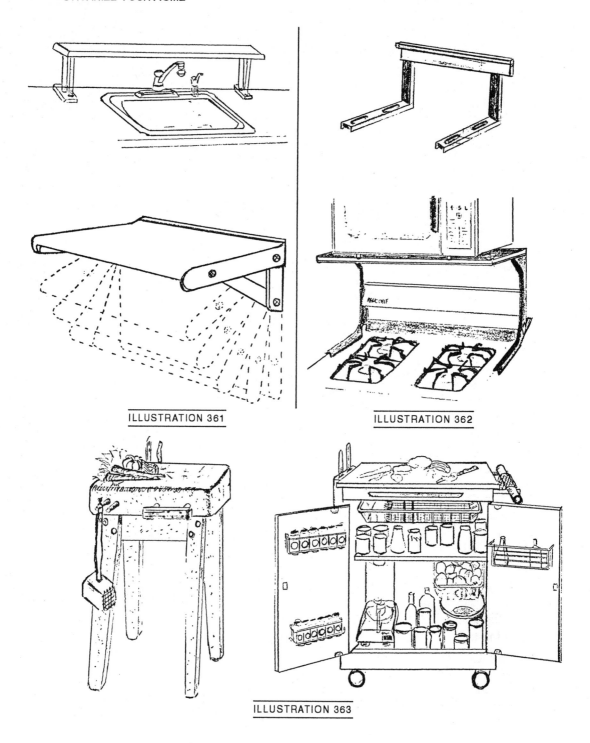

ILLUSTRATION 361

ILLUSTRATION 362

ILLUSTRATION 363

ILLUSTRATION 364

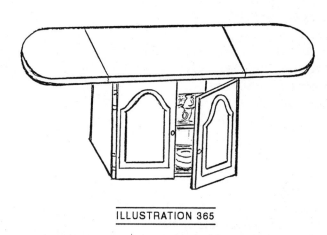

ILLUSTRATION 365

other apparatus that goes with a food processor. The racks are generally wall or door mounted, and they're worth investigating (illustration 364).

The food processor could just as easily occupy this depicted cabinet space (illustration 365). This cabinet not only has alot of storage space, but it also includes work space on the top with two drop leafs so that it can even be used as an eating table.

How to Command Counterspace

Once in a while we decide to beautify certain aspects of the kitchen; not an organizing expedition,mind you, just a little touch that brightens or that makes us feel the kitchen is new and improved. If we were looking to spend our money on a whim, why not purchase the bookcase on the bottom of illustration 366. It not only puts cookbooks in their place, but it also includes two drawers for holding the recipes that are probably roaming around lost. Additional recipe card holders are shown in illustration 367.

Why leave anything lying on the countertop if it can be moved to an attractive, imaginative, and suitable site somewhere else?

Certainly the books and magazines we keep in the kitchen don't deserve residency

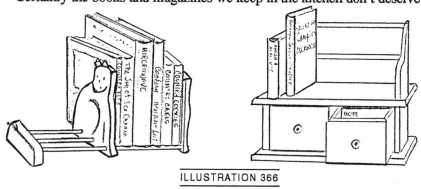

ILLUSTRATION 366

on countertops, the most exclusive and prime piece of real estate in the entire kitchen. Some alternative locations are suggested in illustration 368.

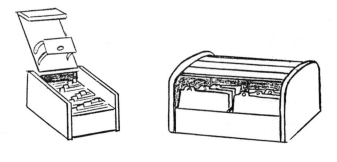

ILLUSTRATION 367

To those who insist on storing their cookbooks and gourmet magazines on the countertop may I suggest the magazine rack depicted in illustration 369. It is made of lucite, which naturally blends with any decor. These racks are also available in wood, woodgrain, leather and cardboard.

Being a nag and perfectionist makes it impossible for me to resist suggesting that these racks be placed on shelves, which also come in lucite. Install these shelves approximately 15 inches below the ceiling on any available wall. Arrange the encased magazines to get visibility, and regain your counterspace!

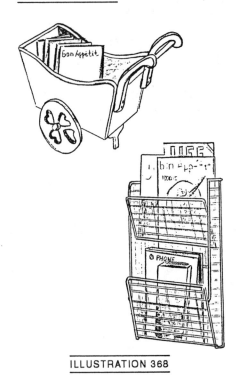

ILLUSTRATION 368

How to Fabricate Flat Surfaces

Once all the flat, level surfaces, countertops, tabletops, and shelves in the kitchen have been crammed with our assorted belongings (many of which do not belong in the kitchen at all) we begin to contemplate ways to alleviate the clutter.

Few of us are fortunate enough to have a wine cellar, but the wine racks in illustrations 370 and 371 are extremely useful. The one in illustration 371 is by far the better space manager of the two. It will fit almost anywhere because each unit comes apart. It can be stacked any way you like.

This wine rack in illustration 372 has the advantage of being a carton-type container (so that it's readily picked up and transported to any location). The cartons can be stacked

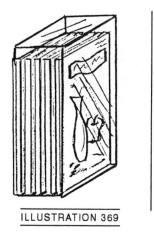

ILLUSTRATION 369

on one another to create a
modular unit of any shape or
size you like.

The cartons are plastic
and, although this particular

ILLUSTRATION 370

wine rack has been singled out for honorable mention, there are many more worthy of
comment and consumer interest.

Needless to say, there are some very important factors that will influence the way we
resolve our obsession with amassing merchandise.

First of all, validate whether or not the item is necessary. Is it essential to daily exist-
ence? Can it be discarded or donated out of the house forever? The possessions that
remain should be grouped into categories to determine which storage solution will satisfy
their demands.

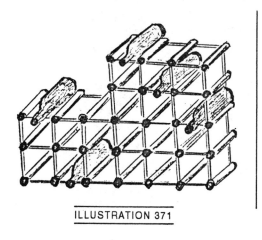

ILLUSTRATION 371

ILLUSTRATION 372

Second, that choice must coincide with either vacant wall space, empty floor space or space that can be reclaimed.

Some of us are so unfortunate that our kitchens are approximately the size of a ship's galley.

Resigning ourselves to midget-sized appliances or collapsible tables and chairs isn't such calamity if we simply keep our wits about us. Illustrations 373 and 374 depict some space savers that might come in handy in small kitchens.

How to Flatter Floors

Two of the largest contributors of bulk and unsightliness in our kitchens are cleaning items and the trash can (illustration 375).

Since trash is such an untantalizing and tasteless topic, it's time we took care of it once and for all. It isn't going to just disappear from our sight and smell unless we give it the vehicle(s) to do so (illustration 376). Recycling seems to be the modern answer.

Choose a center for recycling that fits your floor space. Many such centers are equipped to bundle up old newspapers as well, but make sure it specifically handles the items you regularly discard (illustration 377).

There are as many products for storing vegetables as there are containers for collecting trash.

The four-drawer unit (illustration 378) is well-designed, convenient, and attractive, plus it keeps the various vegetables or fruits separated. The taller version is just as appealing, yet it adds a top layer for increased serviceability.

This model of a vegetable bin (illustration 379) is more common than the others. Most bins of similar size and shape are either screened with wire on all three doors or are solid wood.

ILLUSTRATION 373

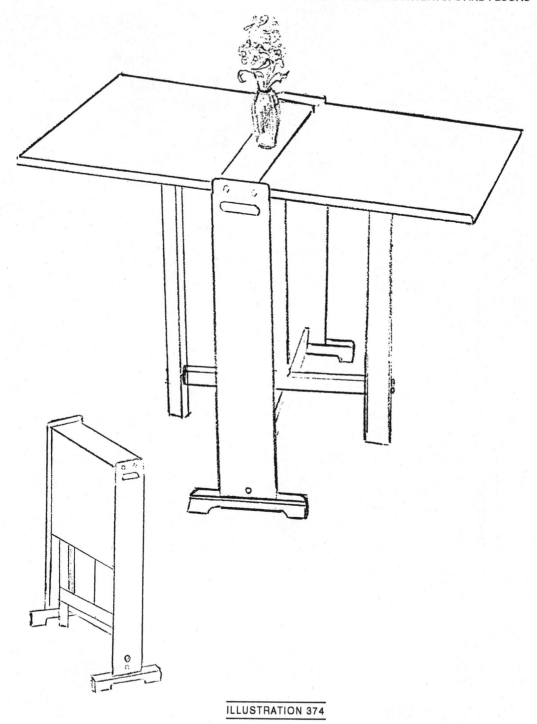

ILLUSTRATION 374

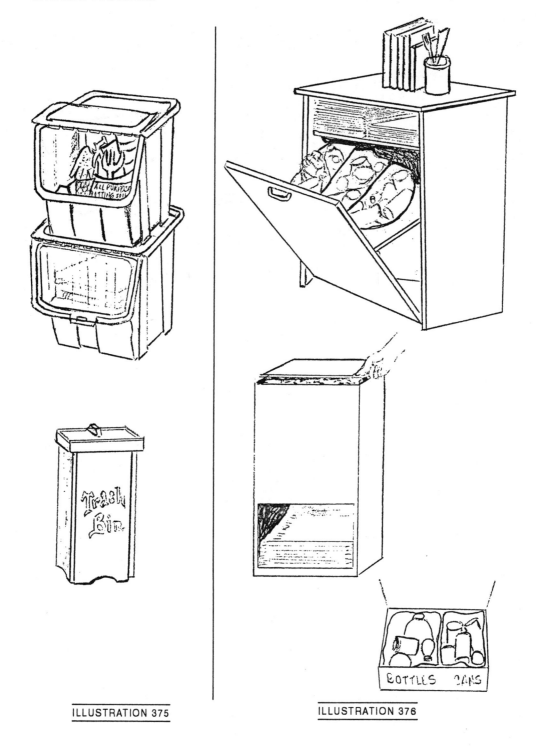

ILLUSTRATION 375

ILLUSTRATION 376

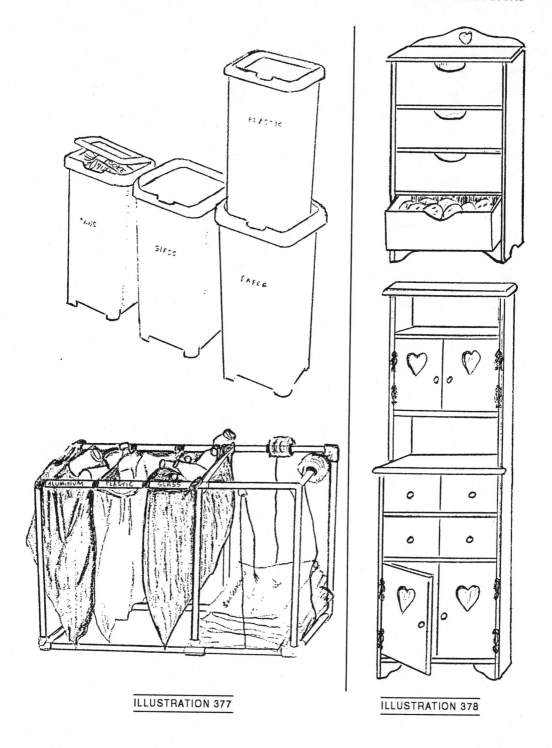

ILLUSTRATION 377   ILLUSTRATION 378

ILLUSTRATION 379

THE KITCHEN

WALLS

✔ How to Hang the Heavies

✔ How to Handle the Hodgepodge

How to Hang the Heavies

We have discussed how pots, pans, and skillets can be hung, stood, and stored within the cabinets of the kitchen, but imagine the space we'd acquire if we evicted them and gave them a nest on the wall (illustration 380).

Naturally we'd need a wall that's well sized, readily available, and centrally located.

The type of rack employed is crucial to success, and should the walls be unusable, there's always the option of using a ceiling rack instead (illustration 381). Depending on the height, this ceiling rack might supply an extra shelf, too.

Plenty of other racks are available (illustration 382) to hang your kitchen utensils conveniently on a nearby wall.

How to Handle the Hodgepodge

A system of hooks is easily installed and works rather well as long as you consider both the intended wall and the burden the hooks will carry (illustration 383).

This all-encompassing display system (illustration 384) is initiated by first installing

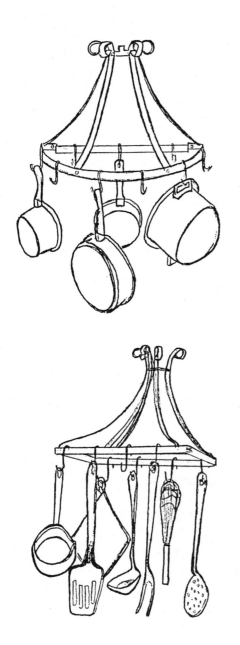

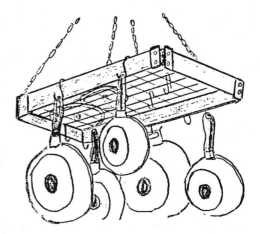

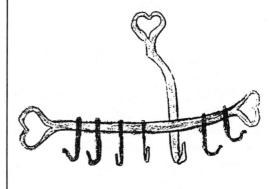

ILLUSTRATION 380

ILLUSTRATION 381

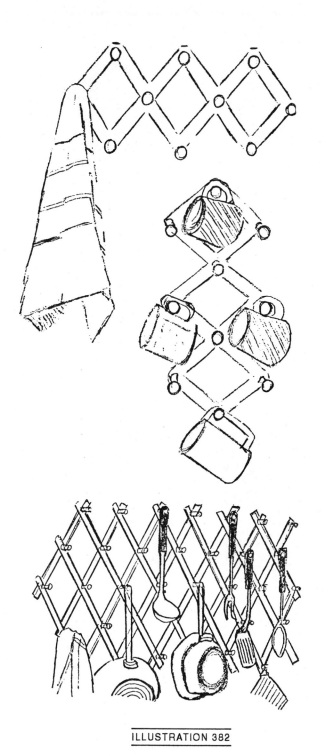

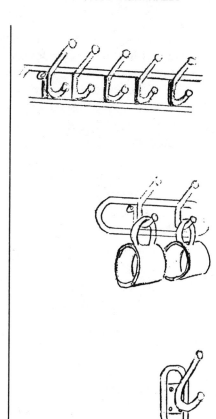

ILLUSTRATION 383

the modular, slotted base. Add
to the base whichever specialty organizer is needed by
simply hooking it into the slots
on the base unit to develop a
customized storage system for
the wall. Combine as many or
as few of the attachables as the
base allows, and use as many
or as few of the bases as the
wall space and your budget allows.

Drawing 1 is the base

ILLUSTRATION 382

unit, 2 shows the spice containers, 3 is a paper towel rack, 4 is a wax paper rack and 5 is a multipurpose tray or shelf. Items 2 through 5 attach to the base unit (installed under your cabinets or on a wall).

It's possible with this system to devise a uniform wall plan that serves many functions. (See illustration 385.)

Drawing 1 is a breadbox while 3 holds pasta and such. Items 2 and 4 are a bulletin board and a battery-operated clock. Item 5 is a magnetic strip for knives, metal utensils, or other types of utillity items like scissors.

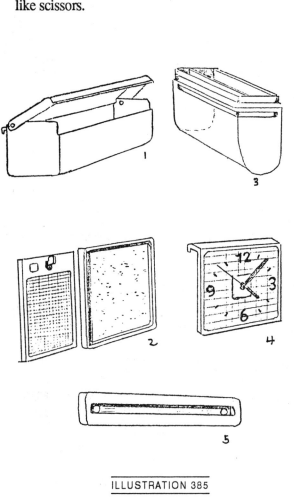

ILLUSTRATION 385

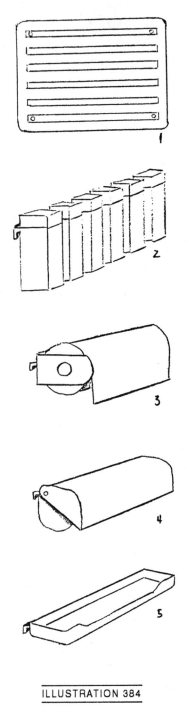

ILLUSTRATION 384

The modular system wouldn't be complete without offering a set of hooks for handling either our keys or dish towels (illustration 386).

This modular unit can orchestrate every conceiveable kitchen event. There are other products that do the same thing, but they offer a more limited range of options. The paper towel rack is a high-quality wooden item that also provides a shelf. The utensil rack, which also mounts on the wall, is far less versatile.

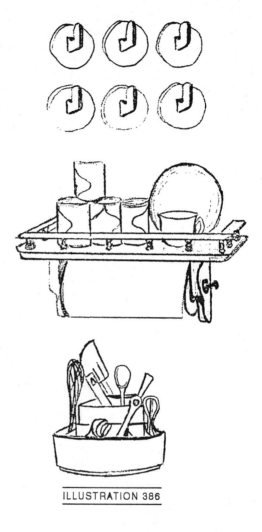

ILLUSTRATION 386

THE KITCHEN

THE REFRIGERATOR

- ✔ How to Beckon Beverages
- ✔ How to Free the Freezer
- ✔ How to Facilitate the Fridge

How to Beckon Beverages

Here sits our massive refrigerator and we ignore it, while frantic organizing activities go on all around it. Yet it probably deserves our attenion even more than the kitchen cabinets and shelves, since it's nothing more than a larger, colder version of a cabinet with shelves. We open and close it many times per day, but we make no effort to organize its contents!

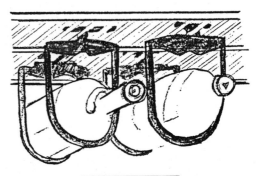

ILLUSTRATION 387

The refrigerator shelves, although they are usually adjustable, present the same problems as the shelves in a cabinet. A substantial number of inches are wasted above the articles sitting on the shelf. The only way this wasted refrigerator space can be salvaged is to find products that use those inches above the items on the shelf (illustration 387).

With excessively tall bottles gone from the shelf in the refrigerator, the shelf can now be raised to a level more in keeping with the heights of milk jugs and cartons of orange juice.

If, however, the refrigerator in your kitchen needs to contain huge quantities of liquid refreshments year round, the top shelf should always be positioned as low as it can go.

Manufacturers have marketed a vast variety of beverage containers and a large variety of beverage dispensers and organizers (illustration 388).

People may prefer their soft drinks in cans or two-liter bottles, but in either case, racking them up for convenient restocking, retreival, and dispensing is a major breakthrough in maintaining order in the refrigerator (illustration 389). Unquestionably, the rack on top that automatically rotates the coldest can to the front during the restocking process offers a distinct advantage. The rack shown in the middle pushes the coldest can to the back during restocking.

ILLUSTRATION 388

How to Free the Freezer

How many times have you pulled the newest frozen entree from the freezer instead of pulling out the oldest one first? Or do you always have numerous bags, packages, and zip-locs partially filled with the same food because you open a new one every time you need something?

There is a very simple solution to this dilemma, and once again it's merely a matter of sorting the food into groups and putting the groups together.

Using bins or containers is the most satisfactory solution since an entire category of food can be removed for better accessibility, visibility, and convenience. Both the unit is removed for restocking or when the unit is removed to obtain what's inside, you spare immeasurable amounts of time and frustration.

Believe it or not, it's quite helpful to purchase frozen foods in similarly sized and shaped packages. Generally, a consumer is interested in the price, the brand name, and the nutritional content of the product and not the size of the box. However, by paying attention

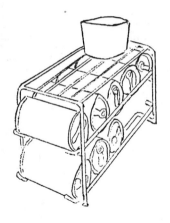

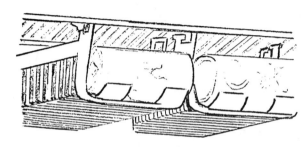

to the size of the container you can maintain an easier system for controlling and organizing the freezer.

Although this drawing (illustration 390) combines an ice tray with a shelf above for frozen food, there are variations that serve food only.

Of the various specialty racks and trays for freezer storage, the basket seems to be the best (illustration 391). It serves the purpose more proficiently because it can be removed entirely from the freezer to gain better insight into what it contains. It's easy to not only restock the basket, but also to rummage through the contents for selection as well.

How to Facilitate the Fridge
All that outside space on the refrigerator is rarely taken advantage of. All we do is to stick a bunch of itsy-bitsy magnets all over its surface. Instead try attach-

ILLUSTRATION 389

ILLUSTRATION 390

ing something more useful to the refrigerator (illustration 392).

Before we move on to other topics, it would behoove us to evaluate a mechanism for moving our refrigerator out of our way when needed.

The ability to clean behind and beneath the refrigerator may not cause the same degree of panic as when all the ice cream's melting onto the floor, but it shouldn't be a subject that's completely shunned. Theoretically, if the refrigerator could be swung into motion with minor exertion, you will be more inclined to periodically roll it away from the wall to wipe out the cobwebs, crumbs, and food particles that have been living there comfortably for some time (illustration 393).

ILLUSTRATION 391

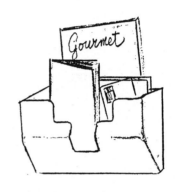

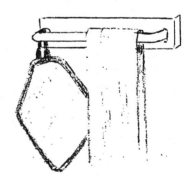

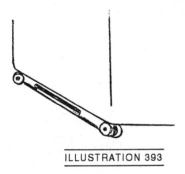

ILLUSTRATION 393

ILLUSTRATION 392

CHAPTER TWENTY-FIVE

THE PANTRY

✔ How to Parlay Pantries

✔ How to Unify Utilities

How to Parlay Pantries

An approach that is overpoweringly successful in providing additional shelf space without ever touching the existing shelves of the pantry is to install wall or door racks. These will not only take care of any overload, but they are better suited to the majority of items frequently found in a normal pantry (illustration 394).

The pantry shelves themselves can then remain free for larger, bulkier articles, like extra sets of dinnerware, drinking glasses, serving bowls, and platters.

These racks are either 12 inches or 18 inches wide. The tallest ones at 72 inches with eight shelves (each five inches deep) can actually free up at least two of the existing shelves in the pantry.

The shorter versions can significantly improve the pantry though they only have two, three, or four shelves. There's also a unit for the corner, truly utilizing every single inch of the pantry (illustration 395).

The canned goods and boxes are best presented for visibility and accessibility when they are on a rack.

With many sizes of racks on the market, it's simply a matter of selecting the one that fits the wall or door best.

The shelves that are already installed inside the pantry may require some updating or improvements. There's no time like the present to investigate the different types of shelving available.

Illustration 396 shows one of the best ideas to come off anyone's drafting board in years. Not only does it fill in the corner space, which is almost always unproductive, but it also turns it into a totally functional area. It also has adjustable shelves.

Don't ignore any of the doors leading off the kithen, into the garage, or basement. A rack works to convert a door into a miniature and handy pantry onto itself (illustration 397).

The products that work best are those that subdivide a shelf into compartments. A system of drawers attached to the underside of the shelves or any type of stack shelf that sits on the shelf is a good idea in the pantry (illustration 398).

The pantry floor is usually the place to store vegetable bins.

There's nothing wrong with this at all. However, the problem begins when we look at the various bin-type containers (whether they have wheels, are stackable, or whether they have openings with lids).

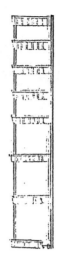

ILLUSTRATION 394

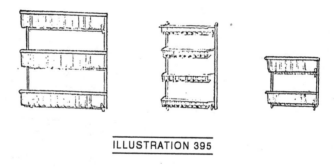

ILLUSTRATION 395

Sorry to be the bearer of bad news, but whatever item is placed at the back of one of these bin is gone for good, unless you want to remove everything from the front to get to the rear (illustration 399).

A product that wasn't previously mentioned is the padded dish and glass saver that stores breakables. The advantage in using them is that they keep categories together.

It doesn't matter if glasses are extra-tall or if there are sugar bowls, cream pitchers, platters and serving pieces galore—these packs are diverse enough to package anything (illustration 400).

It's advisable to store table extensions or leafs in protective sleeves or cases, too. It's a frightful expense and shame to refinish fine furniture.

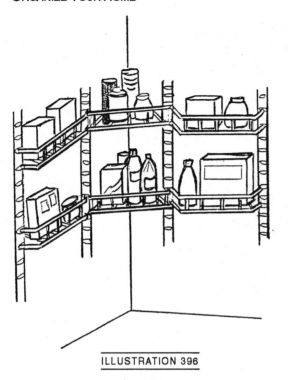

ILLUSTRATION 396

If we have spare or special sets of dinner-ware, it's more than likely that we have spare and special sets of silverware as well. If they weren't

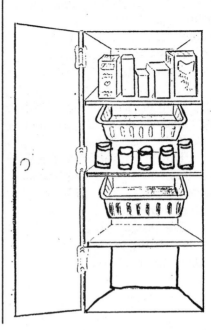

ILLUSTRATION 397

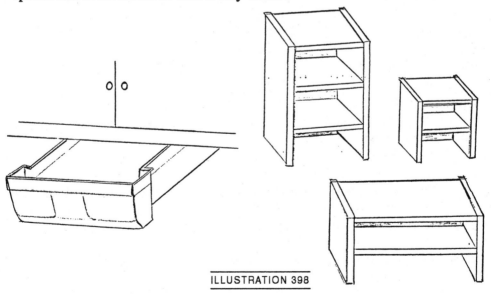

ILLUSTRATION 398

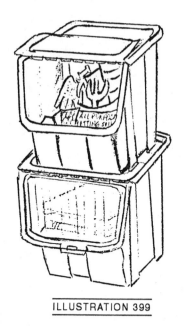

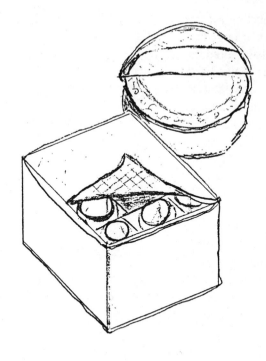

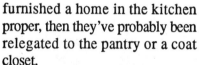

ILLUSTRATION 399

ILLUSTRATION 400

furnished a home in the kitchen proper, then they've probably been relegated to the pantry or a coat closet.

Placing these spare sets of silverware in buffered boxes is a grand idea. Should the sets in question have value, a hand-made carrying case will make them easier to store (illustration 401) and easy to carry to the table when needed.

Very often we own a certain set of silverware for picnic purposes only, but we never thought to put them in the perfect place for permanent storage—the picnic basket or hamper. The hamper simply stays on the shelf (or in the garage) until the next church social or reunion picnic.

The holiday placemats, napkins, rings, tablecloths, candlesticks, centerpieces, and Santa Claus mugs should be stowed away from the mainstream of activities, which means barring them from the pantry all together. Because these items lie dormant for long periods of time, they need to be protected from dust. So gather up some zippered

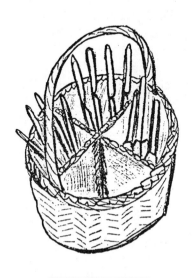

ILLUSTRATION 401

blanket or sweater cases or large zip-loc bags. Fold the items gently inside and carry them to the garage, base-ment, or attic.

For those linens that are used frequently, the pantry is a proper resting place. Consider under-the-shelf-drawer systems,

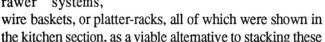

ILLUSTRATION 402

wire baskets, or platter-racks, all of which were shown in the kitchen section, as a viable alternative to stacking these items in piles.

How to Unify Utilities

A very distinct category consists of our household cleaners, mops, sweepers, and vacuum cleaners.

This vacuum attachment caddy (illustration 402) keeps control of the situation. Its compactness permits its placement most anywhere.

There isn't a definite etiquette involved in choosing which closet or room should welcome the vacuum but cer-tain locations are more realistic, logical, and sensible.

Any closet or space in the house has potential, if it's conveniently located (although the main objective is to find an area that holds *all* the accompanying apparatus. Otherwise, if vacuum cleaner is separate from hoses, we will become confused and unfocused, spending time we can ill-afford tracking down various attachments.

We can alleviate this hassle however if locations are specifically assigned for every item, and the functions they perform are listed on our duty roster.

More often than not, the shelves of a closet only ex-tend 12 inches from the back wall, but the closet itself is

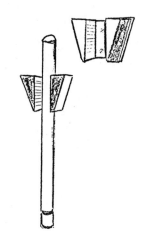

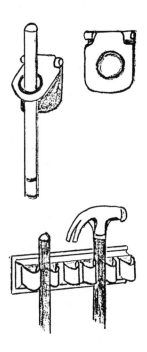

ILLUSTRATION 403

ILLUSTRATION 404

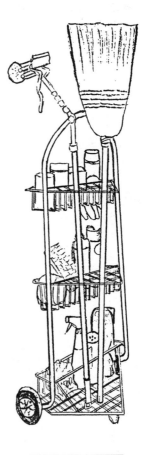

ILLUSTRATION 405

22 inches to 24 inches deep, which leaves us with up to 12 inches of space at the front of the closet to play with.

Many typical cleaning aids and household aids fit nicely on a system of clamps in this space (illustration 403). These systems can be made to fit any space and any item. Therefore, combining them horizontally or vertically can allow us to keep track of even the tiniest attachments.

It would be a rare home in which we couldn't find a closet, wall, or door that could receive these devices for hooking or clamping our mops, brooms, and household tools firmly.

Once we have handled our tools by hanging them on hooks, we can turn our attention to how to camouflage the unsightly appearance of the upright vacuum itself. Sometimes there is just no closet room for it. Covering the sweeper in a costume that conveys either our sense of humor or our good taste is an especially appealing option when it boils down to either this method or showcasing a naked vacuum (illustration 404).

In the rare home in which there truly isn't a closet, wall, nook, or cranny in the entire house that can contain even a minimal amount of utilities, we need to make our own stand for containing our cleaning materials.

This particular cleaning trolley (illustration 405) is portable, which allows us to stand it in the garage or stairwell if need be.

CHAPTER TWENTY-SIX

THE LAUNDRY AREA

✔ How to Deploy Detergents

✔ How to Detain Dirties

✔ How to Drip Dry

✔ How to Banish Ironing Boards

How to Deploy Detergents

The washer and dryer can be as lonely as the Maytag repairman if their fabric softener friends, their detergent acquaintances, their Clorox colleagues, their presoak companions, and their clothes hanger buddies are forced to endure long-distance relationships.

This particular shelf unit (illustration 406) is appealing because it not only keeps tabs on those items but it also comes in widths to fit over any machine. It's self-supporting and therefore portable (meaning no screws or installation and no permanent holes in the wall).

Variations of this unit have either more shelves, are taller or they have a rod on the side for hanging.

When installation isn't a deterrent or when the walls behind the appliances aren't concrete, installing a ventilated shelf/rod system is a relatively painless way to obtain shelves and rods for hangers and clothes (illustration 407). It certainly improves our makeshift methods of old (using clotheslines, ropes, parts of the plumbing, water heater, or furnace,

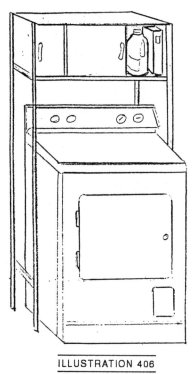

ILLUSTRATION 406

ILLUSTRATION 407

windowsills, wires, or whatever is available).

When space is at a premium, as it often is around the washer and dryer, it's a wise person who converts even the most unlikely corner into an area of productivity. (See illustration 408.)

Minimal amounts of space can be dealt with effectively when the proper product is available to fit the space, as in the case of this tall unit that's only 12 inches wide (illustration 409). Finding 12 inches of space is certainly an easier task than needing to find twice that amount, which is the amount of space needed for the majority of shelf units on the market.

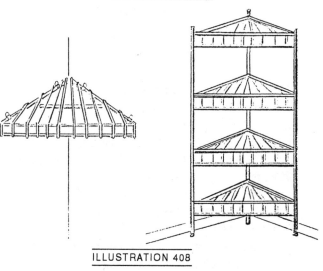

ILLUSTRATION 408

Quite often, a laundry facility has at least 12 inches of space between the appliances and the wall.

This unit is a single structure made out of steel. Many of these units are stackable as well, so the unit can go as high as the ceiling if you want. Very few of the stackable are made in anything other than plastic.

When the room around the automatic machines is less restrictive, different types of aids can be employed.

This four-shelf, freestanding unit supplies a plentiful place for folding and holding clothes or for detergents (illustration 410).

The type(s) and style(s) of laundry-room aids selected should meet the specific needs you have. This crate-on-wheels, for example, could serve as a hamper on top and a bin for storing detergents at the bottom.

ILLUSTRATION 409

How to Detain the Dirties

The two wire baskets shown on either side of the washer and dryer in illustration 411 add an extra touch, since they also have a work space for folding clothes or treating stains and spots. It also creates a neat appearance to the laundering facility.

The pull-out multiple baskets can be used to sort soiled clothes and household linens into light or dark, either as they are deposited or just before washing. The smaller baskets might simply stow such things as hand-washables, gentle cycle delicates, or garments that need some sort of attention.

When money isn't a problem, and you're

ILLUSTRATION 410

the kind of person who dreams of perfection and pleasant surroundings, this modular system is the ultimate solution (illustration 412). It not only grants the wish for beauty, but it provides shelf space and hanging space.

One of the most common sights in houses is the standard laundry basket or the dirty clothes hamper.

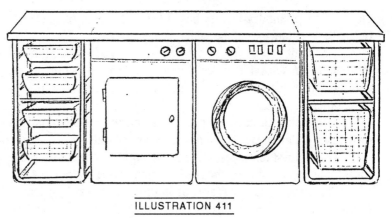

ILLUSTRATION 411

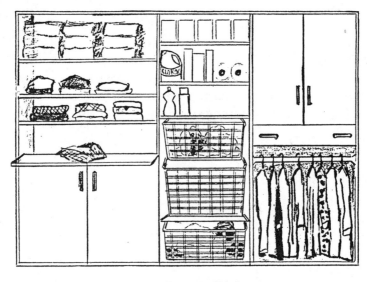

ILLUSTRATION 412

The laundry cart (illustration 413) is probably the most ordinary hamper for dirty clothes, after plastic or woven laundry baskets. However, the cart is a deceitful stealer of space, since the space below the cart is totally wasted.

Imagine what this space could be used for if the hamper weren't sitting on legs.

Laundry baskets can hold huge amounts of our dirty belongings.

A sorting center such as this one (illustration 414), is understandably better because it's taller than a basket, it has a larger capacity, and our belongings are seldom found spilling onto the floor.

A much-improved version of the sorting center is a center made of wood. It can be seen at the local lumberyard. The top lid lifts up to reveal three compartments inside for keeping the darks separate from the lights. The third cubicle is for the overload or fine washables.

It comes in different woods to match your decor.

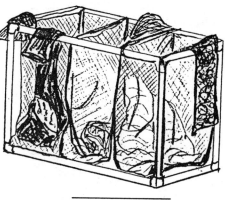

ILLUSTRATION 413

How to Drip Dry

The unit (illustration 415) can provide a surface for drying long or large garments like dresses, robes, or even linen tablecloths.

A specially designed device that makes the drying process for garments painless, inexpensive, and simple is

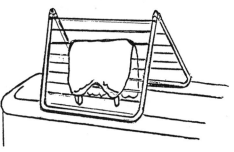

ILLUSTRATION 414

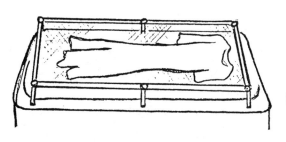

ILLUSTRATION 415

ILLUSTRATION 416

shown in illustration 416. It is space conscious as well.

We can't ignore caring for the clothes properly. These hanging racks (illustration 417) will prolong the life of your clothes.

This stand (illustration 418) is suitable for garments that hang dry. It can be folded down compactly for storage in even the tightest places. It is good to use when the clothes comes out of the dryer or off the ironing board.

The over-the-door rack could be indispensable if there wasn't any

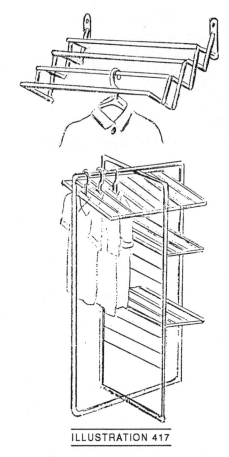

ILLUSTRATION 417

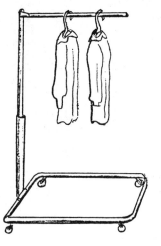

ILLUSTRATION 418

other way to hang clothes near the dryer or ironing board. Its drawback, quite obviously, is that it can't function without a door.

How to Banish Ironing Boards

What a troublesome and cumbersome contraption an ironing board is, but certainly it's more neccessary today than it was in the 1960s.

The old-fashioned ironing board doesn't have to defy our need for a pleasant environment. It doesn't need to stand in the middle of the room, fall from the closet each time the door's opened, or be propped in the corner.

We can treat it for what it is; a hard-working, industrious, necessity of life, ugly and awkward as it may be. All ironing boards are not created equal.

Those ironing boards constructed with Y-shaped feet instead of a T-bar at the bottom (illustration 419) can't be hung from a rack, so they're left floundering in the corners of the house. The T-bar models find their final resting place in a rack.

The second drawing depicts an ironing board that moonlights as a chair, which would be seemly in a person's first minuscule apartment. Otherwise, most professional ironers insist on a full-size board, so that tablecloths or voluptuous skirt tails can be pressed properly.

The types of ironing boards in il-

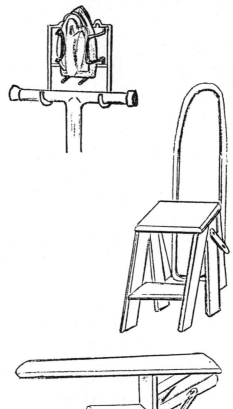

ILLUSTRATION 419

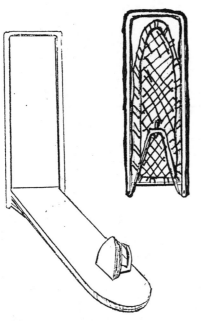

ILLUSTRATION 420

lustration 420 seem to be the newest rage.

The idea is to have an ironing board that is as near to full-sized as possible, while still being able to fold it up or down.

These models mount on either a door or a wall.

The ironing board in the box (illustration 421) slides out of sight. The box itself has shelves for starch and the iron too.

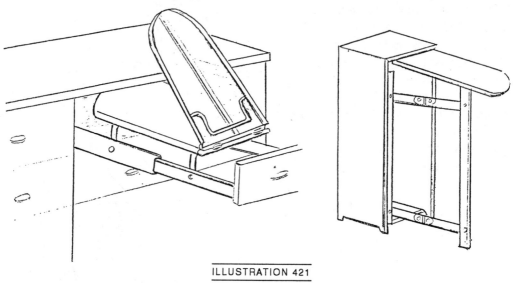

ILLUSTRATION 421

The ironing board in the drawer is pushed out of sight, but the drawer is useless for anything else.

This ironing board (illustration 422) can be folded into nearly a handkerchief size for storage purposes, but it's quite adequate for the chores required of it. Be careful choosing the table top, desk, or floor on which it will be used, however. Even though this ironing board might not let the steam leak through, it's

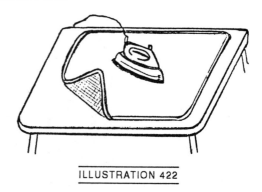

ILLUSTRATION 422

not worth the chance, especially if the surface is a piece of fine wood or carpet fibers that could melt.

The helpfulness of a shelf that attaches to the edge of the ironing board holding either the iron or the starches, fabric sizers, needles, thread, or any tool that aids the ironing process is a practical addition. Some units also have a cord-controller (illustration 423) that keeps the iron's snakelike activity down to a minimum. The cord is placed out of harm's way, so it can't knock anything off the board, rewrinkle the just-pressed garments, or contribute to accidents or burns.

Along the same lines is this pinching bracket (illustration 424) that grabs the edges of the ironing board to form a miniature clothes rod. This rod receives the newly pressed garments. If it were near the washer or dryer as well, just-washed clothes could be put on a hanger and hung from this stream-lined rod, for either drip-drying or pressing.

Unless it's secured properly, the weight of the garments will cause this rod to sag.

Ironing boards aren't often replaced, but the pad and cover are, and it usually takes a miracle to make either of them snug around the edges of the board.

Either the manufacturers have never measured the average size of most ironing boards or the boards themselves vary in size more than we've ever been lead to believe.

ILLUSTRATION 423

These elastic fasteners (illustration 425) will make any pad and cover fit any board. They are easily removed and reapplied when the covers are washed or replaced.

ILLUSTRATION 424

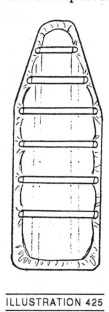

ILLUSTRATION 425

THE GARAGE AND BASEMENT

✔ How to Glean the Good, the Bad, and the Ugly

✔ How to Breed Built-Ins

✔ How to Tackle Tools

✔ How to Guard Garden Equipment

✔ How to Welcome Walkers

✔ How to Neutralize Nuisances

How to Glean the Good, Bad and Ugly

Basements, garages, and attics are the world's largest lost-and-found depositories.

How much of this stuff is actually essential to our well-being, and how often do we go looking for it?

Everyone stores stuff they never use but can't bear the thought of parting with. One solution is to rent a second garage. This pursuit has grown to such gigantic proportions lock-and-store rental units have an entire listing in the yellow pages.

It's OK to rent a U-Haul to haul away unneeded items. Or turn your treasures into cash, by holding a yard sale. Or call up the local Goodwill, Amvets, or Salvation Army.

Whatever the course of action, get those things that aren't used, at least periodically, away from those things that are used regularly and routinely.

The good things that remain, can be organized in a relatively effortless and painless way with the first priority simply being to pick them up off the floor. Thereafter, it's a matter of following step-by-step logic.

How to Breed Built-Ins

After getting the paint cans, aerosol sprays, buckets, boxes, bags, automotive supplies, mulch, flower pots, camping gear, boots, extra lamps, holiday decorations, and shoeshine kits sorted into descriptive categories, it's time to store them on shelves. Shelves are not necessarily the best for everything, but they are the easiest and least expensive storage method for the types of items just listed.

Heavy-duty steel shelf units are readily available and easily assembled. They are made to handle the bulkiest, heaviest items. They range in size from 30 inches wide to 42 inches wide, 12 inches deep to 24 inches deep, and 59 inches high to 71 inches high. Gunmetal gray is not the only color available: many manufactures offer an assortment of designer colors (illustration 426).

The shelving units themselves can then be modified as needed. One of the ways this is achieved is by incorporating a system of pull-out drawers on the underside of the shelves (illustration 427).

Use as few or as many as needed.

It's much easier to keep a box or drawer organized than it is to keep an entire shelf in order.

After arranging the items from the garage or basement onto the self-supporting steel structure, take a minute to admire the results.

It's a smart move to drape some sort of protective cover over the whole structure. If the method of draping adds even the tiniest bit of hardship to the process of seeing and reaching, it isn't an appropriate shield. The transparent vinyl cover-up pictured in illustration 428, is a good solution to this problem.

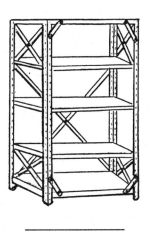

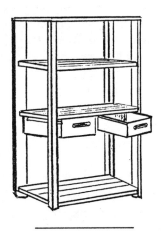

ILLUSTRATION 426

ILLUSTRATION 427

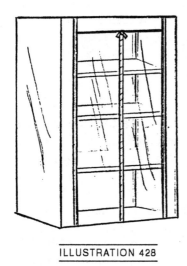

ILLUSTRATION 428

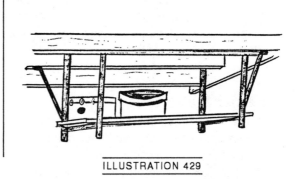

ILLUSTRATION 429

When an item is too large to be stored on a shelf, there is a way to get it off the floor and up into the region of the rafters. However, it would be terribly inconvenient to heft a heavy anything up and down and up and down very often, so consider things along the the lines of spare strips of lumber or camping gear that's only inspected (not used) once every two years.

This hanging shelf with brackets or rafter rack (illustration 429) is expandable. It fits most any ceiling in the garage, basement, or attic. The metal brackets can be lengthened or shortened. Attach it to either closed or open ceiling beams.

Moving along to more specific storage solutions, we should seriously consider a prefab workbench, like the kit model shown in illustration 430. Everyone has hammers, screwdrivers and pliers. They are never here, there, or anywhere visible when we desperately need them. A storage bench helps.

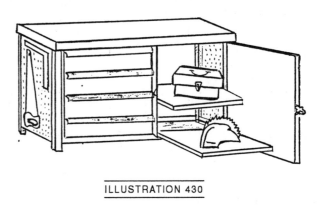

ILLUSTRATION 430

A workbench isn't essential, but wouldn't it be an ultimate goal for anyone to have this modular system (illustration 431), giving us a well-defined work area, plentiful cabinets, drawers, shelves, and utility space for storage, plus a well-lit and accessible place to hang tools.

The key element here is the assigned placement of tools.

Arranging the tools near any flat, level work surface is simply a sensible way to create a workshop. You can use crates and bins to build a less durable and weaker work area, but a work area all the same (illustration 432).

With a little forethought, the bin-and-crate method could supply a multitude of functions. They aren't indestructible, however, so weigh the merits of an initially cheaper version that will need to be replaced against the units that are higher priced but last a lifetime.

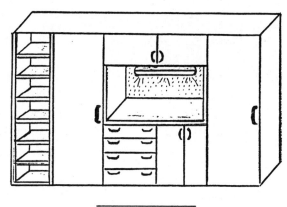

ILLUSTRATION 431

How to Tackle Tools

Positioning and installing tool racks on a wall keeps our hand tools together in one predetermined place

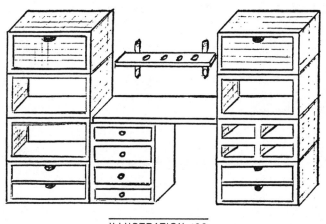

ILLUSTRATION 432

The handle or handles of each tool drop down into an individual hole or slot for safekeeping and speedy recoveries. The second rack in illustration 433 swings away from the wall when in use and hugs the wall when it's not in use.

The carry-it-with-you tool case is a handy portable conveyance. The screws, nails, tacks, tapes, tape measures, nuts, bolts, and washers are contained in the eight transparent drawers located along the bottom on both sides. The screwdrivers, hammers, pliers, scissors, mallets, and handsaws stand in the wide-mouth openings on the top or they lie above the drawers on the flat shelf that spans the unit itself (illustration 434).

This unique tool-tote (illustration 435) is made of heavy-duty canvas or denim for an authentic look, and the pouches and pockets are reinforced for lasting endurance. It comes complete with the hardware for hanging it on a wall or door.

ILLUSTRATION 433

ILLUSTRATION 434

Assuming we have roofs and gutters and that it snows in our neck of the woods, or we have lawns, and possibly flower beds, then our little blue-bibbed buddy won't help us handle the hoes, rakes, ladders, water hoses, shovels and spades.

The strip rack shown in illustration 436 is for longer handled tools, oblong and irregular shapes, and the heavier, bulkier objects we encounter. It provides prongs that support the item at it's useful, serviceable end. The disadvantage in this rack is that the objects can't be hung in the least amount of space.

The strip rack can't adjust. Once the tools are hung, there is idle, empty wall space between items. Whereas an in-

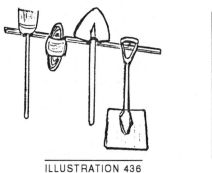

ILLUSTRATION 436

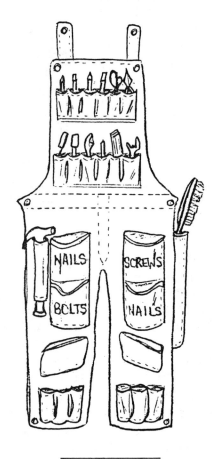

ILLUSTRATION 435

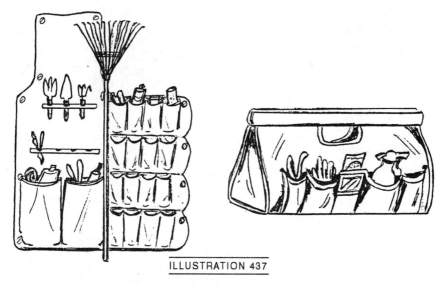

ILLUSTRATION 437

dividual system of hooks would conform to individual needs without wasting space.

How to Guard Garden Equipment

Any gardener would enjoy storing their equipment in either this gardening glove or portable canvas tote (illustration 437).

Everyone has a garden hose. Needless to say, every conceiveable idea for rolling the garden hose into neat loops has been made into a contraption, all of which are sold in the local hardware store (illustration 438).

Remember the crates we mentioned earlier? What a way to create a greenhouse for repotting, arranging, pruning, snipping, and nipping the buds on our flowers (illustration 439).

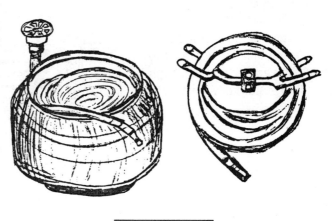

ILLUSTRATION 438

How to Welcome Walkers

However our boots become muddied, it's nice to know the muck won't be tracked all over the garage or mud room and into the house. With so many kinds and styles of mats it would be silly to let the mud inside when prevention is just a step away. Step onto this boot tray (illustration 440). The edges curve upwards, keeping the slop from melting or dribbling over the edges and onto the floor.

Mats and mud-catching methods, even one like this Astroturf brush pad (illustration 441), are fine as far as they go.

Practicality and preventative measures in this instance might call for drastic defenses, such as covering particularly vulnerable portions of the floor with rubberized tiles.

They can be squirted with the garden hose or removed to the backyard for a thorough scrubbing, although removal is

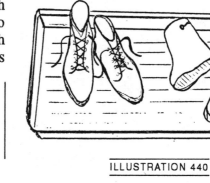

ILLUSTRATION 439

ILLUSTRATION 440

ILLUSTRATION 441

seldom necessary. (See illustration 442.)

By allowing boots to clean themselves, we've eliminated one chore from our list of many. This method for boosting boots, lets the gunk drip off of the boots. (See illustration 443.)

How to Neutralize Nuisances

Newspapers are considered a necessity as they're being read. But after the newspapers have served their purpose, we usually abandon them or stuff them in the bottom of the bird's cage.

Containers and controllers of newspapers vary greatly, from fine quality wooden crates to skimpy metal racks with extended vertical arms, but most usually are equipped with a ball of twine for bundling the stockpile into a manageable and toteable stack (illustration 444).

Another common creator of clutter and uncleanliness is the 25-, 50- or 75-pound bag of dog food we move around from place to place.

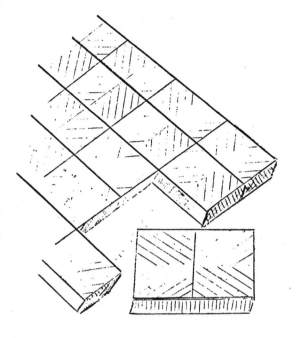

ILLUSTRATION 442

We are likely to be rather fond of our pooch, so resolving the doggie food dilemma rates high. This wall-mounted but portable dispenser is suitably sized for a sheepdog's food (illustration 445).

What do we do when overnight guests visit? Alternatives to the cumbersome folding cot exist.

Folding beds have

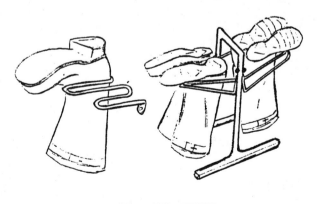

ILLUSTRATION 443

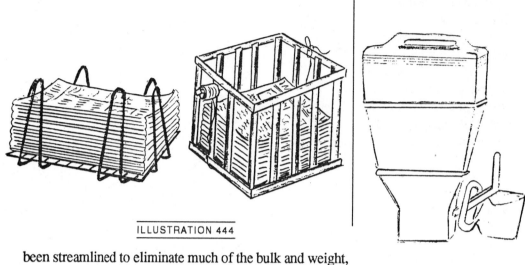

ILLUSTRATION 444

ILLUSTRATION 445

been streamlined to eliminate much of the bulk and weight, while retaining the comfort features. This inflatable mattress, complete with air pump, demands minimal space since it sits compactly on a shelf after it's folded into its original vinyl case (illustration 446). The cushiony mattress has a large sleeping capacity whereas the cots are always sized for single-sleepers.

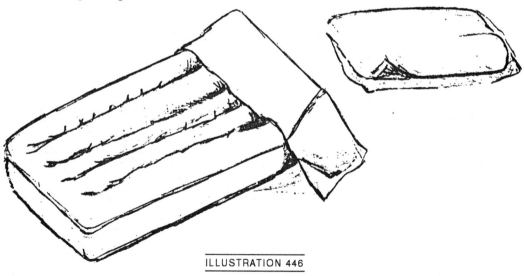

ILLUSTRATION 446

Yes, we accumulate trash in other places besides the kitchen. Putting it in its correct container initially is far more sanitary and sensible than sorting through it again in the garage, prior to the scheduled pickup (illustration 447).

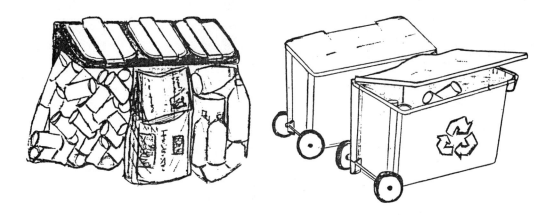

ILLUSTRATION 447

Undeniably, keeping the trash in a cart that rolls to the curb eliminates sweat and toil.

The biggest complaint with the recycling centers that hang on the wall is that the bags are flimsy and weak. Check out any such unit thoroughly to make sure it accepts heavier-gauged replacement bags.

Recycling our aluminum cans and containers has almost become a habit in this day and age. This makes can crushing a must. Position this crusher in a logical and convenient spot (illustration 448).

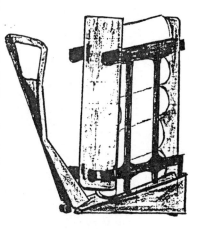

ILLUSTRATION 448

CHAPTER TWENTY-EIGHT

SEASONAL AND SPORTS EQUIPMENT

✔ How to Look at Leisure

✔ How to Gladden Glad Tidings

✔ How to Reason with Seasons

How to Look at Leisure

It is upsetting and frustrating to watch cherished possessions slowly disintegrate and self-destruct before our very eyes.

Many of the hooks that were shown previously for storing ladders and the like are extremely effective for hanging luggage from the ceiling beams in the garage, basement, or attic. This not only gets luggage off the floor to protect against wetness and mildewing, but also helps them to retain their original pristine shape.

Hang them individually if there's sufficient space. Or put the smaller pieces inside of the larger ones and hang the consolidated unit on one hook (illustration 449).

These hooks are also good for hanging bicycles.

Getting the bike out of the way lessens the likelihood of demolishing it when we're backing out of the garage.

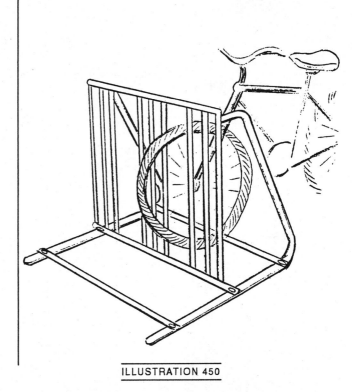

ILLUSTRATION 450

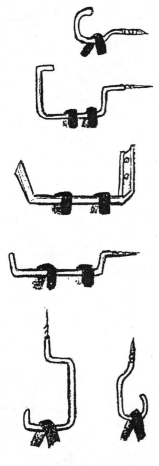

ILLUSTRATION 449

Doing damage to the bicycle itself isn't the only reason to get it out of our path. We often receive our fair share of nicks, bruises, and bangs because of the bicycle and its protruding parts.

A bike or two or three is a wanton waste of floor space no matter where it happens to be.

Bicycles have obviously become a recognized nuisance because a number of storage methods have been devised.

This bike rack (illustration 450) is typical of playgrounds and school yards, yet the ease it offers is great for the cyclist who goes out everyday or when there's floor space to spare.

This pole (illustration 451) for storing bikes needs either an out of the way corner or floor space that measures the length of the bike. This pole simply moves one bike off the floor to place it above another. If you only have one bike, use two hooks to hold it against the wall or hang it from the ceiling at little cost to either the pocketbook or the available space. In other words, cost effectiveness isn't the pole's greatest merit.

Similarly, this rack (illustration 452) holds two bikes on a steel structure that is braced well.

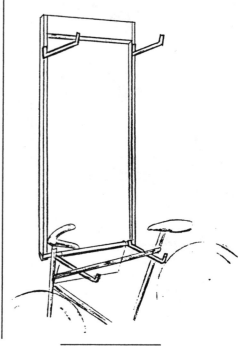

ILLUSTRATION 452

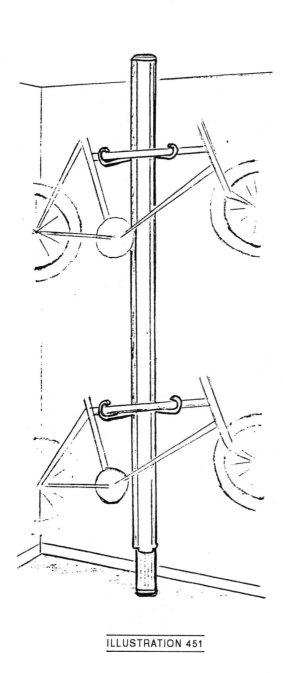

ILLUSTRATION 451

Certainly the expenditure for this rack is higher than for the single hooks it would take to accomplish the same result, but otherwise they're comparable.

The massive volume of golf bags, ski boots, and other paraphernalia we've become addicted to has led to a horrendous quantity of organizing products to choose from.

Taking a look at the sports equipment that can be hung or stored, we should decide whether it's worth the expenditure or whether we're able to improvise our own version that will achieve the same beneficial results.

For instance, the backyard hacker can readily tee off at a moment's notice, when the golf clubs, golf bags, golf shoes, and golf balls are instantly accessible (illustration 453).

The same applies to those who want their tennis racquets and balls organized, available, and in prime condition.

The drawing at the top of illustration 454 portrays a rack that serves up more than tennis balls, since it has extra nooks and notches for baseball gloves, baseball bats, hockey sticks, or other gear.

The skiers are singled out by the makers of ski racks. This rack (illustration 455) is for skis and ski poles only.

The ski rack depicted first in illustration

ILLUSTRATION 453

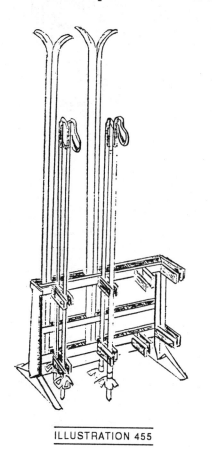

ILLUSTRATION 455

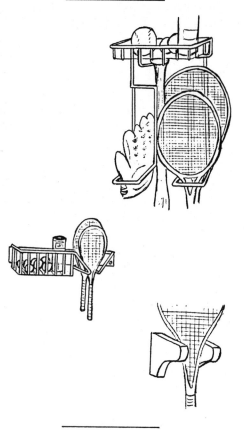

ILLUSTRATION 454

456 is capable of carrying only the skis and the poles, but it has taken them off the floor and hung them on a wall.

This second rack combines storage for the skis and poles with a place for sitting the ski boots as well. Since they are always used together, it makes sense to store them together.

How to Gladden Glad Tidings

We all look forward to different seasons and the special occasions they bring.

We're happy to have amassed a wonderful assortment of streamers, door wreaths, centerpieces, and exterior displays, yet we seldom smile with the same enthusiasm when we start storing them away.

The first priority with seasonal items is sorting them into categories and then putting them in easily accessible and labeled boxes. The boxes themselves should be divided as much as possible, so that the items on top don't

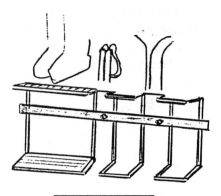

ILLUSTRATION 456

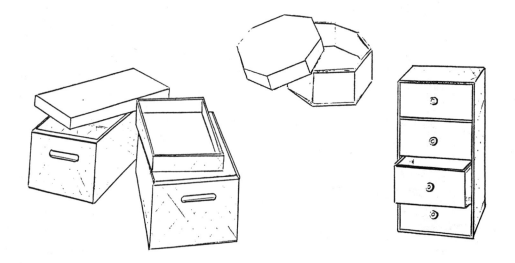

ILLUSTRATION 457

have to come out before we're able to see and reach the articles on the bottom.

The ultimate box for accomplishing this style of storage is a unit with drawers or, at the very least, a lift-out top tray that keeps the upper section of the box separated from the bottom (illustration 457).

Furthermore, an appropriately sized and shaped wreath box protects and maintains door hangings in mint condition (illustration 458).

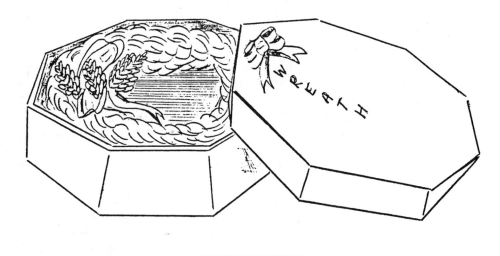

ILLUSTRATION 458

It's possible that certain wreaths, wall decorations, centerpieces, and other products can be stored very simply by encasing them in plastic and hanging them on hooks from the walls or ceiling. This is only a feasible solution if we have wall or ceiling space to spare.

By keeping our holiday categories separate in a grouping or cluster of containers that are clearly marked, we have devised a method to the madness, and we'll enjoy the seasons with a sense of peace.

We may find we have to store a vast array and tremendous quantity of gift-wrap and decorations, ribbons, bows, and tags.

If this is the case, this gift-wrap organizer (illustration 459) consolidates the materials we purchase.

The ability to stock all the pertinent paper paraphernalia, plus scissors and strings, in a single unit that can be hung on a wall, stored on a shelf, or concealed in a corner or closet is well worth the ten-dollar price tag. Most any version available is completely equipped with a drawer, a dowel for spools of ribbons, a compartment for squares of paper, a slot for rolls of paper, and a shelf for ribbons and bows.

How to Reason with Seasons

We're exceptionally fortunate folks if we have a spare closet for storing our seasonal garments.

When a rod or closet isn't a reasonable expectation in the existing household domain, consider correcting the situation by bringing in a portable stand for hanging seasonals (illustration 460).

This is an ususual approach, but certainly one with merit when the area isn't wide enough to accomodate the wider lengths of most hanging racks.

With this rack allowing many of the garments to be moved to higher levels, they aren't hanging side by side

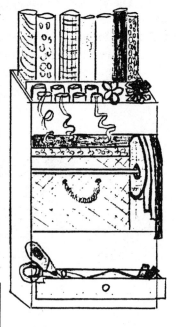

ILLUSTRATION 459

anymore, so less width is needed, yet the same number of garments have been given a place to hang (illustration 461).

The only drawback to storing seasonal clothing this way is making sure we adequately protect them from dust, dirt, and moths, since we won't actually see them again for a number of months.

Prospective stands should have the ability to cover the garments they contain. It's helpful when the cover is transparent because it's so much quicker and

ILLUSTRATION 460

easier to spot-check belongings.

Hanging out-of-season clothing is the only dignified approach our costly and even our cheaper articles of clothing justly deserve (illustration 462). Probably even more incentive for keeping the clothes on hangers is the ordeal we endure when we don't: removing the garments from the hangers, folding them, stacking them, and arranging them in box(es) or bag(s).

Now that it's been made patently clear the benefits to be gained by leaving the seasonal clothes hanging, it's worth mentioning one particular self-supporting stand that's rather interesting. It resembles a cabana structure for changing clothes, although it isn't quite large enough to step inside. It contains a clothes rod and it's attractive enough to use as a decoration in the house. Needless to say, this same serviceability can be acquired were we willing to shell out a substantial portion of our savings to pur-

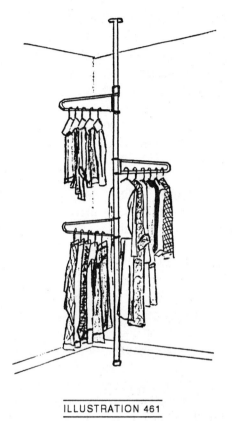

ILLUSTRATION 461

chase a finer piece of furniture, better known as a wardrobe, armoire, or chifforobe.

The seasonal storage we try to include in the basement or garage would benefit by utilizing an instant closet, but it would definitely need to be covered by a cloth or plastic in either of those areas.

Although we found instant closets to be less than satisfactory as our primary source of hanging space, they're adequate for storing seasonal garments.

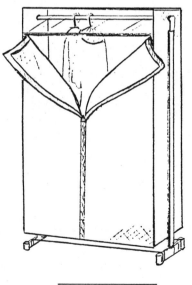

ILLUSTRATION 462

Open the package and assemble the kit. They are available in a wide variety of sizes, so it should be a fairly simply chore to measure the available space and purchase an instant closet that fits that space (illustration 463).

If personal budgets can't be reconciled to either of these options, there is an alternative route that is seldom considered, yet tackles the matter economically.

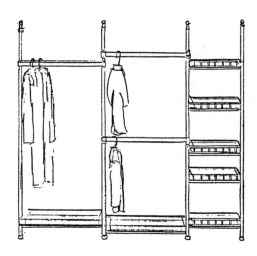

ILLUSTRATION 463

Find an area in the house that supplies sufficient space for one of the inexpensive self-supporting clothing racks. Its relatively unsightly appearance can then be concealed behind a screen divider, and again the screen can consume as much or as little of your cash as finances allow. Purchase a screen or make your own customized one to coordinate with the room's decor and the dictates of the space (illustration 464).

Sometimes, we're hesitant to part with past favorites because we're certain they will be stylish once again or that we'll lose enough weight to wear them again. So we hang on to massive mounds of materials that may or may not see the light of day in this lifetime. We're obliged to find some sensible spot to store them, and it would be totally appalling if that spot were a clothes closet.

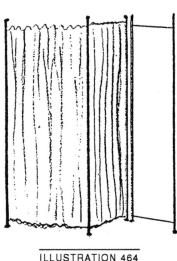

ILLUSTRATION 464

In this instance, it's permissible to store them in this rodded cardboard carton or the cedar-lined garment bag, but the bag better roost from rafters and not a closet rod (illustration 465).

The products available with cedar-linings, such as garment bags, chests, or shallow, under-the-bed units are costly. It's completely a matter of personal preference and budget whether these containers are justifiable (illustration 466).

If storing seasonal clothing in boxes is your only option, invest in an assortment of boxes or quilted vinyl zip-top cases that will supply uniformity and standardization to the system.

Protect the clothing that is destined to spend time in boxes; otherwise the garment eventually released will in no way, shape, or form resemble the original garment (illustration 467).

As in all of life, compromise is general-

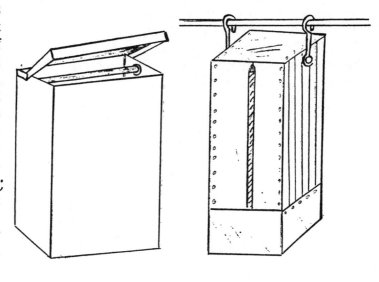

ILLUSTRATION 465

ILLUSTRATION 467

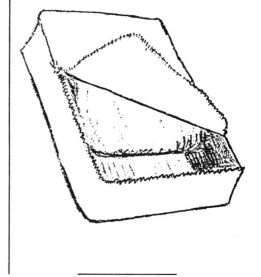

ILLUSTRATION 466

ly unavoidable, and succumbing to the box method of storage is just that, a compromise. Yet in order to make it as effective as possible, a few rules should be followed.

First of all, find a place for storing the boxes that is sensible, logical, and safe.

To offset the possibility of mistaken identity, place only a specific category (like sweaters) in boxes of one color. The garments that would normally hang would go in boxes of a different color, enabling us to know the contents inside without sticking on adhesive labels.

Pack the clothing correctly, spending the time and energy required to create uniformly folded garments. It wouldn't be a bad idea to encase them in protective fabrics or completely cover the box itself to block and hinder bugs from finding a way in.

Packing the clothes properly could be accomplished in a variety of ways or by choosing a box with drawers or interior dividers, making it much easier to classify the contents. This way in the event of an emergency, we could find the poodle skirt or 1940s-style trousers for our class reunion without rummaging through the faux fur boa and elbow-length lace gloves we sometimes pull out for New Year's Eve (illustration 468).

ILLUSTRATION 468

FINAL NOTE

So—we come to the end of the book. We've examined innovative approaches to organizing clothes closets, drawers, linen closets, coat closets, bathrooms, children's areas, kitchens, laundry areas, garages, work and play spaces, and basements. I hope the preceding march of liberation through your home has helped you to conquer clutter in your living space. With good categorization, assigned placement, thinking ahead, and, above all, the habit of making conscious choices about the way your home is set up, you really can give your house or apartment a dramatic "makeover" in short order.

Good luck!

Index

A & E Consumer Products
P.O. Box 190
League City, TX 77573
(Clothes hangers, extra hooks, plastic
shoe racks, pull-out drawers,
show/sweater boxes, tie racks.)

Action Products Co., Inc.
Box 100
Odessa, MO 64076
(Step stools.)

Basic Line, Inc.
17 Industrial Dr.
Cliffwood Beach, NJ 07735
(Clothes hangers, coat/hat rack, plastic
bins, plastic shoe rack.)

Beacon Plastics
126 N. Groesbeck
Mt. Clemens, MI 48043
(Clothes hangers, door/wall shoe racks,
over door hooks, plastic shoe racks,
shoe/sweater bags, stack shelves.)

Cabinet Aides
Amerock Corp.
4000 Auburn St.
P.O. Box 7018
Rockford, IL 61125
(False front sink, pull-out trash unit,
roll-out storage unit, slide-out
baskets, under-cabinet utilities.)

California Closets Co.
6409 Independence Ave.
Woodland Hills, CA 91367
(Modular units.)

Chadwick-Miller, Inc.
10 Pequot Industrial
P.O. Box 9106
Canton, MA 02021
(Acrylic rack, belt rings, brass tissue
pole, open-end hangers, padded hangers,
paper clips, scarf rack, shelf divider,
shoe/sweater bag, stemware rack.)

Closet Components and Accessories, Inc.
7130 NW 36th Ave.
Miami FL 33147
(Baskets, hardware, laundry, ventilated
drawer, wall/door racks.)

Closetmaid Systems, Inc.
Clairson International
720 SW 17th St.
Ocala, FL 32674
(Stack shelves, telescope tie rack,
tilted shoe rack, ventilated
shelf/rod.)

Debbinaire Way
422 McCreary Ct.
Cincinnati, OH 45231
(Honeycomb cylinders.)

Dial Industries, Inc.
1538 Esperanza St.
Los Angeles CA 90023
(Baskets, crates, stackable drawers.)

Grayline Housewares
1616 Berkley St.
Elgin, IL 60123
(Bag racks, beverage rack, cup racks,
freezer trays, hang-on baskets, iron
rack, lid racks, plate racks, sliding
pan rack, towel racks, trash racks,
vacuum racks, wall/door racks, wrap
racks.)

Hirsh Company
8051 Central Park Ave.
Skokie, IL 60076
(Ceiling rack, file cabinet, laundry
tower, modular units, steel shelves,
workbench.)

Independent Products (IPC)
420 Moyer Blvd.
West Point, PA 19486
(Belt ring, clothes hangers, cubby
holes, hooks, paper clips, silverware
tray.)

K-C Products Company, Inc.
1600 East Sixth Ct.
Los Angeles, CA 90023
(Drawer units, shoe/sweater bags.)

Lee/Rowan Company
6333 Etzel Ave.
St. Louis, MO 63133
(Carousel shoes, clothes hangers,
coat/hat rack, door/wall shoe rack,
drying rack, extra hooks, free stand
shoe rack, hanging racks, stack
shelves, tie racks, tilted shoe racks,
ventilated shelf/rod systems, wall/door
racks.)

Rubbermaid, Inc.
1147 Akron Rd.
Wooster, OH 44691
(Drawer organizer, shoe/sweater box,
slide-out shelf, stack drawers, step
stool.)

Schulte Corporation
11450 Grooms Rd.
Cincinnati, OH 45242
(Coat/hat rack, drawer iron board,
tilted shoe rack, ventilated
shelf/rod.)

Shelfco, Inc.
4750 NW 15th Ave.
Fr. Lauderdale, FL 33309
(Ventilated shelf/rod.)

Stack-A-Shelf
160 Columbia St. SW
P.O. Box 10
Waterloo, Canada N2J3Z6
(Modular units.)

Stanbel Spacewares, Inc.
100 Tapley St.
Springfield, MA 01104
(Bakeware rack, breadbox, drawer
organizer, swing shelf, telescope
slacks rack, under cabinet drawers.)

Sterilite Corporation
P.O. Box 524
Main St.
Townsend, MA 01469
(Shoe/sweater boxes.)

Sun Hill Industries, Inc.
Glendale Commerce Park
48 Union St.
Stamford, CT 06906
(Extender rod [chain].)

Tamor Plastics Corp.
11 Penn Plaza
New York, NY 10001
(Clothes hangers, extra hooks,
shoe/sweater boxes, shoe rack, stack
shelves, tie racks.)

Tucker Housewares
354 Central St.
Leominster, MA 01453
(Crates, drawer organizers, drawer
units, plastic bins, shoe/sweater
boxes.)

Whitmor
350 Fifth Ave., Suite 1410
New York, NY 10118
(Storage bags.)

Wilhold (Hugh H. Wilson Co.)
222 Packer St.
P.O. Box 247
Sunbury, PA 17801
(Covered hanging rack, shoe/sweater
box, storage box.)

Zenith Products Corp.
200 Commerce Dr.
Aston, PA 19014
(Bathroom shelves, shower racks, tow
T-bar.)